(continued)

The ELL Writer

Moving Beyond Basics
in the Secondary Classroom

CHRISTINA ORTMEIER-HOOPER

Foreword by Thomas Newkirk

Teachers College, Columbia University
New York and London

Published by Teachers College Press, 1234 Amsterdam Avenue, New York, NY 10027

Figure 2.1 is reprinted from *Journal of Second Language Writing,* volume 6 number 1, P. K. Matsuda, "Contrastive rhetoric in context: A dynamic model of L2 writing," pp. 45–60, copyright 1997, with permission from Elsevier.

"Puzzles" by Myrna Nieves reprinted by permission of the Publisher. From Karen Ognulnick, *Language Crossings: Negotiating the Self in a Multicultural World,* New York: Teachers College Press. Copyright © 2000 by Teachers College, Columbia University. All rights reserved.

Library of Congress Cataloging-in-Publication Data

Ortmeier-Hooper, Christina, 1972–
The ELL writer : moving beyond basics in the secondary classroom / Christina Ortmeier-Hooper, Teachers College, Columbia University.
   pages cm. — (Language and Literacy Series)
   ISBN 978-0-8077-5417-7 (pbk.)—ISBN 978-0-8077-5418-4 (hardcover)
   1. English language—Study and teaching (Secondary)—Foreign speakers. 2. Language and languages—Study and teaching. 3. Language education. I. Title. II. Title: English Language Learners writer.
   PE1128.A2O76 2013
   428.0071'2—dc23   2012045959

ISBN 978-0-8077-5417-7 (paper)
ISBN 978-0-8077-5418-4 (hardcover)
Printed on acid-free paper
Manufactured in the United States of America

20 19 18 17 16 15 14 13   8 7 6 5 4 3 2 1

For Wisdom, Therese, Ken-zhi, Paul, Miguel, Vildana,
and all my second-language students who continue to inspire me

and

To my family, especially my parents, Lothar and Waltraud

Contents

Foreword

For years there was a ritual in Durham, NH for would-be writers. We would contact Don Murray, our local writing guru, and ask him to read a draft. He would invariably agree and invite us over to his house, to his basement office, where he would lift his glasses to his massive forehead, hold our precious words inches from his face, speed read, and ask us all the same question:

"What is this about?"

At first it felt insulting. "What is this about?" It's obvious, look at the title. But it was a good writing question—and a good reading one, a good starting point. So what is *The ELL Writer: Moving Beyond Basics in the Secondary Classroom* about? In particular, where is the "beyond" that Christina Ortmeier-Hooper promises to take us?

At the heart of this book (which, by the way, has a big heart) is a paradox, a tension that reverberates throughout. To assist any group of students, that group must be identified and named. But this identification, these labels, can actually work to the disadvantage of the group being "helped." They emphasize separateness and difference. They stigmatize. The labels tend to constrain them; they stick with these students as they are moving forward in their language development, advancing to become more proficient users of English.

The ELL students Ortmeier-Hooper introduces us to—Wisdom, Ken-zhi, Miguel, Vildana, Therese, Paul—want to be mainstream. They see themselves as serious students, often high achievers in the countries they came from, and struggle to maintain that identity. They are making a huge bet on this country. But the ELL label marks them as different and, as they well know, differences are regularly perceived as deficiencies.

Some of the accommodations these students receive work to their disadvantage. Tracking can keep them from academically challenging work that might prepare them for their dream of going to college. In some cases they are assigned to lower level classes, often with students less ambitious than they are, with the promise they can work their way up to higher levels. But they are not given the academically challenging work that would *enable* them to move up. They're stuck. The research is clear on this—tracked students rarely change tracks.

The writing instruction at this level often takes the form of decontextualized skill work (i.e., worksheets) and what Ortmeier-Hooper calls "survival genres," formulaic writing models that may help them get by on tests, but fail to develop real analytic thought. They are "overscaffolded," so programmatic that the writer has no experience of a process for expression or exploring a topic—no real composing. By making things simple and highly structured, this instruction actually makes it harder for students to get a foothold, to find a personal purpose for writing.

In the splendidly practical second half of the book, Ortmeier-Hooper lays out principles and practices that can help these writers. While acutely sensitive to the emotional and linguistic challenges these students face (she has a great section on "feeling stupid" in a new language), she ultimately makes the case that these writers need what all writers need. They need to feel a relationship with their teacher. They need purposeful, explicit, rhetorically based assignments that draw on the interests, passions, and career goals of students—what Anne Dyson (1993) calls a "permeable curriculum." They need real audiences for their work. They need writing conferences. They need responses that focus on issues of meaning and do not fixate on errors, and they need sensitive evaluation that is respectful of effort and progress.

In his poem "A Servant to Servants," Robert Frost has two workers describe their difficult situation, and one of them concludes:

He says the best way out is always through.
And I agree to that, or in so far
As that I can see no way out but through

This insight, I feel, is the "beyond" of this fine book. That there can be no shortcut, no simplification, no reduction to formula—all of which keep these students from real, meaningful work. The only "way out is through": taking on legitimate and authentic writing tasks, with wise support and help.

Thomas Newkirk
University of New Hampshire

REFERENCES

Dyson, A. (1993). *Negotiating a permeable curriculum: On literacy, diversity, and the interplay of children's and teachers' world.* Urbana, IL: National Council of Teachers of English.

Frost, R. (1969). A servant to servants. From E. C. Lathem (Ed.), *The poetry of Robert Frost.* New York, NY: Henry Holt.

Breaking the Ice

And you may ask yourself—
Well . . . how did I get here?

—David Byrne, "Once in a Lifetime"

This book has been a journey for me as a teacher and a writer; it emerges from my ongoing questions and experiences as a public school teacher, and more recently, as a compositionist and teacher educator, working with linguistically and culturally diverse students. As a secondary school teacher, I taught students who represented more than 16 countries. Most of them were newcomers, but some had been in the United States for 2 to 3 years. In that classroom alone, the students spoke over seven different languages. Spanish was the most prominent, followed closely by Serbo-Croatian. Many of my students were on public assistance and eligible for the free-lunch program. Many of their parents did not speak English, and they worked nights, sometimes two shifts in a row, trying to make ends meet and provide for their families. The students had a wide range of immigration and educational experiences. Some had exceptional language and literacy skills in their first language, and it was only a matter of time before those skills transferred to academic English. Others had been moved back and forth between the United States and their homelands so often that they lacked strong academic literacy skills in both languages. Still for others, their schooling in their first language had been interrupted by poverty, war, or extended stays in refugee camps. Some students had been exited from ELL programs in elementary school, only to find themselves struggling with the increasing academic reading and writing demands of middle school and placed back in another ELL classroom.

My training as an English Language Arts teacher with additional certification in ESL did not prepare me for the difficulties my students would encounter with writing. I had studied the works of Nancie Atwell (1987), Linda Rief (1991), Tom Romano (1987), Donald Graves (1983), Peter Elbow (1973), and Donald Murray (1982, 1990). I had taught writing successfully for native-English-speaking students with results and enthusiasm. But I learned that first language writing pedagogy didn't always work for my students' experiences as second language writers, particularly for those students who had struggled with (or had never really experienced) academic reading and writing in their first language. Although I had taken courses on ESL teaching and second language acquisition, writing was never really discussed in great detail beyond grammar and vocabulary building. No classes on working with second language writers were offered when I was pursuing my education degree. So I blindly taught my ELL students, modifying strategies from books on teaching writing to native English speakers to fit what I knew about second language acquisition. But I remained deeply concerned because there was just so much about these students' writing and their approaches that was unique.

The problem was that everything I knew about writing and English as a Second Language (ESL) told me that writing needed to be an essential, integrated part of their English language development. Writing—being able to convey thoughts, ideas, narratives, and opinions on the written paper—was an essential skill and ability that my students would need if they were to succeed academically. None of the books on writing that I found provided me with a sense of these students as writers. I wondered how they saw the writing instruction and the act of writing in English, and how I might develop teaching practices that would help them become more successful writers. I wanted to know more.

Over the past decade, I have been working in schools with teachers and with students to find ways to meet the needs of second language writers in secondary schools. I returned to graduate school and stumbled upon the burgeoning field of second language writing, which included researchers and teachers from across the world who taught writing to second language students and professionals. Most of their work concentrated on college and university students, but some of their findings made me see my ELL students in new ways, understand their writing, and have a better sense of what I might do as their teacher to help them become confident, savvy writers. I conducted research among U.S. immigrant student writers transitioning from high school to college. I worked with bridge programs that helped ease those transitions and collaborated with fellow teachers to consider some of the best practices for teaching writing in secondary school classrooms. Finally, I embarked on a 2-year qualitative study of adolescent second language writers in U.S. high schools. Case studies from that project provide the portraits of young writers in this book and profile their challenges and their achievements. This book is the culmination of that journey, but it is also a starting point for new conversations on the culturally and linguistically diverse student writers in our English Language Arts classrooms.

ACKNOWLEDGMENTS

My deepest appreciation goes to the students featured in this book. Their many hours of conversation, candid reflections, and sharing of their work have made this project possible. I thank Emily Spangler, my editor, whose comments and insights helped me to revise and strengthen the book. My dissertation advisor, Paul Kei Matsuda, encouraged this project and my ongoing efforts to bridge the gaps between secondary and college writing studies. My teacher, and now colleague, Tom Newkirk, taught me that my main goal as an educator should always be to follow the "good work" and let it lead me. I thank him and all my colleagues at the University of New Hampshire for their encouragement and support. This book would not exist without the steadfast support of Michelle Cox, Laura Smith, John Lofty, and Kate Tirabassi, who read and commented on early drafts.

Most importantly, I thank my husband, Tom, for his encouragement and love throughout my research and writing process. I am grateful for my beautiful sons—Sean, Zachary, and Johnathan—who patiently let Mom write on weekend mornings, collected and stapled draft pages from the hallway printer, and cheered me on.

Finally, I dedicate this book to my parents, Lothar and Waltraud Ortmeier, who remind me through their stories and their lives what it means to come to a new country, to learn a second language, and to imagine America as a place of opportunity and promise.

CHAPTER 1

Who Are English Language Learners (ELLs)?

Understanding Labels and Moving Beyond Them

> The fastest growing group in the American population is immigrant children. For many of us, they are our students now; for others of us they are on their way to our classrooms. An astonishing one out of every five children in the U.S. is an immigrant or a child of immigrants. . . . We can no longer be content with saying, "the ESL teacher will take care of all those kids."
>
> —Randy Bomer (2005), past president of NCTE

STARTING POINTS

"Ms. O, am I always gonna be ELL?" asked Fanika, 14, as she looked over my shoulder and I began to sign off on her high school registration form. Her question was one that I heard often as a middle school ELL Language Arts teacher, especially as my students completed their middle school years and headed off to high school.

We were in a basement classroom; there was a wall that divvied up the old science classroom into two classrooms. The wall only went about three-quarters of the way across, and although it provided a visual buffer between the two classes of students, noise easily filtered from one side of the wall to the other. This wall was built when the school administrators realized that there weren't enough classrooms to support the growing number of English language learners (ELLs) and their teachers. It, along with the outdated textbooks, and our place in the basement of the building, spoke volumes about the position of ELL students in the school.

1

I sat at my desk, and I heard the beginning-level students on the other side of the wall learning the words for fruits and vegetables and the language needed for their upcoming field trip to the grocery store. On my side of the wall, my 8th-grade intermediate ELL students were working away, building story mobiles for the books they had read as part of their book clubs. At the single computer in the room, two students worked on captions, defining key plot turns and describing characters in their books. They were busy; there was a constant quiet chatter as they brainstormed and considered the design of their mobiles and the written text that would accompany them. One at a time, the students approached my desk for a brief conference on their projects and to hand in their high school registration forms. It was April, and the end of their middle school days was approaching.

"Ms. O, am I always gonna be ELL?" asked Fanika again, bringing me back to the moment. Fanika, with her shoulder-length brown hair and embroidered blue jeans, was outspoken and bright; she carried with her a desire to go to medical school and become a doctor, a dream packed up along with the rest of her life when she fled war-torn Bosnia. Fanika's greatest difficulties in English were with writing. She spoke English beautifully and was an avid reader. But she still struggled with her academic writing, scoring below competency on the writing portion of her last English proficiency exam. Overhearing her question, her classmates looked up from their projects. There were 16 students in the classroom, and seven different languages spoken among them. Some of them had been in United States for as little as 8 months; others had been here for close to 3 years. They were all eager to know my response. It was their question as well.

WHY THIS BOOK? ELLs IN THE
ENGLISH LANGUAGE ARTS CLASSROOM

Fanika's question, particularly as it relates to writing, the teaching of writing, and academic achievement, has become the driving force behind this book. English language learners, like Fanika, do not remain in ELL classrooms, but they often hold onto the label of "ELL" long after they leave sheltered classrooms. For many of them, their concerns over their competencies as English users are enhanced by struggles with writing. Historically, we have often talked in terms of ESL classrooms, bilingual classrooms, and so-called mainstream classrooms, as if these classroom spaces and the students within them were distinct spaces without overlap. But today's schools and classrooms reflect what literacy specialist Kerry Enright (2011) has termed the "New Mainstream" student population, one that is more linguistically and culturally diverse than we have ever seen (p. 87).

Recognizing and responding to these New Mainstream students has become an important mandate for English teachers working in 21st century. In our classrooms today, we see students from a variety of socioeconomic backgrounds, educational experiences, and home circumstances, but we are also seeing an increasing number of culturally and linguistically diverse students. The U.S. Census Bureau (2009) reports that students who speak a language other than English in the home make up 19.2% of the U.S. population. According to the U.S. Department of Education, more than 5.5 million English language learners are in our K–12 schools (NCELA, 2008). Strikingly, these numbers are not just indicative of large cities or states like California, Arizona, Florida, and New York. Although these urban areas continue to see large numbers of linguistically and culturally diverse students, states with smaller populations and historically more homogeneous populations are also seeing a shift. In my current state of residence, New Hampshire, the number of English language learners has increased over 200% in the past 10 years (U.S. Department of Education, 2008). States like Utah, Iowa, Indiana, and Vermont have seen similar trends, and statistics suggest that these demographic shifts will continue in the years ahead.

In the past decade, English Language Arts (ELA) teachers have found increasing numbers of these students in their classrooms. In the English Language Arts classroom of the 21st century, the lines between native-English-speaking and non-native-English-speaking students are increasingly blurred. Students may be native English speakers who were raised in bilingual or multilingual settings. They may be learning English for the first time or they may have had years of English lessons in other countries. For some teachers, this classroom demographic is not new; they are used to working in districts and neighborhoods where the majority of the students speak a language other than English in the home. For other teachers, it is a new trend. They work in more homogeneous districts and neighborhoods, in which many of the students are native English speakers, except for a small group of English speakers of second languages. In both scenarios, the ability to work with these students as readers and writers has become an essential part of the work of ELA teachers.

At one point or another, all English language learners move into mainstream classrooms. The movement of English language learners into mainstream ELA classrooms depends on individual districts, school demographics, and other factors specific to the local context. The very nature of English language learning suggests that these students are indeed always in motion, particularly when it comes to their placements and their English proficiency levels, which can seem to fluctuate when new genres, new expectations, new grade levels, and new content material are introduced.

When these students arrive in our classrooms, many mainstream teachers feel underprepared to work with them, particularly when it comes to their writing needs. As educators and administrators, we know that the reality of the 21st-century ELA classroom necessitates that every teacher must be prepared to work with these student writers. English educators Boyd, Ariail, Williams, Jocson, Sachs, McNeal, Fecho, Fisher, Healy, Meyer, and Morrell (2006) note:

> Never in the history of education in the United States has there been a more urgent need for educators to join forces to create literacy classrooms that meet the needs of linguistically and culturally diverse students. (p. 329)

From our teaching experience, we know that even those ELLs with high proficiency in oral language and strong literacy skills will still need instruction and assistance when it comes to their written English. Years after being exited from ELL programs, their writing may continue to have traits of their crossover into English. Wherever these students fall in terms of their proficiency levels and their experiences, it is increasingly important to acknowledge that they can no longer simply be sent to the ELL teacher with the assumption that with "just a few more days, months, or years" of special services, they will perfect their written English. As Randy Bomer, past president of NCTE, noted in the quote that opens this chapter, we can no longer say that the ELL teacher will take care of "all those kids." Those kids are our kids. Teaching these students to write for a range of purposes and academic expectations is an inextricable piece of what it means to be an English Language Arts teacher in the 21st century.

WHO ARE ELL STUDENTS?
A RANGE OF STORIES AND CIRCUMSTANCES

Every ESL student will enter the classroom with his or her own story. Through journal articles, research, educational policies, and our school policies, we have become familiar with a range of terms for these students: ESL, ELL, CLD, LEP, bilingual, and more. The terms are confusing, even for the most experienced of teachers. Teachers who work with second language students in the K–12 schools have seen a steady shift and movement among the terminology used to describe these students, their programs, and their teachers. For example, 16 years ago, when I was first working with second language students, *bilingual* or *ESL* were the terms of choice. *ESL* meant "English as a Second Language," a term that suggested that there was indeed competency and knowledge of a first language. Then, a few years into my teaching career, the term *ESOL* ("English speakers of other languages") took hold. It was subtle shift but it suggested that (1) these students were English speakers, and (2) it acknowledged that they had competency in another language.

But at the same time, testing, assessment tools, and internal school documentation asked bilingual and ESL teachers to write up reports on LEP students (Limited English Proficient). The term *LEP* was often the most problematic for students, because it suggested to them that they might have "limitations" on multiple levels; it seemed to question their cognitive abilities. Often, the term *LEP* was relegated to reports. Programs and students continued to be identified in the hallways of the school by the term *ESL*.

The No Child Left Behind (NCLB) act included references to both Limited English Proficient (LEP) and English language learners (ELLs). NCLB also coincided with the renaming of the U.S. Department of Education's Office of Bilingual Education and Minority Languages, now known as the Office of English Language Acquisition, Language Enhancement, and Academic Achievement for Limited English Proficient Students (OELA). At that point, many schools and teachers began to use the term *ELL* to describe their students and their programs. More recently, some districts have started using the term *Culturally and Linguistically Diverse* (CLD) to describe their multilingual student populations. The fluctuation in terms is representative of various political changes over the past 20 years, as well as a series of ongoing debates on the nature and purpose of language instruction, both at the national and state levels. For example, in the past 15 years, the state of California has moved from using *LEP* to *ELL* and, most recently, from *ELL* to English learner (EL). These shifts in terminology speak volumes about how these students are perceived and the kinds of language programs (two-way immersion, bilingual, ELL, tutoring, and so forth) that are made available to them. Those shifts continue to occur. Most recently, the growing global economy has led to higher numbers of non-native speakers using and working in the English language within international contexts. This phenomenon has led many ESL teachers to begin using the term *English-as-an-International-Language* (EIL) in order to acknowledge the transnational use of English and English variations outside of the United States. I've included a brief glossary of common terms and acronyms often used in conversations on second language students at the end of this chapter.

Throughout this book, I have chosen to use two terms: *ELL* and *L2* (second language) writer.[1] *L2 writing* and *L2 writer* are terms that are taken from the field of second language writing, and I use them here because my work is situated in that field of study. I use the term *ELL* with some hesitancy, though. It is a term that will be familiar to many teachers, and for that reason, it is useful for discussing the student writers in this book. However, I'm also greatly aware of the limits of the term, which suggests that these students are permanently "learners of English" and perpetual novices, and neglects to acknowledge their emerging, and often quite proficient, identities as multilingual language users.

UNPACKING THE LABELS:
LEARNING MORE ABOUT OUR STUDENTS

The demographic trends that I noted earlier have familiarized many teachers and administrators with the terms used to describe these students. For example, the terms English language learner (ELL) and Limited English Proficient (LEP) are used under many federal and state guidelines to discuss, assess, and label those students who are learning English as a second language in our K–12 schools. What all of these labels fail to acknowledge and illustrate, however, is the range of educational backgrounds and linguistic diversity that these students bring with them into our classrooms. Similar arguments have been made by researchers García and Kleifgen (2010), who advocate the term *emergent bilingual,* which recognizes the linguistic strengths of these students.

The shifts in terminology illustrate some of the tensions that emerge from the ways the labels shape our understanding of these students. The labels, and the ways we use them, can unintentionally negate some of the differences that exist around the ways individuals learn and the unique circumstances, both educational and personal, that have led students to our classrooms. The terms can mask important distinctions and individual experiences in ways that also mask these students' strengths. Certainly, as teachers and teacher educators, we need to find some common vocabulary to discuss our students, but sometimes the labels define these young people in a very singular sense, when they see themselves with multiple layers that sometimes coexist and sometimes conflict. To some extent, these terms are necessary and I use them in this book in order to share these students' experiences. But I stress the importance of seeing the individuals and possibilities that exist beyond the labels.

In the pages that follow, I unpack the details behind this range of learners. I begin by exploring some of subcategories that exist when we begin to talk about the multilingual writers in our classrooms, looking specifically at the following kinds of students: international, immigrant (or foreign-born), refugee, international adoptee, generation 1.5, migrant, and U.S.-born.

International Students

International ELL students may be students on exchange, often with quite strong English skills, but limited experiences with American cultural norms. They often stay with host families or relatives who are already connected to the school through other children in the family. International students may also include the sons and daughters of corporate executives, engineers, and other specialists who work in the United States for brief 1- to 2-year periods.

Often, international students studying abroad have had access to excellent educational resources in their home countries, and they have spent time studying English in these settings. They may be more familiar with "textbook English" and grammar terms, but they may have limited experience with classroom discussion, American culture, and lengthier writing tasks. As part of cultural exchange programs, these students often view their time in America as temporary, and their plans to return to their home countries influence how they perceive their time in American schools. For example, students who are hoping to build upon their experiences in American schools in their future professional lives or whose schooling may be more invested in the educational aspects of their experience than students who come to the United States primarily for a cultural experience or traveling.

Immigrant (or Foreign-Born)

Immigrant students represent one of the largest categories of ELLs in our schools. Suárez-Orozco, Suárez-Orozco, and Todorova's (2008) landmark longitudinal study of immigrant students in America provides teachers with a comprehensive look at this student population, revealing the complexity within this group and the ways in which language and immigration impact their schooling. Most of these students are or will become permanent residents or citizens of the United States. Unlike their international peers, they do not see their time in the United States as temporary, and they do not have a plan to return to a home country. These students and their parents are seeking a better life in America in terms of economic opportunity and educational opportunities, familial ties, and often with respect to their personal liberty and freedom. Their educational backgrounds vary widely. Some may be the sons and daughters of doctors and engineers and may have studied at some of the best schools in their home countries. They have had access to English classes, computers, and a range of literacy experiences. Others have had a strong education in their home countries, but only a few conversational English courses. Still others may have less-than-adequate schooling in their home countries due to socioeconomic constraints.

Perhaps the most important point here is that each immigrant student's experience and background is distinctive. Even two students coming from the same extended family or the same town in their home country will have unique sets of circumstances that influence their lives in and outside of the classroom.

Immigrant student populations are often described in more specific terms in the research and literature on English language learners. These terms include *refugee, generation 1.5, foreign-born,* and *adoptees*—each of which I describe in more detail below.

Refugees

Every year throughout the world, there are millions of people who are displaced by famine, war, and civil and political conflicts. Some people are forced to leave their homelands to escape persecution and possibly death. In recent years, refugees have come to the United States from war-torn regions like Vietnam, Bosnia, Croatia, Iraq, Afghanistan, Congo, Somalia, and the Sudan. There have also been groups of families who have sought asylum in the United States because they are fleeing religious or political persecution. Wisdom, one of the students highlighted in this book, and his family offer one example of the kinds of political persecution that bring refugees to the United States.

Some refugees have spent years in refugee camps, where schooling was limited. Malnutrition and poverty may also have limited their educational opportunities, and some may never have experienced school at all. Others had strong early years of education that were disrupted by their country's instability. In many cases, it may have become too dangerous to go to school, or schools may have been bombed or abandoned. As one of my middle school students, a refugee from Bosnia, once told me, "You don't have good teachers during war. Sometimes you don't have teachers at all."

For those refugees coming from refugee camps and war-torn nations, there is always a toll. These students and their parents may suffer from post-traumatic stress disorders. One Congolese student noted that he had difficulty concentrating and thinking during school because he could not block out some of the horrible, bloody scenes that he had witnessed in his village. In the United States, many refugee resettlement communities have social workers, local agencies, and other community organizations who work with the refugee families. Teachers can reach out to these local community resources to learn more about the backgrounds of local refugee students, their countries, the kinds of strife that they may have encountered, and their current needs.

Adoptees

International adoptees enter the United States at a range of ages. Although their adoptive parents are often native English speakers, the adoptees may have limited or no experience with English. Much depends on their birth country and their access to literacy experiences as young children. Issues of attachment, trauma, and other concerns may complicate their language development. Adoptees may be eligible to receive ELL services, particularly if English was not their first language in their birth country and they arrived in the United States as older children.

Generation 1.5

In recent years, the term *generation 1.5* (Bosher & Rowecamp, 1998; Harklau, Losey, & Siegal, 1999; Roberge, Harklau, & Siegal, 2009) has resonated in discussions of immigrant students in secondary and higher education. Generation 1.5 students immigrated to the United States during their teenage years and completed at least some of their secondary schooling in U.S. schools. The term refers to the fact that these students often find themselves between generations. If their parents are defined as first-generation immigrants, and their younger siblings or their own future children are defined as second-generation, these adolescents are squarely in the middle.

Over the past decade, *generation 1.5* has become a popular term among secondary teachers who have witnessed the complexity of these students' experiences, including arriving in a new country, balancing school and home expectations and struggles, learning a new language, and being an adolescent. The term has also been problematic, as it has begun to blur the individual experience and literacy backgrounds of these students. Our one-size-fits-all use of the generation 1.5 label, like many of these terms, has made it difficult for teachers to sort out the complex, perhaps even contradictory, responses and reactions that we may receive from these students in the classroom (Matsuda & Matsuda, 2009; Ortmeier-Hooper, 2008).

U.S.-Born

While the term *generation 1.5* refers to those students who enter the United States as teenagers, U.S.-born English language learners are often their younger brothers and sisters. In many cases, U.S.-born ELLs are born to families in which parents or guardians speak only limited English or English is not the dominant home language. As a child, I fit into this category. I was born in the United States, but my sisters and parents were immigrants from Germany. In my early years, German was the dominant home language. Only as I grew older and my family learned English did English became the primary language in our household. For many children of immigrant families in the United States, particularly those with multiple or older generations in the home, their home language will remain a strong influence in their households as the language used to speak to grandparents, parents, and often in the neighborhoods in which they live. Their home language is a gift—a gift of culture, a way to connect to their families and neighbors, and often, an aptitude for multilingualism in an increasingly globalized economy. For this reason, their home language is not a hindrance but, rather, a resource; home (or heritage) languages for these adolescent students are intrinsically linked to their identity and their language development.

COMPLICATING LABELS AND ISSUES OF ADOLESCENT IDENTITY

For all the kinds of English language learners that we see in our classrooms, individual stories and experiences guide their decisions, influence their language proficiency, and impact their perceptions of school and English. We use labels and categories to begin to make some sense of their needs, but we know from working with our students that labels and categories only take us so far. As Linda Harklau noted in her scholarship on immigrant and generation 1.5 students,

> Learning in a second language is not simply the accrual of technical linguistic abilities but rather it is intimately related to identity how one sees oneself and is seen by others as a student, as a writer, and as an ethnolinguistic minority. (Matsuda, Canagarajah, Harklau, Hyland, & Warshauer, 2003, p. 155)

For all their complexities as English language learners, these students are also complex because they are teenagers. Adolescence, more generally, is often marked by confusion, resistance, and change. Young students wrestle with the ways in which they define themselves and issues of identity. As teachers, we may focus on ELLs' language proficiency, cultural background, ethnicity, and so on, but all of these students, regardless of how they came to English and the United States, are still struggling with the challenges of growing up and finding their identities within the contexts of their schools, friends, neighborhoods, and families. They are wrestling with not only how they perceive themselves but also how others see them.

The issues that arise from learning a language and negotiating the age of adolescence form an intertwining double helix that forges these students' identities in the classroom and in the social spheres that exist in the hallways and public spaces of our schools.

Students like my former student Fanika, who was worried about being constantly viewed as "ELL," worry about the ways they are perceived by others. Fanika, for her part, wanted to grow beyond the label of ELL because it seemed to limit her options as a student. In another example, in one of my high school classrooms, a 14-year-old Thai student entered wearing a Tommy Hilfiger hat and asking, "Do I look American enough today?" With his playfully delivered question, he voiced underlying concerns about what "an American" looks like, and if he could indeed be accepted into various social groups and the larger U.S. culture. On another day, I overheard 17-year-old student Jose saying to his native-English-speaking peers: "I may be Puerto Rican but that doesn't mean I don't speak English," purposefully pulling out his U.S. passport as a way of establishing his appropriate placement in a mainstream classroom. Simply put, the complexities of adolescence, language learning, and secondary school experiences impact these students' identities in high school classrooms and also beyond them.

Jane, 18 and a first-year student in my college writing class, told me that she resisted the label of "ESL" at all costs throughout her high school years, stressing that she reached out to join cheerleading, the honor society, the newspaper, and the prom committee, not wanting to be defined against the backdrop of her linguistic profile. As Jane explained,

> I didn't like ESL. I didn't like how she [the teacher] made it seems like it [ESL] was your only identity. . . . Like I think they try to make that [ESL identity] apparent to other people. And maybe some people don't feel like that's who they are as a whole person. Like it's a part of them, but it is not the most important. (Ortmeier-Hooper, 2008, p. 409)

As Jane's comments suggest, there is ambiguity in the way English language learners express their identities in our classrooms. They often seem unsure of how they want to represent themselves. In our work with these students, we often miss the social and identity-forming implications of the labels that our schools assign to students. For multilingual students like Jane and the others in this book, the labels of "ELL" and/or "ESL" often refer to a great deal more than just language skills or placement. They carry social, academic, and personal implications.

In the chapters that follow, the implications and challenges of these labels remain an important backdrop to the stories and writing experiences of the students featured in this book. My goal is to help us understand the unique characteristics of second language writing and writers while, at the same time, taking a closer look at some of the individual adolescent experiences behind the theory and the labels.

MEET THE STUDENTS

Since the rest of this book takes a more thematic approach, I want to provide readers with a chance to get to know some of the students featured throughout this book. All students, cities, and schools are identified by pseudonyms.

The six writers featured in this book were part of a larger qualitative study of second language writers. I had initially met the students through a summer program where I did workshops and assisted with curriculum design. For close to 2 years, I met with the students after school and also observed them in their school contexts, including their ELL, ELA, and other content-area classrooms. The students attended two different schools in Mill River, a northeastern city of more than 300,000 people with refugee and immigrant communities that have grown exponentially since the early 1990s. The district's students spoke over 40 languages altogether, and at Mill River North, the comprehensive high school on the north side of the city, over 25% of the

2,000 students spoke a language other than English in the home. In contrast, Mill River South, the second high school on the outskirts of the city, was more suburban in nature and had only 35 ESL students (less than 1% of the school's total student population). That difference was reflected in the ELL programs offered at each school; North had a large ELL teaching staff, while South had a single ELL teacher.

All of the students in this study were in mainstream courses. Ken-zhi, Therese, and Miguel received direct ELL-specific services, including ELL language development courses. Paul and Wisdom were fully mainstreamed and were indirectly monitored by ELL staff through their report cards. Tutorial support was available for them, but they chose to attend study sessions with mainstream teachers instead when they needed additional help. In the middle of his first year, Miguel transferred to Mill River South, where his ELL support consisted of a single study hall with the ELL teacher.

The study documents Paul's, Therese's, Wisdom's, Miguel's, and Ken-zhi's school writing experiences throughout their first 2 years of high school through interviews, observations, writing samples, and other ethnographic means. Vildana, the sixth participant, was a junior at the Mill River South high school. Her participation began at the end of her junior year and continued into the early months of her senior year. Many of her interviews and writing samples were conducted and collected during the summer, while she attended a bridge program for prospective college applicants.

Snapshots of the Students

Miguel, age 15, came to the United States from the Dominican Republic to follow his mother, who had been working here for a number of years to prepare for the arrival of Miguel and his younger sister. He had been in the United States for about 18 months at the start of the study.

Ken-zhi, (also called Ken), age 16, came to the United States from Taiwan with his mother, father, and younger sister. He had been in Mill River School District for about 11 months at the start of the study. Both of his parents worked at a local restaurant and did not speak much English. They had come to the United States to give their children more educational opportunities.

Wisdom, age 14, was from Nigeria. He spent 2 years living in a refugee camp in Benin before arriving in Mill River with his older sister and brother. His mother and a number of his older siblings remained in Africa.

Therese, age 14, was the most recent immigrant in the study, having arrived in the United States from the Dominican Republic 7 months before the study began. Her parents came looking for a "better life" with better job opportunities for themselves and opportunities to attend college for their children. Both of her parents had attended college in the Dominican Republic.

Vildana, age 17, was a refugee from Bosnia. She had arrived in the United States following the Bosnian conflict in the 1990s. She had completed 8 years of schooling in her home country before coming to the United States in 9th grade. She had studied German extensively in Bosnia, but not English.

Paul, age 15, came to the United States from El Salvador with his parents and younger brother. He had been in Mill River for 2 years at the time of this study. In El Salvador he had attended a private religious school, where he did well academically. Paul had a high level of academic literacy in his host language of Spanish. After school he pursued his Eagle Scout badge. He hoped to attend a well-known U.S. university.

Throughout the rest of the book, you will find Meet-the-Students interchapters that provide more vivid portraits of these individuals, highlighting the diversity of their perspectives, goals, educational backgrounds, and immigrant experiences. These interchapters serve as a backdrop to the chapters, which describe students' individual experiences as academic writers and their experiences in the English Language Arts classroom and as writers. In the following pages, we'll take a closer look at what it means for these students to write in their second language and what it means for us as their teachers to create writing classes that broaden our sense of the possibilities when it comes to these student writers.

NOTE

1. In some instances, I have quoted work from authors who use the terms *ESL* or *ESOL* to describe their research. I have chosen to quote those pieces directly and not to change the terms originally used by the authors.

ADDITIONAL RESOURCES

In order to learn more about the ELL students in your district and state, I recommend the U.S. Census Bureau's useful Factfinder application, which provides information about the language communities that surround our schools: http://factfinder.census.gov/home/saff/main.html?_lang=en

In addition, the following books and online publications offer powerful insights into the experiences of ELL writers in our schools and communities:

National Commission on Writing. (2009). *Words have no borders: Student voices on immigration, language and culture.* Retrieved from http://professionals.collegeboard.com/profdownload/words-have-no-borders-2009-cb-writing-comm.pdf

Suárez-Orozco, C., Suárez-Orozco, M., & Todorova, I. (2008). *Learning a new land: Immigrant students in American society.* Cambridge, MA: Harvard University Press.

Valdés, G. (2001). *Learning and not learning English: Latino students in American schools.* New York, NY: Teachers College Press.

Common Terms and Acronyms

In the fields of second language acquisition and English as a Second Language, acronyms and labels abound. Here, I highlight some of the key terms and programs that are often used in the research.

Terms for Students and/or Programs

CLD: Culturally and Linguistically Diverse
EIL: English as an International Language
EL: English Learner
ELL: English Language Learner
ESL : English as a Second Language
L1: First language
L2: Second language

Emergent Bilingual/Bilingual/Multilingual Research Fields

L2 Writing/SLW: Second Language Writing
SLA: Second Language Acquisition
TEFL: Teaching English as a Foreign Language (often used in international educational settings)
TESOL: Teaching English to Speakers of Other Languages

Programs of Instruction

- **Mainstream classes** are regular content-based classrooms, where English learners learn alongside their native-English-speaking peers.
- **Push-in ESL programs** are programs in which English learners are placed in mainstream classrooms with in-class tutorial support. Often, ESL teachers/tutors accompany students into the classroom and offer support to the students in meeting the mainstream teacher's content objectives and completing assignments.

- *Pull-out ESL programs,* according to Peregoy and Boyle (2008), are programs where "English learners receive the majority of their instruction in regular classrooms, alongside their monolingual English-speaking peers. However, they are 'pulled out' of the classroom on a regular basis to receive additional help from an ESL teacher or aide" (p. 24).
- In *magnet ESL programs,* "English learners are taught all subject matter using English as the language of instruction in a class taught by a teacher with special knowledge of second language development. The majority of students in such classes are non-native English speakers with various levels of English language proficiency" (Peregoy & Boyle, 2008, p. 24).
- *Sheltered instruction,* which often can be a component of magnet and mainstream classrooms, includes "those programs in which students are taught subject matter entirely in English. Subject matter instruction is organized to promote second language acquisition, while teaching cognitively demanding, grade-level-appropriate material. Special teaching techniques are used to help students understand English instruction even though they are still limited in English language proficiency" (Peregoy & Boyle, 2008, p. 24).
- In addition, there are a number of *bilingual program* models are available in some schools. One such model is a *two-way bilingual program,* or *dual immersion program,* that brings together monolingual English-speaking students with language minority children from a single language background. Classroom instruction is provided in both English and the minority language, either alternating days or alternating class periods. In this model, both native English speakers and speakers of another language can acquire academic proficiency in a second language, while simultaneously developing literacy skills in their first language. One of the goals of this model is to prepare all students to become proficient in at least two languages and to see bilingualism as an important academic and professional skill that has benefits in a global society and economy. Two-way bilingual classes may be taught by a single teacher who is proficient in both languages or by two teachers, one of whom is bilingual.

Second Language Writing

Puzzles
by Myrna Nieves

I do not know
why I am writing in English
a second language
a wave where spaces open into a void
and you just need
to jump off a cliff

A language where approximate sounds
suggest what I would like to say
A language with blanks
—like in a test—
which my memory will remember
sometime in the future.

—from Ogulnick (2000), *Language Crossings:
Negotiating the Self in a Multicultural World*, p. 11

WHY WRITING MATTERS

Most English teachers acknowledge that teaching students to write well is a high priority. Writing, after all, is a means of self-expression, creativity, and a way to tell a story or explain our thinking. Even beyond the classroom, texts surround us—from novels, short stories, and poetry to textbooks, newspapers, blogs, emails, business letters, proposals, and reports. For today's students, participating in the 21st century means writing and engaging critically with texts in multiple formats and contexts.

In some ways, writing well has always been a language skill that has benefited students in their academic pursuits and in their workplacesand community lives after they've completed their schooling. But these days, technology and the ways in which we communicate (i.e., computer-mediated technology, email, social networks, file sharing across various regions, collaborative workplace initiatives, and more) have raised the importance of writing to a communicative necessity. The National Commission on Writing's (2004) survey of major American corporations revealed that, according to industry leaders, "people who cannot write and communicate clearly will not be hired and are unlikely to last long enough to be considered for promotion" (p. 3). Beyond the workplace and in our communities, the ability to produce texts is intrinsically linked to our ability to be full and participatory citizens in our democracy (Alsup, Emig, Pradl, Tremmel, & Yagelski, 2006). Writing well in English is a threshold skill, necessary for success in the classroom, in the community, and beyond (National Commission on Writing, 2003).

This increased importance of writing mirrors an increasing focus on standardized testing in our schools and academic settings. In most states across the country, mandated assessment testing includes writing as a component. For example, the Massachusetts Comprehensive Assessment System (MCAS) exemplifies the kind of high-stakes, state-mandated testing that requires students to demonstrate their academic writing skills. At many colleges, writing exams and assessments are gateways to upper-level courses, majors, and even graduation. The same is true of many secondary schools, where tracking and written exams are becoming the norm, and "jumping the academic tracks" often requires a demonstration of academic writing skills. For many ELL students, writing remains the most difficult area of the English language to gain confidence in; they may have had limited practice or felt unsuccessful in English writing. These negative experiences can limit other academic opportunities, discouraging them from taking part in broader academic programs in high school and creating obstacles to their pursuit of higher education.

The high-stakes nature of writing has real and immediate consequences for those 5.5 million English language learners in our schools. Writing can open doors for these students, or close them.

THE CHALLENGE OF WRITING IN A SECOND LANGUAGE

Flashback to your years in Spanish or French class, when you moved from fill-in-the-blank or single-sentence responses to your teacher's request for you to write a two-page opinion or narrative in that language. Now imagine writing that two-page paper on mitosis or the causes of the Civil War, and you will have a sense of the challenge that multilingual writers face.

My own experiences with academic writing in my second language came in college, when I spent a year abroad studying at a German university. By all accounts, I should have been well qualified for the writing that would have been asked of me. I had studied German for 3 years, had spoken the language at home with my immigrant parents since I was born, and had completed coursework in German novels and literary criticism. I wrote letters on the latest family events, thank-you notes, and holiday cards often to my German relatives and cousins. At my U.S. university, I had written 2- to 3-page compositions on interviews with my classmates or some aspect of German culture in my German courses. I received high marks on all of these; I felt ready to engage in the German academic world.

In the spring of my study abroad program, I took a literature course on Islamic culture and history. The course, conducted entirely in German and filled with students from around the world, was fascinating and enlightening. The readings were difficult and time-consuming, but doable. The lectures were wonderful. The entire course grade depended on a single 10- to 15-page paper at the end of the semester to be written entirely in German. This academic task shook all of my confidence as a student in ways that I could never have anticipated. I sat in my attic apartment for weeks on end, laptop open and blank pages scrolled out in front of me. The subject matter was not easy, and although I knew what I wanted to write about, somehow I could not find the words. All the sophistication and nuance that I could muster in my English language was lost when it came to my German writing. As a literature major, I knew how to write these kinds of papers. I knew the arguments that I wanted to make and I knew the word choices that I wanted to use, but all in English. In German, I fell silent. I sat with a paper and pencil, trying to brainstorm and draft in German—one painstaking paragraph at a time, losing sight of my larger goals of argument. Then, as the piles of crumpled paper accumulated in a metal wastebasket by my table, I switched to English, trying to draw upon what I knew, reasoning that I could just translate it all later. But the sophistication in my native language never made it to the German version. My arguments and observations were reduced in all sorts of ways. All sense of my voice, my self, my confidence in my thinking, and my analysis of my topic drained away from me. As I concentrated on the higher-order issues of content, trying to come up with ten pages of cohesive sentences to make my points, all that I knew about German grammar, word order, and even spelling seemed to slip to the back of my mind. I squeaked out ten pages of the most generic, banal paper, riddled with basic errors—ten pages of simple description and simple comparison. I worked on it for weeks, trying to bring the paper to some semblance of what I knew I was capable of in English. By term's end, I handed in the paper to my professor, tired and defeated, frustrated that he would think I had gained so little from his class and his lectures. I got a C- for my work.

Years later, I would overhear my ELL students telling similar stories of frustration and defeat, as they tried to show their knowledge and thinking skills in their English compositions.

BICS, CALPS, AND ACADEMIC ENGLISH

Research on second language writing tells us that writing in a second language is often the most difficult communication skill for second language users to master. Jim Cummins (2001) and other second language specialists distinguish between basic interpersonal communicative skills (BICS) and cognitive academic language proficiency skills (CALPS). BICS are those language skills that we often think of as playground language or cafeteria talk. They are often developed in a year or 2, and they are the first language skills developed by most ELLs. Students who master BICS can give the impression that they are far more prepared and fluent in the English language than they actually are, particularly when it comes to school assignments or academic language tasks. CALPS are the academic language skills that students need in order to succeed in the school setting. Students can take 7–10 years to develop mastery in these areas of English. CALPS include skills such as reading grade-level textbooks in the subject areas, participating in class discussions, synthesizing and analyzing readings, using academic vocabulary, writing in a variety of genres, taking written exams, and more. Often these higher-level competencies are called "academic English," which refers to the scholastic variety of English that we use in schools and the awareness that we are using it (Dutro & Moran, 2003). In recent years, respected researchers like Guadalupe Valdés (2004) have complicated our definition of CALPS by noting that "academic language" is not a singular, monolithic term. As teachers, we are influenced by the academic circles and intellectual practices that are part of our field and our training. So, ESL teachers may have one definition of academic language that includes certain words, phrases, and intellectual activities, and science teachers may have another set of academic language and practices in mind when they use the term. Still, when we hear the term, many scholars tend to share a definition similar to the one put forth by Dutro and Moran (2003). They define "academic language" as

> the language of texts, of academic discussion, and of formal writing. Academic-language proficiency requires students to use linguistic skills to interpret and infer meaning from oral and written language, discern precise meaning and information from text, relate ideas and information, recognize the conventions of various genres, and enlist a variety of linguistic strategies on behalf of a wide range of communicative purposes. (pp. 230–231)

For students, becoming fluent in academic language can be difficult. This type of fluency is about mastering a meta-cognitive awareness of how we use language, the ability to discuss that awareness, and the capability to recognize the skills and steps that we use to complete academic tasks. In the classroom, students demonstrate these skills when we ask them to analyze and/or summarize readings, interpret and extract information from graphs and charts, or evaluate written opinions for persuasive arguments (Dutro & Moran, 2003; Fillmore & Snow, 2000; Scarcella, 1990; Scarcella & Rumberger, 2000). Some students come to know these academic language tasks implicitly through years of schooling, but many students, including ELLs, are unaware of how to demonstrate their knowledge in academic language and do not have a strong understanding of the metacognitive academic vocabulary that surrounds their school assignments.

For example, the end-of-the-chapter questions in a language arts textbook ask students to summarize, analyze, and synthesize their understanding of Harper Lee's *To Kill a Mockingbird*. Some students will be familiar with the term *summarize*, but *analyze* leaves them puzzled. The term *synthesize* raises the stakes even higher. Students might ask what the difference is between *analyze* and *synthesize*. How do I know when I am completing one and not the other? For ELL students, their unfamiliarity with academic English terms can be compounded by a lack of background knowledge. Students may know very little about the historical and cultural contexts of certain books, themes, or references. Many ELL writers will assume that they are the only ones in the classroom who don't understand or have questions about these historical or cultural contexts, and as a result, they may be hesitant to ask questions.

Cognitive overload, that overwhelming feeling of processing too much information at once, can also make academic writing tasks seem more difficult. For English language learners, the multiple levels of cognitive processing that need to occur simultaneously in an assignment like the one above can leave students unsure of where to begin, forgetful of the skills they may have mastered in the past, and unable to fully process (or complete) the assignment at hand. In my own research with adolescent writers, one student, Therese, described this phenomenon, noting in interviews that when she experienced difficulty in writing English, she became worried, overwhelmed, and simply "stopped" putting her words on paper. Research-based evidence from the field of second language writing reveals she is not alone. In fact, there are many distinctive processes and challenges that second language writers experience. In the next section, I'll explore these "knowns" that have been documented in the research on L2 writers.

"THE KNOWNS"

Second language writers often come from contexts in which writing is shaped by linguistic and cultural features different from their native-English speaking (NES) peers. Beliefs related to individuality versus collectivity, ownership of text and ideas, student versus teacher roles, revision, structure, the meaning of different rhetorical moves, writer and reader responsibility, and the roles of research and inquiry all impact how student writers shape their texts.

—CCCC Statement on Second Language Writing and Writers, November 2009

In the past decade, research and discussion on second language writing has flourished, particularly at the college level. Evidence-based recommendations on instructional practices, teacher training, and writing assessments, like those noted in the Conference on College Composition and Communication (CCCC) on second language writers provide one starting point for learning about working with L2 writers at the secondary level. Research from scholars in the field provides another. My goal in the pages ahead is to summarize some of the major findings and understandings from the field of second language writing in order to establish a baseline for understanding the needs of ELL writers in our classrooms.

To begin, let's consider some of the similarities between native English writers and non-native English writers. Research tells us that both types of writers set goals for their writing tasks and create a plan to meet those goals. We also know that, whether English is their first language or not, many students struggle to become proficient writers. We know that all writers tend to rely on strategies that have worked in the past. For ELL writers, these can include strategies that were used when writing in their first language. Many student writers have not had much practice with a variety of writing situations, academic or otherwise. These inexperienced writers tend to rely on a "what's next" approach, looking only at the next word, the next sentence, or the next paragraph, with little thought to the larger plan for their piece of writing. They often find it difficult to cognitively "hold on" to these larger plans while attending to the immediate writing at hand. Cognitive overload can also be an issue here. When inexperienced writers encounter a new genre, larger planning issues, or a new topic, these challenges compete with lower-order concerns such as sentence structures, grammar precision, and spelling. Often, these challenges produce writing that seems less accomplished and less effective to readers and teachers.

But despite these similarities, I want to stress that there are definitive differences between English language learners and their native-English-speaking peers when it comes to their approaches and experiences with writing in English. Quite simply, writing in a second language is unique. In his landmark overview of L2 writing research, Tony Silva (1993) maintained that all writing teachers should have an understanding "of how and to what extent [L2 writing] differs from L1 writing" (p. 191). He noted that such differences need to be acknowledged and considered if we are to teach L2 writers effectively and fairly (p. 203). To help teachers begin to understand the nature of L2 writing, Silva identified the following characteristics as unique to L2 writers' texts and their composing processes:

Planning

- Second language writers tend to do less planning, both in the global sense (the large view of the piece) and in the local sense (at the sentence level).
- Second language writers tend to do less goal-setting when writing; they may have a difficult time both articulating their goals for a particular composition and achieving these goals in their writing.

Generating Material/Invention

- Second language writers devote more time to simply generating material, which is a more difficult and time-consuming process. They take more time to decide on a topic and to generate language with which to write about it, and many of their ideas do not actually make it onto the written page. The result is that they may run out of time and energy to "translate" (literally or figuratively) their ideas onto the page.
- Transcribing text (the physical act of writing text down) is more labor-intensive and less fluent for L2 writers. They are more concerned about wording and have more difficulty with vocabulary. They tend to stop and start more as they compose. As a result, they generally write at slower pace than their native-English-speaking peers. In classroom writing situations, this characteristic often means that the texts of second language students are shorter and their ideas appear less developed than those of their native-English-speaking peers. Their ideas and intentions may, in actuality, be more sophisticated than what is visible on the written page.

Written Page

- L2 writers tend to use shorter and vaguer words in their texts. Their texts may show less variety and sophistication in vocabulary, syntax, and sentence structures in comparison to native English speakers.

- L2 writers tend to write shorter compositions, either due to the slower pace of composing or because they write with a sense of caution, fearing that too much writing leaves room for them to make too many errors.
- L2 writers tend to make more errors overall than their native-English-speaking peers. These errors can be with syntax, verb choices and tenses, or articles and nouns.

Revision and Review

- L2 writers tend to review their texts less, rereading and reflecting less on their writing. Often, time plays an issue here. With so much time needed to generate and simply compose the initial material, L2 writers often have less time for rereading and then setting goals for revision. Time is a factor that becomes evident in other areas of revision and review as well.
- Many second language writers, particularly those with limited writing experience, revise less than native English writers. They may be unsure about how to go about revision, have little practice with concrete revision strategies, and be hesitant to "mess with" a text that was labor-intensive to create. They may be unsure how to prioritize and set goals for their revision. Often, they focus more on grammar, mechanics, and spelling than on expansion, the addition of details, or addressing a specific audience.

The Role of Culture

Often, our expectations of writing are culturally driven and heavily influenced by our culture's values and traditions. Robert Kaplan, a linguist, first noted what is called contrastive rhetoric (see The Study of Contrastive Rhetoric textbox, following this list on page 25, for more details).

- For students from other rhetorical traditions, the ways in which North Americans look for writers to make their arguments, tell a story, or reveal their opinion may seem foreign. More important, L2 writers may write in ways that reveal their own rhetorical traditions, which may not fit the expectations of North American readers. There is often a tendency for teachers to see these choices as "wrong" or ill-chosen, rather than as a reflection of cross-cultural differences.
- L2 writers may be unfamiliar with concerns about plagiarism or mystified by the importance we place on citing sources and acknowledging the "ownership" of ideas and texts. In many ways, the principles behind citation practices are uniquely American, driven by a national

cultural identity that places great emphasis on the individual, on ownership, and on new ideas (Currie, 1998). Even if L2 writers learn the formal structures of MLA or APA citation styles, they may have difficulty understanding their importance without first understanding the cultural pieces that are behind those practices and rules.

- Some second language students who are more recent arrivals to the United States may be unfamiliar with references to popular culture. For example, a writing assignment that asks students to comment on the Late Night battles between David Letterman, Jay Leno, and Conan O'Brian may resonate with some students, but others will be unfamiliar with the references and find it difficult to find a way into the topic.

- Culture and past experiences can also play a role in a student's ability to tackle a writing topic. Some students may come from cultures and traditions where discussing personal topics is unsettling and impolite. Some personal essay topics may prove difficult for students, like Wisdom, who lost family members to the political strife in his home country. Others may welcome the opportunity to write about their own lives. In argumentative or persuasive writing, students may come from traditions where critiquing or forming opinions about the work of a published author or teacher is discouraged as disrespectful. Still others may come from traditions where the students' classroom writing is penalized for reaching beyond the classroom content.

CONTEMPORARY RESEARCH ON L2 WRITERS IN SECONDARY SCHOOLS

Many of the "knowns" that I have summarized above come from L2 writing specialists working with international and resident English language writers in colleges and universities. Research on adolescent L2 writers has remained limited (Leki, Silva, & Cumming, 2008) until fairly recently. Historically, research on L2 writers in K–12 schools focused on the emergent literacy practices of children in the early years of elementary school. The work of Carol Edelsky (1986) and Sarah Hudelson (1989), along with Guadalupe Valdés (1999, 2001), has provided great insights into the practices of these younger bilinguals. On the other end of the spectrum, scholars like Linda Harklau (2000), Mark Roberge (2009), and Gwen Gray Schwartz (2004) have considered the transitions of multilingual writers as they move from high school into their first year of college. But research on adolescent L2 students while they are in middle and high school settings has historically been more limited. The studies we have seen, and those that are emerging, confirm that many of the writing characteristics and challenges, discussed above as "knowns," are also evident in adolescent ELL writers.

The Study of Contrastive Rhetoric

The theory of contrastive rhetoric is a new concept for many English teachers. Contrastive rhetoric (CR) has its roots in a landmark article published over 40 years ago by linguist Robert Kaplan (1966). Kaplan's landmark article, "Cultural Thought Patterns in Inter-cultural Education," posited that rhetorical patterns in the writing samples of students and professional writers were culturally influenced. Kaplan examined 600 texts written by non-native English speakers, and he generalized (complete with "doodles") that Romantic language speakers tended to use more tangents and digressions in their writing, that Asian writers tended to circle their topics and be more implicit in their writing, and that English speakers were more linear and direct. Kaplan's initial work has not been without criticism. Those infamous doodles visually characterized entire cultures of writers into simplistic lines and sketches that overlooked intercountry regional differences and the ways that cultures can change over time (Severino, 1993; Zhang, 1997). In addition, the doodles were widely circulated, often without an understanding of the limitations of the study and Kaplan's own concerns about the limited, exploratory nature of the piece.

Today, second language writing specialists do agree that culture can influence writing, rhetorical approaches, reader expectations, and genre (Connor, 2003; Hinds, 1987). Ulla Connor (1996) argues that "language and writing are cultural phenomena" and "each language has rhetorical conventions unique to it" (p. 5). In the United States, the genres that we teach—from personal narrative to thesis-driven arguments to op/ed pieces—have conventions and expectations that are influenced by our North American culture, values, and history. When we encounter ESL student writing that does not seem to follow these cultural norms or genre expectations, we may judge these student essays as being off-putting or lacking clarity. We often fail to see the students' work through the lens of alternative rhetorical strategies, or even worse, we may jump to conclusions that the students' thinking is unclear. Knowledge of contrastive rhetoric can help teachers see some of their concerns with their L2 students' writing in light of cultural and rhetorical traditions that may be very different from the ones taught in U.S. classrooms.

However, an overzealous belief in contrastive rhetoric can lead teachers to make assumptions about their student writers, viewing these students as simple products of their national culture and national education. As Matsuda (1997) argued, "No two people from similar backgrounds share exactly the same experience" (p. 53). There are additional influences on a writer besides culture—including educational background, out-of-school literacies, online literacies, socioeconomic status, writer's personal identities, and other personal experiences (Kubota & Lehner, 2004; Matsuda, 1997). Matsuda's dynamic model of L2 writing (see Figure 2.1) offers a productive way for ELA and ELL teachers to think about how culture impacts rhetorical styles, writing strategies, and teacher response.

In Matsuda's dynamic model, a person's written text becomes the meeting point between reader and writer. Matsuda emphasizes that ideally the writer (student) and the reader (teacher) enter a "bidirectional exchange" in which the teacher also becomes aware of how her culture, language, and education are influencing her reading of an L2 writer's text. This model acknowledges the range of experiences that can influence an L2 student's writing. Matsuda (1997) explains this complexity further by offering the following example of a Japanese student writing a letter to an editor:

> Her background as a writer is much more than growing up in Japanese culture, speaking the Japanese language, or being educated in a Japanese school system. Her decisions as a writer may perhaps be influenced by, for example, her experience as an editor of a high-school newspaper in Japan. Her religious view may also affect how she reacts to the particular issue. She may try to present herself more indirectly if the editor she is criticizing lives in the same residence hall as she. Furthermore, she may approach the task of writing with more confidence if she has some prior experience in writing argumentative letters for the same newspaper. (p. 55)

In the end, research from this subfield of contrastive rhetoric continues to broaden our understanding of how writing and writing instruction takes place in other parts of the world. For teachers, it is valuable to learn that the expectations we have of certain genres are not universal. As Jennifer, one of my student teachers, recently wrote:

> It is extremely valuable for individual teachers to be able to recognize in their students' writing rhetorical patterns other than those valued in the American educational system and to be able to think in terms of differences rather than errors or inexperience. Introducing the principles of contrastive rhetoric can broaden teachers' perspectives on writing and make them more flexible, more adaptable, more perceptive, maybe even more compassionate.

FIGURE 2.1. A Modified Version of Matsuda's Dynamic Model of Contrastive Rhetoric

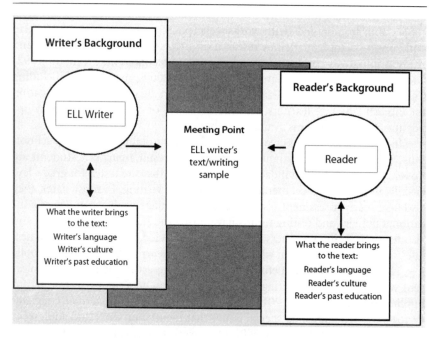

But new complexities and factors also impact the experiences of adolescent L2 writers at the secondary level (Ortmeier-Hooper & Enright, 2011). As Leki, Silva, and Cumming (2008) have argued: "Of all the contexts in which L2 writing occurs, high school is probably the most fraught and the most complex" (p. 17). In middle and high schools, students are impacted by pressures from peer groups, families, media, and their own growing sense of independence. There is also a wider array of students and experiences in these settings. Students may have less choice about their trajectories and the kinds of classes available to them (Ortmeier-Hooper & Enright, 2011). Similarly, secondary school teachers may find their classroom practices influenced by ever-changing educational policies and politics at the local, state, and national levels.

Early research in the 1990s suggested that ELL writers in secondary schools often made only small gains in their writing skills throughout secondary school (Tarone et al., 1993). Seminal research by Linda Harklau (1994a, 1994b) and Danling Fu (1995) found that ELL students did very little writing in their mainstream classrooms. Harklau (1994a) documented that common writing activities for ELL students "were limited to a single word or phrase, in the format of fill-in-the-blank, multiple choice, and short answer exercises" (p. 255). But she also found that students could sometimes find outposts of rich writing experiences, like an ESL classroom in her study that was led by a teacher trained in the National Writing Project. Fu's (1995) ethnographic study of Laotian ESL adolescents explored how students were tracked into low-level classes and "bombarded" with worksheets (p. 205). These studies by Harklau and Fu were complemented by research on successful bilingual programs and reading initiatives conducted by scholars like Freeman and Freeman (1992) and Au (1993). But by the late 1990s and early 2000s, many states, including California, Arizona, and Massachusetts, largely eradicated bilingual education for English language learners, limiting the kinds of multilingual literacy opportunities and programs available to them.

In the 2000s, NCLB increased the level of accountability that K–12 schools must assume for English language learners. As a result, many ELL students are no longer exempt from standardized testing, and they are tested for grade-level skills in math, science, literature, reading, and writing. In most states, they also take yearly assessment tests for English language proficiency. These educational policies and testing trends have raised the stakes for ELL writers and also for their writing teachers, but they have also led researchers to raise new questions about the ways in which ELL students learn to write in our schools.

This renewed, and hopefully sustainable, interest in the needs of adolescent writers among L2 writing researchers and teachers can be seen in recent publications. In 2002 and 2011, respectively, the *Journal of Second Language Writing* (*JSLW*) published special issues that focused on early and adolescent L2 writing (Matsuda & DePew, 2002; Ortmeier-Hooper & Enright, 2011). Ortmeier-Hooper and Enright (2011) pointed to a series of factors—from adolescence to public educational policies—that made the experiences of school-age L2 writers distinct from those of college-age L2 writers. Secondary school issues, from curriculum mandates, testing, local- and state-level educational policy decisions, tracking, peer interactions, and school climate, play an important role in how adolescent authors learn to write. Contemporary research also reflects a growing awareness and concern about how these writers fare over the duration of their school careers and the kinds of in-school trajectories that are available to them. Studies like Enright and Gilliland's (2011) examination of the New Mainstream and the impact of NCLB demonstrate a profound understanding that the writing and writing experiences of L2 writers in U.S. high school settings cannot be understood in isolation from educational policies, standards and assessment, issues of access to advanced coursework, and academic achievement.

Recent research has revealed a great deal more about adolescent students' writing experiences and their writing processes. For example, Kibler (2011) illustrated how ELL students used their first language to negotiate interactions with their monolingual teachers. She found that the strategic use of the first language encouraged multilingual writers to assert a sense of their expertise and ownership when it came to their in-school literacy tasks. At the middle school level, Reynolds (2005) explored how middle school ELL writers had difficulties in developing writing fluency and meta-cognitive understandings of writing, often because they had limited practice with a variety of genres. In another study, Enright (2006b) followed the experiences of Latino ELL high school students and their school's new emphasis on senior writing projects. She found that the standardization of writing instruction, originally developed to aid students in these projects, "presented both opportunities and constraints" for students (p. 41). Enright documented how teachers advocating for ELL writers sometimes unintentionally lowered expectations and narrowed definitions of writing achievement.

Some of the most interesting research on adolescent ELL writers has begun to look at the writing and literacy experiences outside of school, revealing a breadth of experiences. Rubinstein-Ávila (2004), for example, shares the case study of Miguel, whose role as a language broker for his family led to a profound awareness of how writing is used in legal situations, insurance paperwork, and rental contracts. Digital literacies, online writing, and transnational interactions have also been embraced as a point of study for writing researchers (Black, 2005; Lam, 2000). For example, Youngjoo Yi (2007, 2008, 2010a, 2010b) has extensively documented the impact of Korean American immigrant students' use of online literacies, through social networking sites and blogs. Yi (2010b) questions the traditional ways in which we have posited out-of-school writing practices in opposition to academic literacy. Her research findings suggest that ELL writers' out-of-school literacy experiences can reverberate and provide important stepping-stones to their in-school writing practices.

No doubt, the research on adolescent L2 writing and writers will continue to grow in the coming years. But current studies suggest that the writing experiences and practices of our adolescent L2 students are always socially imbued. Educational policies, standards and assessment, home literacies, students' sense of identity, teacher training, issues of access to advanced coursework, and expectations of academic achievement all impact what occurs between the student writer, the teacher, and the written page.

CONCLUSION

This chapter has been about the "knowns" of L2 writing. We know that writing in a second language is unique, in both its process and its challenges. L2 (or ELL) writers have distinctive needs and characteristics in their approaches to writing. These differences need to be acknowledged and understood in our work as writing teachers, because they require us to reflect upon and even reconsider our daily work as teachers and the kinds of pedagogy that we use in our writing classrooms.

In my summary of the research, you may have noticed that many studies described L2 writers in comparison to their monolingual native-English-speaking peers. Historically, L2 writing specialists and English writing teachers have spoken about L2 writers always using L1 writers as the frame of reference. To some extent, these kinds of comparisons seem natural, even acceptable. In many of our classrooms, we often view and respond to the written work of our English language learners alongside the written work of their native-English-speaking peers. We wonder about the differences we see in the texts; we make comparisons. But as I begin to share the stories of the student writers featured in this book, I hope to complicate those kinds of comparisons. A. Suresh Canagarajah (2002), a leading figure in ESL and writing scholarship, has commented:

> We shouldn't be surprised that L2 students fall short when L1 writing is treated the norm or point of reference. . . . How would our interpretations differ if we understood the composing strategies of ESOL students in terms of their own cultural frames and literacy practices? (p. 217)

In the rest of this book, I'll take up Canagarajah's question and his implicit challenge for us to complicate our notions of L2 writers "falling short." The stories and teaching strategies that follow illustrate how their stories further explore these "knowns," but they also raise new questions about the challenges that L2 writers face.

ADDITIONAL RESOURCES

The CCCC Statement on Second Language Writing and Writers is a useful policy statement for all writing teachers. It contains information on best practices, provides teachers with a tool to advocate for changes in their schools, and includes an updated bibliography. The statement is available at http://www.ncte.org/cccc/resources/positions/secondlangwriting.

Research and recent scholarship on second language writers and writing is regularly published in the *Journal of Second Language Writing*. For more information, go to http://www.jslw.org.

Both TESOL and the National Writing Project have websites with useful information on teaching writing to English language learners.

TESOL's site: http://secondlanguagewriting.com/slwis

NWP's site: http://www.nwp.org/cs/public/print/resource_topic/english_language_learners

There are also a number of recent books on second language writing that provide more insights into the ongoing research in this field:

Leki, I., Cumming, A., & Silva, T. (2008). *A synthesis of research on second language writing in English*. New York, NY: Routledge.

Matsuda, P. K., Cox, M., Jordan, J., & Ortmeier-Hooper, C. (Eds.). (2006). *Second-language writing in the composition classroom: A critical sourcebook*. Boston, MA: Bedford/St. Martin's.

Meet Ken-zhi

He plays like an angel. It was amazing. Like a private concert. I've never seen a student like him with so much talent.

—Teacher at Ken-zhi's high school

In one of my initial observations of Mill River North High School, I ran into one of the ELL teachers, who told me of the day when Ken-zhi took out his flute and practiced in the empty hallways outside her classroom. Teachers began to pour out of empty classrooms, drawn to the music that floated up and down, bouncing off the hallway walls. She gushed in her praise; she was not alone. During the fall of Ken-zhi's freshman year in high school, the music teacher took Ken-zhi and some of his peers to a local university for a review of their individual talents by the university's music faculty. The professors were astounded by Ken-zhi's performance, noting that he had exceeded the talents of many of their own university-level music students. They were even more amazed that he was self-taught. In addition to the flute, he also played piano. In the summers, he played with local quartets and chamber music groups.

Ken-zhi arrived from Taiwan during 8th grade. Since his arrival in the United States, his family has been very transient, moving three times, within the city and along its outer limits, during the course of this study. Both of his parents worked at a local restaurant, often late into the evenings, leaving Ken-zhi and his sister on their own. His mother, a secretary in Taiwan, could not find a similar job in the United States because she did not speak English very well. The restaurant job paid the rent, and the family's goal was to provide a good education for Ken-zhi and his sister. The family remained in contact, always through cell phones. After school, Ken-zhi usually headed home to work on homework. He was also an avid computer user and spent many afternoons emailing and IM-ing with his friends from Mill River and Taiwan.

Ken-zhi often seemed older than his years. At almost 16 years old, Ken-zhi was the oldest of the five participants. His younger sister told me that he was "too serious," and that he always told her that she needed to worry more about the future. Ken-zhi was greatly concerned about getting into college and "succeeding in America," as he explained. He worked diligently in school, played in various music ensembles, and had dreams of attending Juilliard in New York City.

In terms of the high school social scene, though, Ken-zhi seemed very young. He was eager to please and watched his peers at every turn, trying to take note of what was cool and what was uncool. He was very aware of who belonged and who didn't and what the various social groups were on the school campus. But Ken-zhi wasn't quite sure how he fit into that puzzle. He loved to chat and gossip, often telling me of the latest school incidents, who got in trouble, along with his concerns about girls and the kids in band. Ken-zhi had a tremendous amount of energy and arrived at each of our interview sessions eager to begin. He took his assignment as a participant and an informant very seriously. He always came with writing, copies of assignments, and a willingness to share. As a writer, Ken-zhi was meticulous. He aimed for perfection in his English, but also in his style.

Meet Therese

> Therese is dropped off at the library by her father. Her hair is pulled back into a tight ponytail, and she is wearing a conservatively styled lavender tank top. She looks a bit worried.
>
> —Field notes, August 2004

When I met Therese, she was the shy girl in the summer bridge program, and I was surprised when she expressed an interest in being a participant in the study. She had moved from the Dominican Republic to the United States only 7 months before the study began. In initial interviews, she was often quiet. She seemed uncomfortable and unsure of what to expect. Often, she would answer my questions with one or two words.

Therese arrived from the Dominican Republic during the winter of 8th grade. Her 8th-grade ELL teacher reported that Therese was a bright, intelligent, curious young lady, beautifully fluent and articulate in her native Spanish. When Therese first arrived in Mill River Middle School, she told her teacher that the "English words hurt her mouth." She had difficulty moving her mouth, jaw, and lips in ways to get the "American sounds" out. It all felt so awkward and stilted.

Therese described herself as a "good student" in her native Dominican Republic. Her parents valued education. Both of them had attended college in the Dominican Republic. Her mother was an architect, and her father was a medical professional. When they arrived in the United States, they had to start over. Her father could not practice medicine in the United States. To support the family, Therese's father, who was also a talented mechanic, had become an assistant manager at a local garage in Mill River. At the time of the study, Therese's mother was still seeking work, but she struggled with English, which made it difficult to find meaningful employment. Therese, for her part, wanted to be a lawyer . . . or an actress. She was still deciding, but she knew that she wanted to go to college in the United States. The promise of a strong college education was the main reason her family had come to the United States. In the Dominican Republic, Therese had studied English only sparingly, during once-a-week classes of basic conversation.

Therese's brother Isaac was 2 years older, and he was a good student. His decisions and his academic success provided an example of what was possible, and he had knowledge of the high school world, peers, and social climates that Therese encountered on a daily basis. Her parents looked to Isaac for insights, and they often positioned him as a role model for Therese and her younger brother. It was through Isaac that Therese became involved in a school-to-work program, a program that gave Therese experience with workplace writing. The program played a strong part in her literacy development and identity roles during her first year of high school.

As time went on, I was struck by the increasing length of Therese's interview responses and her growing confidence. She would talk at length about her experiences as a student and a writer with few interruptions or prompts from me. Sometimes she could step outside herself and see with mature, adult-like eyes the actions of those around her, the realities of the future, and her own actions. Yet she readily admitted that although she could step into that observer role, she lived in her teenage reality, where she made decisions based on the moment, the impulse, her peers, and her own satisfaction. In our talks, she maneuvered between those two perspectives, at one moment speaking with such maturity and insight about her life and her future, and at the next, confessing a crush and a broken curfew. In many ways, her impulses were reflective of the everyday reality of adolescence.

Therese's experiences as an adolescent Latina, in terms of social situations and in the classroom, added dimensions to her experiences in the classroom and in her academic writing. Therese's academic experiences were often more complicated by her social interactions than they were for the male participants in the study. As she became more socially active and began dating, the peer pressures to abandon her academic focus increased and Therese was often conflicted about her decision to stay in school or do well in her classes. Therese was also very proud of her Latina heritage and her heritage language. As we walked and talked on occasions, she would elegantly switch back and forth between Spanish and English, code-switching with ease in her conversation. Sometimes, teachers expressed frustration when she spoke Spanish in the hallways. Speaking Spanish with her Latina friends made her feel comfortable. On one occasion, she noted that speaking Spanish made her feel like a real person, while speaking English often made her feel isolated and unintelligent, a shadow of herself.

CHAPTER 3

Stumbling Blocks—What We See
Identity, Confidence, and Writing Practice

When the student writers in my study faced an academic writing task, there were often moments when they struggled. On the pages, these moments were marked by crossed-out words and incomplete ideas or sentences that simply trailed off. In these textual moments and in our interviews, the students themselves revealed nagging doubts about their competencies in English and as writers. The act of writing in a second language, specifically writing for academic purposes, often reconfirmed (in their eyes) their deficiencies as English users, and the students' self-doubt often reinscribed negative and deficit-centric perceptions of them as "English language learners."

For many of them, being ELL was a label that they found troubling. On one hand, being ELL often created a sense of community between them and other second language students in the school. Their ELL teachers were kind and worked to make the ELL classrooms and corridors welcoming places and safe havens. But the ELL label also marked these students as different from their peers. For Miguel, Therese, Ken-zhi, Paul, and Wisdom, difference seemed too often to be defined as deficit. They sometimes wondered if their high school teachers saw them as the bright, intellectual students they had been in their own countries. As Therese once noted, "I don't have to say that I'm ESL. Because when you say that, people laugh at you. And they think, just because you are an ESL kid, they think you are stupid. And I don't like that." Overwhelmingly, the other students in the study shared Therese's concerns, particularly when it came to the perceptions of their teachers, guidance counselors, and administrators (Ortmeier-Hooper, 2010).

These concerns over their academic abilities and their intellect left them vulnerable to self-doubt, and when they stumbled in their English writing, their frustration, anxiety, and disappointment was tangible. The following "stumbling block" experiences of Ken-zhi and Therese illustrate these moments.

WHAT WE SEE: ERASERS AND INSECURITIES

Ken-zhi engaged in his struggle with English words fully armed. His pocket translator was always at hand. He reported that a dictionary, with pages marked and words circled, sat by his desk at home, ready to be drawn into his battle with writing. A poster in Ken-zhi's upper-level ELL classroom reminded students to "check through to see if you can use any other words—higher-level vocabulary."

It was in achieving that "higher-level vocabulary" that Ken-zhi, like many second language writers, struggled. His meticulous print masked his uncertainty, but his papers showed the wear of erasers rubbing out imperfections in word choice and sentence structure. During the research project, I regularly received copies of Ken-zhi's drafts in progress via email. The drafts were normally accompanied by apologetic emails that were marked by hesitancy, uncertainty, and embarrassment, like this one:

> Hi,
> I finished my paragraph, but it's like . . . I am telling a story, and it's really funny, and it's really bad too, it's like . . . I don't know how to explain, so are you sure you want see my paragraph? Because it's really funny and stupid, looks like I am not writing a paragraph that I suppose to do, looks like I am writing about my life. Get ready to laugh. HA HA HA HA HA

In interviews, Ken-zhi told me that he only let his teachers read his drafts. He was afraid that his friends, particularly native English speakers, would laugh at his writing. He had a fear of being seen as laughable and, in his words, "stupid." Even as he strived to blend in and socialize with his English-speaking peers in the cafeteria and in classroom conversations, he worried that his writing would "out" him and his placement as an ELL.

Ken-zhi's apprehension was coupled by his intense need for perfection in his written work. As I observed Ken-zhi in his upper-level ELL classroom, I was always struck by the prominence of the large, white eraser and mechanical pencil that he placed at the top corner of his desk during the opening minutes of each class. The importance of that eraser to his written work became obvious as he worked on an essay describing the short stories of Edgar Allan Poe. As his teacher looped the classroom, she asked students to pull out the introductory paragraph, which they had written the night before. Surveying his draft, Ken-zhi began furiously assailing his neatly written text with that eraser, removing every trace of his words.

When the teacher stopped at Ken-zhi's desk and asked if he had completed the assignment, he replied, "Yes, but I just erased it." The teacher, confused, asked, "Why?" and Ken-zhi explained, "Because it's bad."

The teacher pulled back from his desk, taken aback by his almost masochistic willingness to erase his work so fully, before sharing it. She told the rest of the class that they would have the class period to work on their next two paragraphs. She then quietly told Ken-zhi that she wanted to see "some of his writing before he [left]" for the day to ensure that he was making progress.

In the hour that followed, I observed Ken-zhi as he wrote. I saw how regularly he paused. He wrote and then he erased, sometimes whole sentences and whole paragraphs, sometimes just a word or two. He reworded the same line or phrase multiple times, each time carefully erasing the previous attempt so that there was no evidence of his earlier attempts. On occasion, he pulled out his translator and looked up a word or two. At one point, he worked on a single sentence—writing, erasing, rewriting, erasing again, writing again—for over 15 minutes. His ELL teacher, witnessing his frustration, stopped by his desk and tried to help him move forward with the assignment by writing a sentence at the top of the page, suggesting that he use it in place of the sentence that was troubling him.

The importance of the eraser in the hands of many second language writers is duly documented in research on second language writing. Fu (2009) has explored the ways in which fears of error and lack of vocabulary can stilt the writing fluency of young ELL writers. Raimes (1985) found that inexperienced college-age L2 writers had difficulty completing individual sentences without hesitation, and they often interrupted their writing to return and reread the writing prompt. More experienced L2 writers had less difficulty with individual sentences, but their sense of fluidity and fluency hit a roadblock as they moved out of one sentence and began to compose the next. The same was true as they moved from one paragraph to the next. Additionally, Raimes described how students often retreated to the safety and security of completed paragraphs, editing those extensively and then limiting the further development of their drafts. Often, they lost many of their original ideas in the process. The lack of development and loss of ideas is frustrating for many second language writers, who notice how little the writing on the page represents the ideas in their minds (Fu, 2009).

WHAT WE MISS: BENEATH THE ERASER

Let's get back to Ken-zhi in that classroom, though—because there is often more than meets the eye in these moments, too. Ken-zhi's frustration was obvious from both the teacher's vantage point and my own. But the how and why for that frustration surprised me.

Often, when we see students like Ken-zhi attack their words with erasers or the "delete" key, we may assume that these are solely acts of uncertainty—concerns over a verb tense or spelling or language usage. We may assume that students are embarrassed or afraid to take risks, as one teacher speculated during this study. Given Ken-zhi's emails and other expressions of doubt in our conversations, I don't doubt that these concerns played a role in his writing experiences. But Ken-zhi's discussion of this episode with the eraser in his English class surprised me; it wasn't about vocabulary, verb tense, or grammar at all. His interludes with the eraser were rhetorical and concerned his audience and purpose.

In the discussion that immediately followed the class, I sat down with Ken-zhi, his paper in hand, and asked about his erasures. We looked over what he had written and rewritten during class time. He told me that he found this writing assignment difficult but he couldn't express what he wanted to say. He explained, frustrated, "In Chinese, it would be easier. I know the words."

But I learned from Ken-zhi that his frustration was not simply about vocabulary. If the problem were the vocabulary, Ken-zhi argued, the translator would have helped him. For Ken-zhi, the difficulty was in capturing in English the emotion that he wanted to express in his writing. For this piece on Edgar Allan Poe, he wanted to make a certain impact on his readers through his words; he was searching for an ending that would echo the terror and fear that Poe's writing evoked. I asked him if it might help to write in Chinese first, to get some of his ideas down on paper. Ken-zhi shook his head adamantly, explaining: "It just doesn't translate. This is really hard. Really hard." In our discussions, Ken-zhi tried to articulate the problem as he saw it. He felt that the conclusion of the essay ended too abruptly. As he said over and over, "It ends too quickly . . . it ends with nothing."

There is often more to ELL writers' texts than meets our eyes. As I thought about that conversation with Ken-zhi, it dawned on me that the "lack of words" that troubled him not only stymied his ability to express his sentiments, but also his ability to be rhetorically savvy. For Ken-zhi, a student with a good sense of his audience and purpose in this piece of writing, the greater sense of frustration came not from a lack of vocabulary, but from an inability to reach his audience rhetorically. As an author, he was striving to engage with his readers with his prose.

The teacher's suggested sentence, scrawled at the top of his page, though grammatically correct, did not convey the impact that he wanted to bring to his writing. He told me that he wanted a "strong ending" and her suggestion did not help him create one. True, it completed the assignment, and in that sense, perhaps, her goal to move him forward with the assignment was met. Ken-zhi wanted to do more—he wanted to work out that ending so that it worked for his readers. On one level, he was stymied by the lack of English words in his repertoire, but Ken-zhi was more concerned that he couldn't find the level of complexity, the kinds of sentence structures, that would articulate his meaning and achieve his desired effect.

Ken-zhi was trying to write as a writer in that moment. He was struggling with words the way we all struggle for words as writers. He didn't want to settle for the teacher's model at the top of the page that would have gotten the job done but didn't let him express his full intention. In many ways, what Ken-zhi needed in those moments with the eraser wasn't a model of the correct sentence structure, but a sounding board, someone to talk to about his writing. He needed to discuss his intention, his plans, and the effect he was trying to create with a fellow writer (or reader). He needed to orally work through his language choices and options, to see how his work on the page could have the desired impact on his reader. But that moment, read against a backdrop of deficiency and Ken-zhi's status as an English learner, was interpreted as a grammar problem, rather than a rhetorical one. The model sentence at the top of page did the job and completed the final paragraph so that it could be handed in and Ken-zhi could move on to the next assignment.

Many secondary writing teachers note that one of the main goals is to help their students reach fluency in their writing (Kittle, 2008; Robb, 2010). We aim to find the writing equivalent of what Michael Smith and Jeff Wilhelm (2002) have described as "flow experiences," in which students are so deeply engaged in a writing activity that they let go of their internal censors and just write. But building such "flow experiences" for second language writers can prove difficult if we don't stop to listen to them as writers. One of the four main principles of "flow," as Smith and Wilhelm (2002) explain it, is having "a sense of competence and control" (pp. 28–30). But what happens when that sense of competence and control feels out of reach for an L2 writer? In many cases, the ELL writers in our schools feel like outsiders to the English language. Even Ken-zhi, who overall was a relatively confident and ambitious student, worried that his writing would be seen as "funny" or "stupid." They may question our investment in their work as writers, asking, "So are you sure you want see my paragraph?" Even more concerning, they may simply shut down and avoid writing in any language, under any circumstance, because they feel they have lost their voice.

THERESE: LOSING HER VOICE IN ENGLISH WRITING

When Therese began school in the United States, she told her 8th-grade teacher that the English words hurt her mouth. Less than a year later, she sat in a mainstream English classroom, writing an essay on "who she is becoming" and it was the lack of English words that halted her voice and her pen. In an interview, Therese explained what hinders her when she writes for her classes: "I saw a mistake and I felt bad. So I stopped."

Research on second language writers tells us that she is not alone. Composing in a second language is often "more constrained," "more difficult," and slow-going (Silva, 1993, pp. 661–668). Therese's pauses and errors could stop her writing outright because they reinforced her concerns about being a capable student and effective communicator in the classroom. Therese's difficulties with an essay assignment from her English class illustrate these struggles and highlight how these challenges frustrate students and chip away at their sense of themselves as critical thinkers and good students.

The essay was assigned for Therese's lower-level English class. The assignment prompt, written in extensive prose and handed out in class, asked students to consider how they were an extension of certain personality traits. The lengthy prompt asked students to think of a personality trait that they would like to have: honesty, courage, discipline, kindness, creativity, and so on. The directions then asked students to write out the name of their proposed trait at the top of a page and then write a poem or paragraph describing that trait. The prompt continued with the following directions: "Now write out a plan for developing this quality in yourself. Be specific. What actions can you take each day?"

The third paragraph of the prompt then asked students to think about a skill they'd like to learn, such as driving a car, playing tennis, singing, or using a computer. It suggested to students that they describe the skill and then picture themselves using the skill, including the following directions: "Picture yourself having mastered the skill. Then draw a picture of yourself using that skill. Describe what it will feel like to reach the goal and the actions you need to take to develop this skill. Make a plan." The written prompt included no further details about the assignment, but in class, Therese's teacher explained that students should use the prompt and its directions to write an essay about "who they were becoming" as young people in the world, what they wished to develop in themselves as they grew older, and how they planned to achieve their goals.

Students would have an opportunity to write a first draft, to workshop and conference with their teacher, and then complete the final draft. Therese's teacher, an experienced writing teacher, explained that the writing process would take some time, and that the final product would be due in about 10 days. The first draft would be due in 2 days.

When Therese showed me the prompt, I asked her to explain what it meant. She noted that it had to do with the future and figuring out who you want to be. According to Therese, many ELL students in her class had not understood the prompt at first, but her English teacher had taken most of the class period to walk them through the assignment, explaining new vocabulary and the expectations of the assignment. The teacher talked about her own personality traits and even shared her own model essay. As Therese noted with approval, the teacher had explained everything: "So we can get it. And she gave examples with herself."

A day later, Therese handed me her first draft of the essay, which she completed during her study hall and gave to her teacher. She decided to write about creativity. In red pen, she had written out an annotated version of the prompt along with her brief responses (see Figure 3.1). After the picture, she had copied more of the prompt down and written: "I think that I can do something created (creative) every day, like draw a picture in my mind and then put it on a paper." This was her draft of her essay. She was mimicking the prompt's language, pointing to her drawing, and using her mind to create pictures. When I asked her about this writing sample, Therese talked at length about her difficulties with the assignment. She was frustrated. The draft that she handed in to her teacher wasn't her best work, and she knew it. I asked her about the prompt, and she said that she thought it was a good one—interesting and engaging. She liked having to think about these kinds of self-reflective questions. But it was hard.

She told me that her English teacher suggested that she draw out some of her ideas in order to get started, to locate some of the vocabulary she might need. Indeed, the prompt itself encouraged that kind of link by suggesting respondents draw a picture of themselves, as a way to generate ideas for their essays. But Therese found the suggestion difficult, because she didn't like to or know how to draw pictures. As she wrote out the draft, she reluctantly attempted to draw her thoughts, combining her drawings with the rest of her written words. But the drawings she did reflected her lack of involvement: a simple stick figure with two thought balloons, one showing a sunset on the horizon and the other, an ice cream cone. They were the only kinds of pictures she knew how to draw and they felt completely disconnected from her intentions as a writer. In some ways, the pictures she drew just made her feel more incompetent. In our interview, Therese explained:

> T: One of the problems I had was I didn't know how to express myself very
>   well . . . because sometimes I want to say something but I didn't find
>   the words.
> C: What did you want to say?
> T: In that question, like drawing pictures. I don't know how to draw the
>   pictures so I draw an ice cream cone.
> C: What does that represent?
> T: I don't know. It like represent like my imagination. Like this huge ice
>   cream cone with chocolate chips on it.

FIGURE 3.1. Therese's First Draft

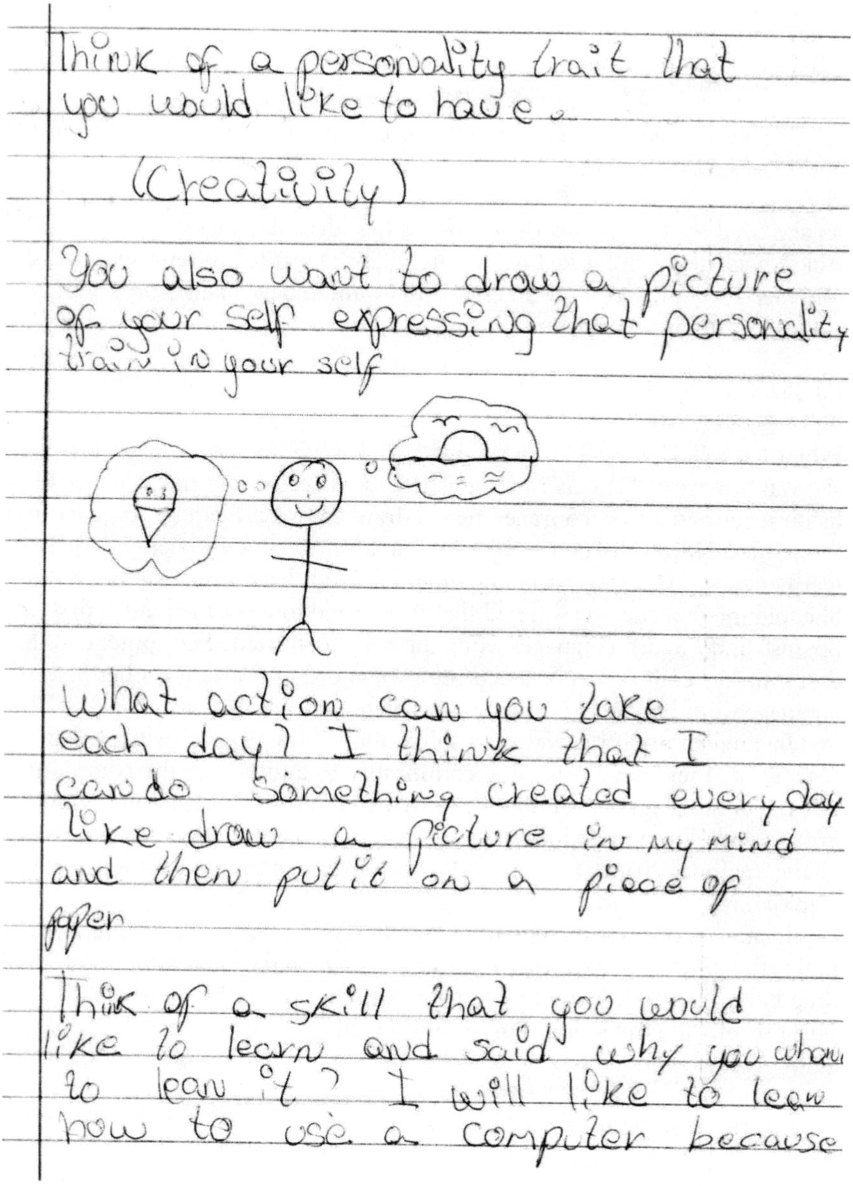

Think of a personality trait that
you would like to have.

(Creativity)

You also want to draw a picture
of your self expressing that personality
trait to your self

What action can you take
each day? I think that I
can do something created every day
like draw a picture in my mind
and then put it on a piece of
paper

Think of a skill that you would
like to learn and said why you whan
to learn it? I will like to learn
how to use a computer because

C: Okay. And then you have a sunset?

T: Uh-huh.

C: So are these things you want to be able to draw?

T: Uh-huh.

C: So do you think you want to be an artist? Is that what you are talking about here [in the writing]?

T: Hmmm. No, not an artist. But like, can make, like some people do stuff so creative. And the only thing that I can draw is the sunset.

As she tried to find the words to discuss her ideas during our interview, she still struggled. When I asked her about what she wanted to represent her, she told me, "I want to like write an essay and I want to have many words on it, like some words that are different."

No Spanish Allowed

When I asked Therese why she didn't try to write her essay in Spanish first, she was adamant: "This is my English class." Therese told me that her English teacher had also encouraged her to draw upon her Spanish language and knowledge. However, Therese rejected that idea. She saw and defined the English Language Arts class as being all about English and English acquisition. She told me that she was worried that if she tried to write in Spanish first, the Spanish and English languages would become "confused." She contended that there was no connection between the two, and that drawing on her Spanish language would not help her to become better at English.

In English teaching, we often think about how people switch linguistic registers as they move from one community to another. In the community, our use of language can shift as we move from our home life to our work life. We can move from more formal language (academic) to more casual language (slang, regional dialect, texting, and so on) multiple times over the course of a given day.

In studies of second language students, "code-meshing" or "code-switching" is the practice of moving from one language to the next, sometimes shuttling back and forth between languages depending on the audience and the purpose of the interaction. For second language students, like Therese, the ability to code-switch comes from her daily interaction with two languages and cultures (Grosjean, 1989).

There are some who might, in essence, agree with Therese—there is no room for Spanish in the English classroom. Indeed, some consistently suggest that the best ways for English language learners to learn English is to "do English," and they express concern that the first language becomes a crutch that prevents students from becoming fluent in their new language. At teaching conferences and in education classes, I have often heard teachers note that "code-meshing" or incorporating words from a native language may confuse young writers like Therese. Teachers and even students themselves worry that the home language will "interfere" with writing in English. For example, many Asian students miss articles in their English writing because they don't use them in their native languages. Other students may have difficulty with English spelling because they are used to a different alphabet or spelling structures in their home language.

However, if we consider Ken-zhi and Therese, who both struggled to continue writing but wanted to express their ideas on paper, there are bigger challenges that we need to be concerned about.

Overwhelmingly, researchers believe the home language can actually act as a transfer mechanism as students learn to write in English. Students with advanced literacy skills in their home language can and do transfer those skills into English. More important, students who feel that they can turn to their home language for support, or who are able to continue to feel confidence in their writing ability in their home language, maintain a stronger sense of that control and competence that Wilhelm and Smith suggested was so important to "flow."

For Therese, her assumptions about "interference" from Spanish proved problematic on so many fronts. Her lack of language and the inability to use complex "words that are different" reaffirmed and solidified her sense that when it came to English, she just wasn't smart. Her own self-doubts about her writing abilities were encumbered further by her reluctance to draw upon the strength of her other language expertise. The lack of any language made her feel like she had nothing to say.

When I suggested an experiment of sorts, a chance to respond to the original prompt in her native Spanish, she was at once reluctant and skeptical. But she was also a bit curious. She worried aloud that using Spanish in her English classroom, even for freewriting, would highlight her "weaknesses" to her English teacher. If the teacher saw her using Spanish, wouldn't she question Therese's abilities as a writer even more?

I asked her to humor my curiosity for a few minutes and try responding to the prompt in Spanish. Doubtfully, she picked up her pen and paper. But as I made copies of her other work, I observed her write nonstop for 15 minutes. There was fluidity and confidence as she attacked the paper with the pen.

When I sat back at the table, she wrote a final sentence and handed the paper to me with flourish. It wasn't done, only a draft, she told me, but she was smiling. She then confidently walked me through the draft in English, pointing out sentences she especially liked and explaining that, as she wrote, she realized that fashion was a key part of how she viewed creativity. Figure 3.2 shows an excerpt from that experiment with writing in Spanish, along with an English translation completed by Therese and me of her sample.

Noticeably, Therese's Spanish essay on "becoming more creative" used more words, those "different words" that she so wanted to be able to use in the English version of the essay. She used more complicated words and sentiments, imagination, and imagery. But even more apparent was the strong sense of Therese's voice. Her discussion of creativity revealed her interest in fashion and design, something that she never articulated in her conversations with me before or in her English version of the assignment. It did, however, coincide with the various fashion magazines that I found her sifting through whenever we met at the library and her evolving use of makeup and hair accessories during the year. As she shared her writing with me, she translated and explained to me in English what she deemed "creative" about herself and how she wanted to expand upon that in the future, meeting the goals of the original assignment. As we talked, there was an "a-ha" moment in which Therese discovered her topic, but also found her own voice and way into the prompt that the teacher had given her. Somehow, through our little experiment with Spanish and the conversation that followed, Therese not only reconnected with her ownership of language, but she also found her voice, a sense of self, and a confidence in her ideas.

CONQUERING STUDENTS' WAVES OF DOUBT

In showing the story of Therese's Spanish writing experiment, I hope to highlight how much is hidden from our view as English teachers. When writing in English, even small obstacles can make ELL writers experience waves of doubt, causing them to question their own intelligence, as if all the aspects of their bright, articulate, funny, and insightful identities in their home language suddenly evaporated when the language changed. Despite her ELA teacher's best efforts to encourage Therese's abilities and talents in her English writing, Therese's experiences as a writer in her English classroom were very much impacted by her sense that she did not own English, that she was no longer that bright, honors-level schoolgirl that she had been just 1 year earlier, and that she was an outsider to writing in this setting.

Considering the Uses of the First Language (L1) to Develop Writing in English

Danling Fu (2009) advocates an understanding of ELLs' writing development that starts not with their English proficiency level but with their first language literacy. Often, in our models of writing proficiency, we gauge ELL writers on a scale that begins at the basic level of words, phrases, or simple unconnected sentences. We create rubrics and proficiency criteria that begin only with very limited English language proficiency and then move to very

FIGURE 3.2. An Excerpt from Therese's Writing on Creativity in Spanish and a Translation to English

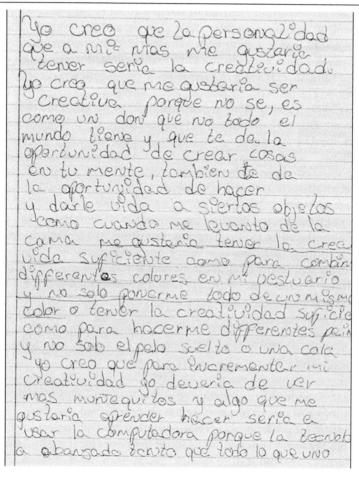

I believe that the personality (trait) that I would like to have is the creativity. I believe that I would like to be creative because it, itself, is like a gift that not everyone has and that you have the opportunity to create things in your mind. Also it gives you the opportunity to do things and to give life to certain objects.

When I get out of the bed, I'd like to have the sufficient creativity to combine different colors in my wardrobe and not only dress in all of the same color or to have the sufficient creativity as to do different hairstyles and not have only loose hair or only a ponytail. . . . .

high English proficiency levels. An alternative model, suggested by Fu, proposes that we evaluate the learning of writing in a second language from a standpoint of "transition." Instead of starting at the beginning of English development, we acknowledge the writing abilities, and, I would add, rhetorical abilities, that ELL writers come with. When we start our understanding of ELL writing development with the student's first language literacy as the starting point, we validate their sense of themselves as competent writers and thinkers (Fu, 2009, p. 21).

Fu's (2009) transitional model of writing development is not the only one that suggests that we look more closely at how using a first language may help students like Therese approach writing in their second language. Janet Bean, Peter Elbow, Paul Kei Matsuda, and others have also raised questions about where and when students' home languages may benefit their writing. They note the parallels to our work with native English speakers, whom we often encourage to freewrite and perform other generative activities. But when it comes to ELL writers, teachers and sometimes the students themselves are hesitant to allow the use of the first language in writing. As Therese's case suggests, there is a concern that somehow "using Spanish," or any first language, will be at a detriment to the English the student is trying to master. But as Bean, Matsuda, Elbow, and their coauthors (2003) noted in their article complicating this concept:

> The question was not so much whether or not to invite students to write in a mother tongue different from standardized English, rather, when and under what conditions might it make sense to do so? (p. 226)

Teachers are torn by competing goals. We want to see ELL writers master verb endings and transitions, but we are also concerned that their writing is too simplistic for grade-level expectations or doesn't truly reflect the depth of their ideas. We worry about our obligations to prepare for them for assessment tests, college essays, and "future fluency." Yet, as Bean (2003) reminds us,

> A teacher who takes future fluency as the sole exclusive goal is likely to decide that students should always compose in standardized English—and simply accept the price that must be paid for work exclusively on this goal: a considerable delay not only in comfort and fluency in language but also in the richness and complexity of writing. (p. 232)

Sacrificing "richness and complexity of writing" is something that should concern all English teachers. These sacrifices can have long-term repercussions for our students' sense of confidence and prowess when it comes to their writing skills and their overall academic success. ELL students can benefit from opportunities to use their first languages as a means of developing their voices on paper, to explore topics and ideas, to freewrite, or to work on initial drafts. Even in our more academically challenging writing assignments, where we aim to teach students a sense of formality and authority in their writing, it can be good practice to allow students to make use of their first language in order to develop their ideas (see Figure 3.4).

But what happens when students refuse to use L1 on their own grounds? What should teachers do? Therese's struggles with her essay illustrate what often happens with ELL writers when they become frustrated with their inability to express their ideas and thoughts in their writing. They shut down. They stop writing. Or, perhaps even more accurately, they stop caring about what they write. The inability to access vocabulary, to "find the right words," starts to play a soundtrack of doubt, one that can frustrate and dishearten second language writers. The written product that they produce does not feel like a true reflection of who they are, what they are capable of, or what they believe. Using their first language as a starting point, either when they get stuck or when they first begin to brainstorm, can assist many ELL writers in gaining a stronger sense of voice and purpose in the early stages of a writing assignment. It is helpful for teachers to talk to their ELL writers about how, when, and why using a home language might be helpful.

I should note that for some students whose home dialect or language is not commonly used for writing, an invitation to write in their home language can be problematic. Some students may have strong oral fluency in their home languages and less experience with writing in those languages. For example, I had two students from the Sudan who were unsure how to write in their native Dinka language and had limited experience with writing in Arabic, the language that was taught in Sudanese schools. In another instance, I worked with a young woman, born in Mexico, who spoke Spanish at home, but rarely wrote in that language. In cases like these, the suggestion to write in a home language may frustrate the student further.

Bean and her coauthors (2003) also remind us that invitations to write in the home language require a certain level of trust and rapport between student and teacher. Often, ELL writers wonder about their teachers' beliefs and convictions on the issue of language use and English. They are hesitant to take us up on our invitations to use a home language if they feel that it might impede their progress, their grade, or their standing in the teacher's eyes. If individuals in their schools or in the surrounding towns and cities seem unsupportive, or even antagonistic, toward the use of languages other than English, these issues and apprehensions may also sway students. But questions about using a home language in one's writing do not have to end the conversation between teachers and students. Those questions could begin the conversation.

FIGURE 3.4. Inviting Students to Write in Their Home Language: Some Guiding Questions for Teachers

---

Bean et al. (2003) suggest that teachers, often in conversation with their students, consider a number of variables when inviting students to use their first language, including:

1.   What kind of writing is the goal?
2.   Who is the audience?
3.   What is the learning goal for the writing on this particular occasion—practicing for future fluency in standardized English or drafting for a present text in standardized English that captures the students' richest thinking and strongest voice?
4.   What is the political or psychological context for an invitation to write in a home language—particularly with regard to stigmatization and identity?
5.   What is the process by which students move from exploratory writing or early drafts in a home dialect or language to a revised and final version in standardized English?

CONCLUSION

The variables suggested by Bean and her coauthors offer teachers a way to talk to ELL students and acknowledge them as real writers (see Figure 3.4). Conversations like these create opportunities for student writers to realize that all writers have options and make decisions about their writing based on their purpose. We might allow students to "experiment" with their writing and writing process, encouraging one assignment to be started in the home language and then asking them to reflect on that "experiment." We might create opportunities, particularly in personal narratives, for students to cross the borderlands (Anzaldúa, 1987) in their writing, incorporating words and images from their home language. In short, we might open up their writing, their concerns about writing, and their writing options to discussion and find a place in our writing instruction that moves beyond rote practices and beyond their nagging self-doubts about their abilities as students and thinkers.

Teachers also need to consider how the cultural contexts of our school hallways and overheard comments at the local shopping mall about "why don't they just learn English" influence students' actions and decisions when it comes to their English writing. Sometimes those overheard comments stifle the very voices that we are trying to cultivate on the written page. Indeed, our own concerns about helping students master the basic skills of English usage, grammar, and punctuation may lead us to overlook conversations about more complex issues of tone, voice, and intention. Perhaps we assume that we can't have those conversations yet with ELL writers, not until these students master the basics. When Therese and Ken-zhi hand in their academic English writing assignments to their teachers, the papers show only the most obviously visible markers of their struggles and "problem areas" as English language learners and writers. Often, these are the moments, the artifacts, upon which administrators, teachers, and guidance counselors base many of their assumptions about the academic abilities and talents of second language writers in high schools.

But these judgments often overlook a wide range of rhetorical skills, writing talents, and competencies that second language writers can develop and bring with them into their academic writing. The danger is that these one-dimensional assessments can seem accurate, making teachers see only the weaknesses of ELL writers, not their strengths. The result is often a constrained and limited writing curriculum, in which (1) lessons become predominantly focused on forms, grammar drills, and procedures; and (2) students have little time to practice their writing and work on lengthier, more involved writing assignments. When there are fewer sustained opportunities for English language learners to engage with writing as a critical thinking activity, it becomes more difficult for them to see themselves as creative, smart, and rhetorically savvy communicators.

ADDITIONAL RESOURCES

The following books offer additional insights into the writing development of secondary school ELL writers, particularly as they move across languages, and deepen their skills as English writers.

Fu, D. (2003). *An island of English: Teaching ESL in Chinatown.* Portsmouth, NH: Heinemann.

Fu, D. (2009). *Writing between languages: How English language learners make the transition to fluency, grades 4–12.* Portsmouth, NH: Heinemann.

Reynolds, D. (2009). *One on one with second language writers: A guide for writing tutors, teachers, and consultants.* Ann Arbor, MI: University of Michigan Press.

Meet Miguel

Miguel is outgoing, polite, confident, and utterly charming. Early this year, when the bus route was not settled, he twice walked from his house on the other side of the city to the middle school, once in the rain.

—Recommendation for summer bridge program
written by Miguel's middle school ELL teacher

Rain or shine, Miguel loves school. For him, school is a place of validation, involving caring teachers and social activities. Miguel is tall with a mop of curly black hair and a continuous smile. He loves baseball, David Ortiz, and video games.

Miguel had been in the United States for only 18 months when the study began. His mother had lived here for a number of years before that, preparing for her children's arrival, finding steady work, and becoming proficient in English. During that time, Miguel and his sister stayed behind in the Dominican Republic with his grandmother. His parents were divorced, and Miguel's father remained in the Dominican Republic. After the divorce, his father remarried and had children with Miguel's stepmother. Miguel was fond of his father and his younger siblings, but he was fiercely loyal to his mother and incredibly proud of her. They had a close relationship and he respected her highly. She, in turn, wanted him to succeed in school, to stay out of trouble, and to take full advantage of the educational and economic opportunities that he and his younger sister had in the United States.

In the Dominican Republic, Miguel studied English one period a week, during which he learned how to say, "Hello," "Good-bye," "How are you?" and not much else. When he came to the United States, he did not know how to read or write in English. In the Dominican Republic, he noted that he was an "okay" student that teachers liked. He always did his homework.

In the United States, his 8th-grade teachers saw Miguel as charming, likable, and popular. He did his work, and although he did not often get the best grade, his work showed effort and dedication. He picked up oral English quickly and was able to express his thoughts, but he continued to struggle with reading and writing in English. Miguel tested as a low-proficiency reader and writer on his 8th-grade English proficiency test. By the end of 9th grade, he had made some gains as a reader, but his writing scores fell. On his writing assessment from a summer school bridge program, his summer school teacher commented, "Miguel copied the supporting details randomly into his writing, instead of using them to support his own thoughts." Indeed, his skills in academic reading and writing were the weakest of all the student participants and he struggled the most as the academic demand increased in high school.

But, despite his struggles with reading and writing, Miguel paid attention in class, tried to complete all his homework, and showed respect for his teachers. These were qualities that won him much praise from his teachers. He was also the most willing to please, and in some ways, the most passive of all the study participants, willing to do and accept whatever his teachers told him to do. While other students in the study expressed some resistance to their academic placements, questioned their teachers, and thought about inequities, Miguel was hesitant to criticize and eager to please. He loved his teachers and his school. He wanted to be a "good boy," to stay away from gangs, to be safe, and to stay in school. At home, he liked to work on home improvement projects with his uncles, including painting and electrical work. He thought he might become an electrician, but he also told me that he would like to go to college to learn about business. In the year following the study, Miguel proudly became a U.S. citizen.

Midway through the study, Miguel transferred to another high school in the district, Mill River South. His transfer provided me with an interesting opportunity to observe his identity and academic writing experiences in another school setting, one that had far fewer second language students and only one ELL specialist who had little training in teaching writing. Miguel struggled with his writing throughout the study. His new ELA teacher at Mill River South was unsure of how to work with him; he was her first ELL student and she relied on the ELL teacher to help him with his writing and other English assignments. But his Mill River South ELL teacher didn't see herself as a writing teacher. She was more of a tutor. She helped him with his work by simply correcting the errors, rewriting entire sentences, and fixing the misspellings. Then Miguel would copy the corrected written work, never asking why changes were made, and hand the new pages in to his mainstream teachers. Throughout the school year, Miguel received only limited instruction and experience with writing. By the end of his first year, he saw himself as a non-writer. He was concerned that his end-of-the-year test scores in writing had not improved, and his grades on any kind of assignment that required writing were often poor. He began to question the importance of school in his life.

CHAPTER 4

Overcoming the Myth of Sisyphus

And I saw Sisyphus at his endless task raising his prodigious stone with both his hands. With hands and feet he'd tried to roll it up to the top of the hill, but always, just before he could roll it over on to the other side, its weight would be too much for him, and the pitiless stone would come thundering down again on to the plain. Then he would begin trying to push it up hill again, and the sweat ran off him and the steam rose after him.

—Homer's *Odyssey*, Book 11, lines 593–600

If the act of writing in a second language is often a point of struggle for our students, it is also true that much of the writing curriculum that is part of our language arts curriculum can leave many ELL writers (and often their teachers) feeling like Sisyphus. Although they are pushing the rock up the hill with each writing assignment, they feel that their skills as writers are not improving.

THE WRITING PROCESS

As Ann Raimes (1985) and others have pointed out, writing process pedagogies and theories can offer ELL writers an opportunity to see writing as exploratory. The process approach, with its emphasis on recursivity and revision, can, in theory, offer them a chance to work through the writing stumbling blocks that I mentioned in the previous chapter. Yet it's important to acknowledge that writing process pedagogy is often an unknown for many ELL students coming into U.S. secondary schools. Of all the students in this study, only Wisdom was familiar with the writing process, a concept he'd learned during his time in U.S. elementary and middle schools. Our discussions throughout the year revealed his familiarity with revision and drafts. He shared his 8th-grade writing portfolio with pride, pointing to his reflections on writing assignments and detailed comparisons between first draft and final draft samples.

But for the more recent immigrant students, the methods, meta-vocabulary, and expectations of the writing process were completely disconnected to their prior learning and writing experiences. Ken-zhi, Miguel, and Therese all reported that they could not recall any kind of direct instruction with regard to writing in their home countries. For many of them, previous writing instruction had focused on handwriting, correct sentence structures, recitation, and restating answers from a textbook script. Writing as composing was a new concept.

Yet, even when they came to U.S. schools, these adolescent ELL students witnessed a writing process that was codified and decontextualized in ways that evaporated the values that it might have offered them as writers. This was especially true in the lower-level academic tracks. They had few opportunities to become more critically and rhetorically engaged as writers. Miguel's story illustrates this concern.

MIGUEL AND THE FOUR-STEP WRITING PROCESS

Early in the fall of his freshman year, Miguel sat in his ELA classroom diligently taking notes from the board. He was learning about the writing process. In his notebook, Miguel copied the teacher's word for word. He paid attention to each letter, trying to grasp the concepts as he carefully focused on making sure his words matched the words on the board.

In our interview following the class, I asked Miguel to tell me about these notes (Figure 4.1). He replied, "Well, I don't really know. Because she just put it on the board, and I copy. Because I don't want to miss something." As Miguel and I sat at the local library talking about the notes, it became apparent that he was unfamiliar with the concepts of process that were written out on the pages of his notebook. The steps were shared as part of his teacher's preparation for the upcoming assignment: Write a five-paragraph essay about a fellow student. The assignment had students (1) interview another person in the class, (2) organize the information gained from that interview, (3) compose a draft, and (4) hand in a completed five-paragraph essay. But Miguel noted that the teacher had spent only limited class time discussing the assignment and the new terms. He had never heard of them before, and he was not even sure how to pronounce them. In our interview, he tried to explain the steps to me:

> Okay . . . let's see. Step 1. Step 2. [pause] Well . . . oh, this is about this stuff [points to a list of questions he created for an interview of another student] . . . oh, in this one [Step 3, Prewriting], they say one part that you don't have to worry about spelling, you don't have to worry about spelling. . . . Here is d . . . dra . . . draffing. Oh—this is about the paragraphs—introduction, bodies—that's where you have to put that stuff. . . . In this one [Step 4, revising], you need to worry on spelling and that.

FIGURE 4.1. Miguel's Notes

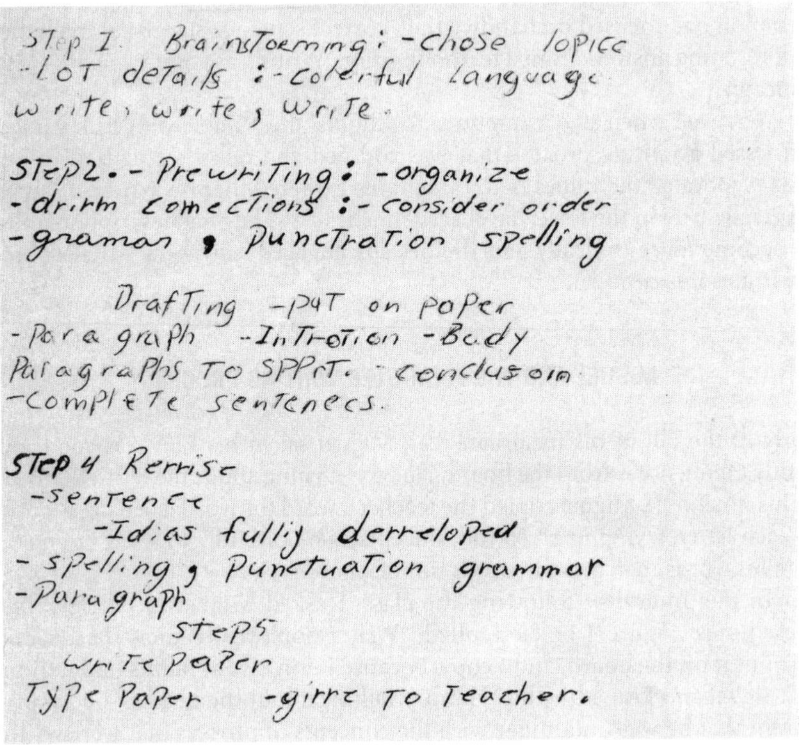

STep I. BrainsToerming: -chose Topicc
-LoT deTails :-colerful language
write, write, wriTe.

STep2.- PrewriTing: -organize
-drirm comecTions :- consider order
-graman , puncTraTion spelling

DrafTing -puT on paper
-Para graph -InTroTion -Body
Paragraphs To SPPrT. - conclusoin
-compleTe senTenecs.

STep 4 Rerrise
-senTence
-Idias fully derreloped
- spelling, PuncTuaTion grammar
-Paragraph
sTeps
wriTe paPer
Type Paper -girre To Teacher.

In the days that followed, Miguel and his peers enacted the steps of the process to compose the five-paragraph biographies. Students brainstormed questions, then interviewed their fellow students and wrote out their interviewees' responses under each of the questions. This was part of prewriting, according to Miguel. Then students used graphic organizers and were directed to place information from the interview into four squares of categories, such as biographical information, things they like to do, and so forth. Miguel explained that using the four-square organizer was part of drafting.

When we met, I asked Miguel what he would do with the organizer and the interview notes. He answered, "Well, then I do, like, an essay with it." When he talked about his plan for forming the essay, he expressed concern that he didn't know what came next. I asked if he knew who his readers for the piece might be; he looked puzzled and replied, "Well, I don't know really." He expressed frustration and a genuine sense of loss as he looked at his notes and tried to figure out what to write. Miguel decided to copy the boxes of sentences out onto the blank page and separate them each by a line "to make them look right."

As he copied the words from the chart into his draft, he explained that he was mostly concerned with following the procedure set out by his teacher. He also knew that he had to have five sections or paragraphs. His notes were all direct transcriptions from his interviewee's answers. So he decided to change all the *I*'s to *she*'s, shifting the first-person voice of the interviewee into the third person. He also decided that it might be a good idea to open the essay by introducing himself to readers. Then he numbered the sections, the chunks of text. His last sentence would be an answer to the question the teacher had written on the board about the experience. He wrote: "Yes, I like the assignment because I like to meat new pieple and learn about their country and family."

Miguel's assignment is a common one, particularly in those initial school months when teachers and students are trying to learn more about one another. Miguel liked having the opportunity to talk to his peers. The assignment also emphasized a learn-by-doing approach. But there were no opportunities to explore how and why these strategies might be useful to writers. For Miguel, those missed opportunities meant that the concepts of prewriting, brainstorming, drafting, and revision became hollow terms.

Miguel's first draft, shown in Figure 4.2, demonstrated that he had understood how this information might be organized. In many ways, it was a good early draft for Miguel. In the first paragraph, he was playful, addressing his readers personally and trying to build interest for the piece, writing: "I didn't tell you that I interview Arso, so let's see what we have to say about her." The early draft showed that he was writing in complete sentences, but his lack of capitalization and end punctuation made it difficult to identify where one sentence ended and another one began. The draft illustrated places where Miguel was still struggling with the English language as a writer. In his ELL classes, he was learning about nouns, verb tenses, and complex sentence structures. His ELL teachers also worked on punctuation, but Miguel didn't make the connection between the exercises he completed in ELL class to his own written texts in the ELA classroom. They seemed completely disconnected.

After the first draft, Miguel took on the fourth step of the writing process: revision. As Miguel noted earlier, the final step was when "you need to worry on spelling and that stuff." Here, Miguel typed his final essay, shown in Figure 4.3, and bulleted chunks of paragraphs. The five-paragraph format and organization of the essay remained unchanged. In the opening paragraph, he rewrote the topic sentence: "My purpose of this is to learn about my classmates, and practic [*sic*] using the writing process to practice writing a 5-paragraph essay." His rewritten sentences mimicked the teacher's chalkboard sentences from the classroom, replacing his original opening. Miguel explained that he felt he had to make the change because the teacher had put the purpose sentence on the board. He assumed that his original opening to the essay was wrong.

FIGURE 4.2. Miguel's Early Draft

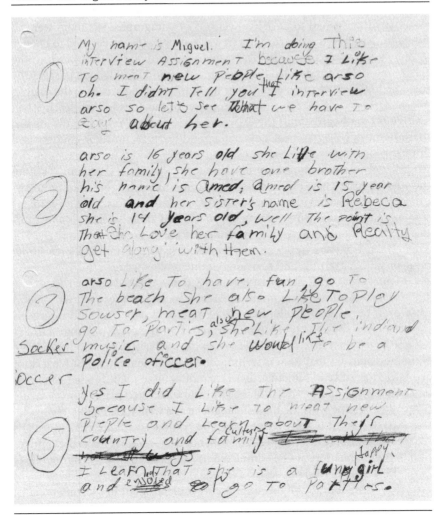

He added a fourth paragraph, telling the story of his classmate and a supermarket encounter, but the details of the incident are difficult to follow. There is little sense of how this story connects to the larger narrative of the essay. Miguel explained that he forgot to include this supermarket information earlier and that he needed it in order to reach the required five paragraphs. His concluding paragraph directly answered a question that the teacher posed in class, but provided no reference to the original ques-

FIGURE 4.3. Miguel's Final Draft

- My name is Miguel I interview arso and my purpose of this is to learn about my classmates and practic using the writing process to practice writing a 5 paragraph essay ..

- Arso is 16 years old she live with her family, she have one brother his name is amed, amed is 15 years old and her sister's name isrebeca she is 14 years old well the point is that she love her family and really get alond with them.

- Arsolike to have fun,go to the beach she also like play sowser, meat new people go to parties, she also like the indiand music and she would like to be a police oficcer.

- When arso was at the super market with her sister a challenge came their way,Arso have been scare before but never like that day, Her stomach felt nervous, she was glad at least wasn't along. it is always a challenge to calm down when you are scared, at the super markt there was a dark boy who was scary, the dark boy began to stare at them in the store. when they left the market he fallowed them. arso told her sister that someone was fallowing them. when they looked back he wasn't around because he was there___ in front of them. so they began to run away from him sa fast as they could. they get home soon as they can , they calm down and the y stare dancing and plaing ...

- Yes i did like the assignment because I like to meat new people and learn about their countri and culture I learned thst she is a happy girl and she like to go to parties...

BY:

tion. What's apparent in that final sentence is that he is only writing for his teacher. His final draft showed no other attempts at revision on the local level (word choices, sentence structures, spelling, verb tenses, punctuation, and so on), the global level (organization, development of ideas, inclusion of details and description), or the rhetorical level (purpose, audience, language choices, and so forth). Miguel was unsure what to do in revision. He had no strategies and little understanding of how to set goals for himself as a writer. The assignment had laid out steps for the writing processes, but Miguel never understood who he was writing for or why.

Strikingly, Miguel's class had little discourse on writing. His ELA teacher was wonderfully adept at creating interactive discussions on the literature the students read, and Miguel was an active participant and listener in these conversations. In his English notebook, he kept lengthy notes on storylines and characters. He would copy out full passages from the classroom's worn paperback books when he wanted to remember a certain character's traits or a plot event. Indeed, other ELL students in the study had similar experiences. They enjoyed talking about their readings, the characters and plotlines they were studying, and the literary conventions that they learned as part of their discussions. They knew the language of these literary conversations and they could articulate their understanding of their readings with these terms.

But the opportunity to "talk" about writing, and the work of writers, did not exist with the same level of depth or enthusiasm. Miguel was not given the chance to think about or discuss writing (his own or others) in a critical way. He couldn't see how writing was an act of communication between readers and writers. He didn't have opportunities to talk about his written work, to share ideas, to listen to other writers, to think about how he might connect with readers, or to set goals for revision. No one shared a writer's vocabulary with him beyond those initial terms of *prewriting, drafting,* and *revising,* and those terms remained hollow and artificial for him. Without those kinds of opportunities to listen and talk about writing, Miguel wasn't sure how to revise in more substantive ways, and the limited notes and instructions on the board weren't enough to help him develop his writing further.

His final draft still revealed many concerns (see Figure 4.3). He was still neglecting capitalization, still unclear about sentence endings and beginnings, unsure of the use of commas, still struggling with spelling and vocabulary, and still struggling with paragraph development. On the positive side, he had written more than 200 words, taken steps to organize his information into quasi-paragraphs, and demonstrated an understanding of how information fit together. He included some good details and had a successful, informative interview.

What is most troubling here for me, for Miguel's teacher, and for other English teachers is the sense that Miguel hasn't made much progress from first draft to final draft. On a global level, there are elements of a narrative apparent in paragraph four, but Miguel does not develop that narrative more fully. The narrative takes some leaps and jumps. There are gaps that leave the reader asking for more details, context, and explanation. On a rhetorical level, he has gained almost no knowledge of how a writer is influenced by his readers, his purpose, and the genre. Miguel does not see any "real" readers for his writing; he isn't a real writer. He isn't aware that this essay is actually a profile, a specific genre used by professional writers in magazines, newspapers, and creative nonfiction. Ironically, Miguel, an avid baseball fan, often read profiles of his favorite sports heroes like David Ortiz and Pedro Martinez in Spanish and English sports magazines. But he hadn't encountered any models of this genre in class and couldn't make the connections. For Miguel, "doing the essay right" is about following those steps, answering the teacher's questions, and getting to that fifth paragraph.

Miguel's final draft showed promise, the foundations of an essay. He had located his topic, selected vocabulary for the piece, and found "nuggets" of an interesting narrative that might be explored further. In short, this second draft could be a place to work on his language or to develop a story more fully. But as soon as he had developed a draft that he could truly work with as a writer and as a learner of English language, the assignment was due, the pages were collected, and it was time to move on.

MIGUEL AND SISYPHUS: L2 WRITING AS A ROCK

I opened this chapter with an excerpt from Homer's *Odyssey*, depicting the unending, disheartening struggle of Sisyphus and that rock. Miguel's experiences with writing remind me of that struggle.

After completing this writing assignment, Miguel went about writing in English as he always had, putting words on paper without considering his purpose or his readers. He didn't draft; he didn't prewrite; he did not make webs or lists to brainstorm. He didn't worry about organization. He didn't think about how paragraphs and ideas might transition to guide his readers. He didn't consider what his readers might expect to see in his writing. He remained caught up in concerns over spelling and punctuation. He didn't worry about readers, just correctors. Writing remained a passive enterprise for him. He awaited the teacher's red marks and then made corrections.

Most of Miguel's classroom time was dedicated to writing what appears on the teacher's board, mostly notes. As a result, Miguel saw the act of writing as an exercise in transcription. And when he did write a longer piece, just as he was ready to engage with his writing, explore his options as a writer, and talk about what he might do next, it was time to move on.

Like Sisyphus, he kept starting over.

HELPING WRITERS MOVE BEYOND THE SISYPHUS MOMENT

Often, when I speak to teachers about Miguel and share his writing, there are moments of uneasiness. We've all been there. We've had moments where writing lessons were cut short, or where we know that certain students haven't made as much progress as we had hoped. When I share Miguel's story with teachers, they comment that his text is not an easy one to "fix," and they worry about the lack of progress that they see as they compare Miguel's first draft with his second and final draft. As one of my student teachers recently exclaimed, "What can I do if there just doesn't seem to be any progress?"

Helping students move beyond the Sisyphus moment is not a magical formula. In this chapter, I offer a few ways for teachers to enrich their current use of writing process pedagogy and further activate the writing and learning of their ELL writers. My goal is to provide some ways to enrich instruction and assignments that teachers may already be using in the classroom. First, I share some of the dangers of teaching writing as a decontextualized lockstep process. I argue that we need to be wary of downgrading the critical thinking aspects of writing process pedagogy into a stale facsimile. Second, I recommend that teachers implement writing instruction that includes more opportunities for students to engage in explicit discussions about their own writing and the writing decisions of others. Finally, I share concrete strategies for helping ELL writers learn how to revise.

The Dangers of Decontextualizing the Writing Process:
Step One, Step Two, Step Three . . .

Across the board, the students in this study encountered writing and the writing process as a series of lockstep procedures and distilled forms. Writing concepts in their courses were presented in ways that were decontextualized, simplified, and empty. The writing process was presented as a simple assembly-line approach where the writer's intentions and the reader's expectations took a backseat to the procedure. In one ELA classroom, the final exam's only essay question illustrated this concern, by asking students to list the four steps of the writing process. They were not asked to write an essay, using the steps, or even asked to consider, in writing, how the steps might benefit writers. It was just the list.

Nancy Sommers (1980) has critiqued what she calls the "linear models" of the writing process that "separate the writing process into discrete stages" (p. 378). The linear models produce "a parody of writing," according to Sommers, "isolating revision and then disregarding it" (p. 378). This "parody of writing" is particularly disadvantageous to ELL writers who need rich, sustained writing experiences and conversations about writing embedded throughout the English curriculum. ELL student writers need time to develop; writing is often the most difficult language mode for them to master. But in order to develop and master writing, they need to be critically engaged with meaningful writing activities that provide sustained time, meaningful assignments, and thoughtful, speculative, class-wide conversations on writing.

Often, teachers tend to frontload writing curricula, focusing a great deal of energy on the inventive part of writing, followed by a single round of feedback and error correction. The result is that we don't encourage students to think more critically about the rhetorical nature of writing. We shortchange writing conversations that provoke critical thinking and decision-making strategies. Students need to learn to step back and analyze their readers and their readers' expectations in order to consider how word choices and language can reflect their purpose. But they often need the classroom setting and their teachers to aid them in setting goals and developing strategies for revision.

A Call for More Classroom Conversation on Writing

Martin Nystrand (1997) has argued for the importance of classroom discourse in developing students' literacy practices. He noted that students need to have opportunities to engage in quality classroom discussions, where they have chances to take on serious, participatory roles that require them "to think, interpret, and generate new understandings" (p. 3). But those roles are often not available to ELL writers. Weissberg (2006) found that discourse interactions between teachers and ESL students were often limited only to direct instruction (from the board to the notebook). Presently, as Nystrand points out, "Most schooling is organized ... for the plodding transmission of information through classroom recitation. Teachers talk and students listen. And the lower the track, we found, the more likely this is true" (p. 7).

Miguel's struggles as a writer were compounded by the fact that the classroom discussion on writing was almost nonexistent. The writing process wasn't presented as a way of opening up an ongoing discussion between teachers and students on the ways that writers write and make decisions. Miguel's teacher and his peers did not discuss how the steps of the writing process might be recursive. They did not talk about the nuts and bolts of how writers actually "do" revision or even the benefits of having multiple drafts. A rich discussion around writing that could have added new depth to their understanding and articulation of their writing processes was missing. And here is the sticking point—Miguel could have contributed to that conversation.

For many ELL students, their ability to "talk" about their writing is at a higher level than the written page of their work may suggest. For example, if Miguel and his teacher had made the connection between the sports profiles that he read in magazines and his assignment, Miguel would have been eager to share what he knew about the style of those pieces. Although some ELL students may be reluctant to speak aloud in class, classroom management strategies that allow time to vet ideas in small groups or with partners often help bolster the confidence of these students and allow them to share their ideas. Marcia Pally (1997), an L2 writing specialist, has argued that if we can "raise students' awareness both that texts take their meaning from communities in which the texts are used, they may more readily see that writing—by others or by themselves—is a series of choices and decisions, an awareness that benefits writers in any language" (p. 296). As readers and writers in their first languages, ELL writers do have experiences with texts, storytelling, audience, characters, and persuasion. But often, they are unsure how to draw upon that knowledge or to marshal it when writing and setting goals for their own texts. They don't know if the insights that come from their out-of-school literacy experiences even have a place in the English classroom. Even if they think there might be some useful connections, ELL writers may need a teacher's invitation and a classroom community where such conversation is the norm.

REVISITING REVISION:
OPPORTUNITIES TO TEACH ELLs TO ENGAGE AS WRITERS

In 2003, the National Commission on Writing published *The Neglected "R" report* on writing in K–12 schools. They concluded:

> If students are to make knowledge their own, they must struggle with the details, wrestle with the facts, and rework raw information and dimly understood concepts into language they can communicate to someone else. In short, if students are to learn, they must write. (p. 12)

The truncated nature of the writing instruction that Miguel experienced in his class meant that revision, "struggling with details," "wrestling with facts," and the recursive, communicative nature of writing were lost to him. For many writers, revision is the stage of the writing process that holds the most powerful opportunity for gaining critical thinking skills (Bean, 2001; Langer & Applebee, 1987). Donald Murray, in his seminal book, *The Craft of Revision* (2003), wrote that "revision is not the end of the writing process, but the beginning" (p. 1). Revision can teach writers to re-see and re-envision their texts (Sommers, 1980). Revision, with its focus on changing texts in order to heighten meaning, can critically engage inexperienced writers with their texts, their intended meanings, and their readers. Revision forces writers to consider whom they see as their readers, identify their purpose with more clarity, and consider how organization, word choice, and genre can affect the meaning and interpretation of their texts. Yet, many ELL writers are unsure how writers go about "reseeing" their texts. Instead, they think in terms of error and "fixing." Miguel's experiences demonstrate how easily students, and sometimes their teachers, can allow revision and editing to coalesce, with editing concerns becoming the predominant goal of second drafts.

At the same time, ELA teachers can be frustrated by the lack of revision in their students' drafts. Students change a single word, rewrite a single sentence, and correct their use of commas. One of the problems may be that we don't explicitly teach revision as well as we teach students about errors and editing.

Many adolescent ELL writers are particularly fearful of revision. If one considers the time and effort that these writers put into just generating the words for their texts, trying to reach a certain page count, and finding the right vocabulary, it is no wonder that they cringe in fear when we speak of revamping entire paragraphs, expanding to add new material, and even worse, deleting sections that may no longer work. Others concentrate on "tidying up," through error correction, misspellings, and punctuation. The hesitancy speaks volumes.

I want my ELL writers to engage in writing more critically. I want them to see writing as a thinking activity, one that requires them to think more deeply and work through problems. I have learned that I cannot simply ask for revision; I need to teach it, providing students with tangible methods for revision, in-class activities, and the time to practice.

So where do I start? Well, I begin by reminding myself of a simple, yet profoundly important realization:

Most student writers do not know how to revise their papers.

Then I teach revision, but I begin small.

Small Starts

In the early days of the fall, I enter the writing classroom with revision on my mind. I share an excerpt from my own work (on an overhead or in a handout) looking at how a draft of a narrative becomes more visceral for readers through sensory detail and rich description. As a class, we talk through these changes and decisions. The lesson builds on previous discussions about expanding our use of detail in our writing, but it also begins the conversation on revision.

I start by introducing a series of small writing prompts to the students, most often focused on literacy histories, so that all students can engage in the topic. Sometimes we freewrite in class to a prompt; other times I may assign one or two prompts for homework. The goal is generative. Students are instructed to write for 5, 10, even 15 minutes on a given prompt. For students, these small writings, of which they write 8–10 of them, are usually interesting musings on a single question or object or descriptions of single moments. The students are not yet fully committed to them, though, so the pieces can become a testing ground for revision strategies.

Each day in class, we take our small writings and I invite students to play with them. I may teach a specific kind of transformation (from personal letter to poem to horoscope, for example). We play with multiple genres—rewriting a scene as a dialogue, or vice versa. As we make these transformations, we spend time discussing and examining the different genres, analyzing how each uses language and how it is used by readers, and discussing its form and conventions. I bring in samples of "real-world" (out-of-school) texts whenever possible to complement the in-school genres. In other moments, I use revision prompts that ask students to go deeper into their small writings by "unburying a story" that may be hidden in a sentence (Cox & Tirabassi, 2008; Rule & Wheeler, 2000). I may also ask them to choose an object or person mentioned in their small writing and write a second piece that richly describes that object or person through metaphor, memory, and detail. (See the sample "Play, Write, Revise" prompts in Appendix A and also online.) The key here is that we play with our language and lose the preconceived notion that writing is a one-shot, correct-your-grammar-and-move-on kind of activity.

In the end, I ask students to bring these small writings together into a lengthier multigenre piece, a strategy that I learned from Tom Romano (2002). The goal is for students to become comfortable with revising their work more drastically than they may have done in the past, and to present them with some strategies for revision. They are receptive because the short writing makes them less tied to their pieces and more willing to take risks. At the same time, the multigenre end product provides students with a sense that these small writings and experiments are not throwaway exercises to toss into the trash bin when the bell rings. Even these small writings can lead somewhere.

I am also able to teach students our classroom's vocabulary of revision through this assignment. We build a kind of classroom shorthand for our discussions on writing throughout the rest of the year. It is not uncommon in early spring to hear students suggesting to one another that they need "to layer in the detail" or "unbury the story" even in their analytical and argumentative essays.

Profiling Our Readers

> Reader profiles are sketches of your readers' tendencies, abilities, experiences, needs, values, and attitudes.
>
> —Robert Johnson-Sheehan, 2010, p. 40

In this revision strategy, I ask students to take a step backward from their initial draft. We take time to think and talk about the rhetorical situation in which the writing is situated, analyzing the purpose, genre, and audience. Often, they see only me, the teacher, as their reader. That's okay, because it leads to interesting questions about what teachers are looking for in writing and how that may vary across their different content classes. For example, does Mr. Keller in Physical Science have different expectations when it comes to their lab reports or research papers? How about Ms. Smith in World Geography?

I then ask students to create a reader/audience profile of their primary and secondary readers. (See the Profiling Our Readers activity in Appendix B.) Even if they see me as the primary reader for a text, I ask them to consider secondary readers. If they are having a difficult time identifying readers, we discuss the potential readers as a class. I want to move them from seeing their writing as flat, one sided, or rote. My goal is to get students thinking about their texts as communicative devices and to consider the kinds of questions they need to ask themselves as writers.

Johnson-Sheehan (2010) tells technical writers: "Don't assume that your readers have the same needs, values, and attitudes as you do" (p. 42). This is a wise rule that I pass along to ELL writers as well. I share many aspects of writing in the workplace with my adolescent writers, and my purpose is twofold. First, I want to expand our vision of writing and genres beyond the academic and the personal. Today, writing and texts are everywhere, and students need to see that writing in emails, workplace reports, and community postings will be asked of them well beyond the classroom walls. Second, I want to echo Johnson-Sheehan's thoughts that knowing your reader is an essential part of communicating effectively.

For ELL writers, activities like this one help them identify and differentiate the expectations of their readers, whom they may often see in very simple terms, lumping readers together in singular, simple categories (e.g., teachers, Americans, and so on), rather than seeing the differences in those categories (e.g., science teachers versus language arts teachers, American teens versus American politicians, and so forth). The activity also creates a way for students to consider the differences between local slang and academic English, between long narrations and bulleted summaries, between text message terms and standard written English, and so on. I hope for them to see writing as a series of decisions, helping them to articulate/decide/defend their goals and choices as writers based on critical thinking and analysis. The goal is to encourage ELL writers to think critically and confidently about writing and their drafts in ways that move beyond verb tense and spelling, so that they gain start skills and strategic approaches to writing, strategies that will aid them as writers in a variety of academic, workplace, and community settings.

Writing About Revision: Developing a Meta-Awareness

Since ELL writers may need practice in learning how to work through and articulate the kinds of decisions and questions that writers ask themselves, I regularly use the following informal writing prompts with my students in order to help them reflect upon different aspects of the revision process, the assignment, their progress, and their goals/purpose. The students' responses also serve as a good way for me to learn more about their individual strengths and challenges.

Thinking About Revision. *Write about what you do to revise your essays. How do you define revision and what does it look like? Try to be as specific as possible and provide some examples.* I often use students' responses to this question as a way to open a discussion on drafting and revision in class.

Analyze the Assignment. *Let's take a look at the assignment. Analyze the assignment for its purpose, audience, and genre. Then, in pairs, summarize your analysis in a short paragraph. What are some ideas that you have for this assignment?* I use this writing prompt as a way for me to gauge how students are interpreting my assignment. It is particularly useful when I work with ELL writers, because I can get a sense of what is challenging for them, where I need to clarify, and what they are planning to do. For ELL writers with limited writing experience, I often use a graphic organizer or chart (with the categories of purpose, reader/audience, and genre) so that they can use shorthand/shorter sentences to articulate their ideas, before we discuss the assignment as a class.

What's Our Progress? *Briefly describe how the writing/drafting is going for you. What area has been really difficult/hard? What sections of this essay/writing assignment do you feel the most proud of and why? What still needs some work?* I may also include some of the following questions in order to help students to plan ahead for their next drafts or assignments: What revision strategies have worked for you as you have been creating the draft? What is your plan over the next few days as you think about your next steps with this assignment?

Answering the "So What?" Question *(courtesy of Donald Murray). What do you want to communicate to your intended readers?* I usually ask students to do this a few times throughout a given writing project, as a way of having them "check in" on their own writing goals and intentions. The goal is to help them see how their thinking and hopefully their writing has deepened over time.

Picking up the Scissors

Another more advanced example of hands-on revision comes from Bruce Ballenger. Ballenger's *The Curious Researcher* (2008) is one of my favorite books for teaching students about research-based and inquiry-based writing. At one point in his discussion of the revision process, Ballenger insists that students bring in their current drafts and take scissors to them, cutting them up paragraph by paragraph. He then walks them through a series of steps and questions that guide students to reevaluate and critically consider the pieces of their cut-up drafts. This would also work with a single paragraph cut apart by sentences to check for coherence, opportunities for expansion, and so forth.

Through class discussion, students establish criteria for identifying core paragraphs, learn to evaluate how their own writing functions by analyzing how each paragraph fits within the larger framework established by that core, and think critically about places where they may need to expand to address holes in their research or arguments. The cut-up pages provide students with a highly malleable version of their first draft, already shuffled beyond recognition. This drastic measure helps them overcome the fear of "tampering" mentioned earlier. The individual paragraphs then become tangible, like a textual version of math manipulatives, easily disassembled and reassembled for a variety of writing situations and expectations. Sometimes students discover entire paragraphs that may be irrelevant or sentences within paragraphs that need reworking. They then begin to bring the paragraphs together with tape, adding in notes or blank pieces of paper where they need to add more. These "Frankenstein drafts" provide the roadmap for the next incarnation of the essay.

I share this last strategy with a hint of trepidation. Even my most accomplished student writers see me show up with a box of scissors and four tape dispensers, and balk at this assignment. For ELL writers, this strategy can feel like the destruction and disrespect of many hours of hard work, so I truly have to "sell" it to my students. Humor helps. So does encouragement and support. I acknowledge the fact that they will probably hate me throughout the class period and even as they go home to reassemble their drafts, and that many of them may decide that I am crazy. But I also talk about my own feelings of running my head into a wall as a writer. I share my own experiences with being unable to see where I need more detail (or evidence) in a given piece, if an argument makes sense, or how to come up with more material. I bring in samples of my own Frankenstein drafts to show them that I have indeed been there. I also ask them to trust me. I should add that this is not a strategy that I use early in the year, and it is also one that comes after we have established a culture of revision in our class.

As they work with their scissors, their paragraphs, and their tape, I circle the room, stopping by the desks of students who need more help or encouragement. I read through their work, identify the core paragraph, and talk through decisions to keep or reject certain paragraphs. In all cases, the strategy of cut-and-paste revision, though often met with initial shock and some strong resistance, leads students to think beyond simple formulas and formulaic writing to a deeper engagement with their own texts and ideas. It helps them move forward with their writing, to get their rock up and over that hill, and to see beyond that "Sisyphus moment."

CONCLUSION

Miguel reminds me that many ELL writers are unsure about the pathways they can take to become better writers. Some ELL writers are very respectful (or wary) of teachers and, as a result, passive. They wait for the English teacher, whom they see as the language owner and expert, to make decisions for them. Increasing our classroom dialogues on writing, teaching revision methods, and moving beyond lockstep procedures and formulas are powerful ways to increase the engagement of ELL writers in their texts. Our goal in working with ELL writers should be to provide opportunities for legitimate participation as writers and thinkers. Discussions on readers, revision techniques, and writerly decisions provide ELL writers with a chance to participate and share their own expertise and experience. (See Chapter 7 for ways to use discussion, along with techniques from systemic functional linguistics, to teach writing.)

Only then can we move these students in from the sidelines—from a place where they may doubt their voices, their academic abilities, and their ideas—to a place where they are encouraged and supported, but also challenged. Often, we see the written page of second language writers, and we aren't looking for the writer; we're looking for ways to help ELL students survive the minimum writing expectations of high school and the tests. But with our gaze so tightly focused on their survival, we miss opportunities—and so do our ELL students. In the next chapter, I'll take up the issue of missed opportunities even further, as I explore the experiences of advanced ELL writers.

ADDITIONAL RESOURCES

These resources and authors come from a variety of writing backgrounds and theoretical stances, but they all emphasize approaches to writing that encourage more socially situated writing assignments, more assignments that encourage writing-as-communication, more "writing-to-learn" activities, and more critical thinking for student writers.

Ballenger, B. (2008). *The curious researcher* (6th ed.). London, United Kingdom: Longman.

Bean, J. (2001). *Engaging ideas: The professor's guide to integrating writing, critical thinking, and active learning in the classroom*. San Francisco, CA: Jossey-Bass.

Ferris, D., & Hedgecock, J. (2005). *Teaching ESL composition: Purpose, process, and practice*, 2nd edition. New York, NY: Pearson.

Johnson-Sheehan, R. (2010). *Technical communication today* (3rd ed.). New York, NY: Pearson.

Meet Paul

Paul slumps into his seat, a wooden chair in the young adult book section of the local public library. When he entered the room, his backpack hung onto his back and shoulders, weighted down by the volume of books and notebooks inside. It now sits at the floor by his side, and he sits across from me, waiting. Of all my case study participants, Paul, with his narrow face and short-cropped black hair, seems the most reluctant participant and also the most ambitious student.

—Field notes

Paul arrived in Mill River from El Salvador when he was 12 years old. His family had come to join an uncle who lived in the area. The family move was due, in part, to the attacks of September 11, 2001. As Paul explained, "After 9/11, things changed in my country. The economy got really, really bad. There were no jobs." In Mill River, both of his parents could find work, and Paul, along with his two older sisters and his younger brother, could attend good schools and go to college.

In El Salvador, Paul had attended a private Catholic school. It was one of the best schools in the country, he explained to me, and his family paid a high tuition for him to attend. Paul received excellent grades in math, Spanish Language Arts, social studies, and religion. In our interviews, he reported that he had done "lots more homework" in El Salvador, much more than what he had to do for his classes in the United States.

As a child, Paul's parents read to him every day. His mother was a dress designer by trade. Her schooling had been interrupted on many occasions due to the civil war. His father had gone to private school and was a trained graphic designer. Both of his parents cared deeply about Paul's success in school, and so did Paul. He knew that doing well in school was a prerequisite for college, and he and his family wanted him to attend the best U.S. college he could. When Paul arrived in the United States, it was late May and the school year was nearly complete, so he did not attend school until the following September. As a result, he missed almost a full year of schooling due to the move, the transition, and the language barrier. He didn't speak much English when he entered the 7th grade in Mill River, where he took sheltered ELL classes in language arts, science, and social studies. He was placed in one mainstream class—math, his favorite subject. In 8th grade, he proudly told me that he took all mainstream classes. His teachers described him as "an excellent student," "a hard worker," and "motivated." Paul liked "being in classes with rest of the kids," primarily native speakers of English. One middle school teacher commented in a letter of recommendation: "Paul demonstrates a strong desire to learn as much as he can as fast as he can." Paul reported that the mainstream classes were "only difficult in the beginning," and he did very well on all his progress reports and exams.

Paul was an active Boy Scout, working toward the rank of Eagle Scout, and he was a keen reader of *Boys' Life* magazine. He was also an avid player of action-adventure and role-playing video games. One morning a week, he attended a teenage Bible group at his church before coming to school. He was a shy, quiet student. Paul could be critical of students that he saw "goofing around" in class. During the school year, he became close friends with Wisdom, another participant in the study, whom Paul identified as having similar academic goals. After school, they often played video games or basketball together.

As a writer and a reader, Paul was confident about his skills. His summer school teacher had seen him as one of the strongest writers in the course, noting that he mostly needed to work on enriching his writing through detail and description. She commented, "He organizes his thoughts well and has strong spelling and grammar skills." He knew how to write summaries and the basic four-paragraph essay. He understood the importance of topic sentences, supporting sentences, and cohesion. Paul wrote easily in English, composing quickly, rarely stopping, and making only a few sentence-level errors. As he told me in our first meeting, he loved writing a good story, usually adventures or mysteries, with strong, action-driven plots, elaborate character descriptions, and character dialogue.

Meet Wisdom

Wisdom, you are a wonderful boy. . . . You were wonderful to teach. In high school you will be a star. Portfolio: A+.

—8th-grade Language Arts teacher, final portfolio

Wisdom, you did it! We are so proud of you! You are a shining star, destined to accomplish amazing things.

—Note from Wisdom's 8th-grade basketball coach

Wisdom clearly leaves an impression in his wake. In our interviews and throughout the high school hallways, he wore an easy smile on his face. He always walked into a room with confidence in his stride and a twinkle in his eye. He loved the banter of a good conversation and was insightful, articulate, and thoughtful. He was extremely politically aware of issues on the larger world stage, but also of the politics that surrounded him on a daily basis. These qualities were not surprising, given his history.

Wisdom arrived in Mill River in the 5th grade, a political refugee from Nigeria. He is the youngest of 11 children. In Nigeria, his father was a leader in their village and a small-business owner. In the 1990s, he, along with other village leaders, led an uprising against corrupt officials in the Nigerian government. In Wisdom's words, the conflict was a matter of "economics," a struggle for the oil-rich province that Wisdom's family called home. As Wisdom explained,

> The president of Nigeria and the government wanted to take the oil from the town and without exchange. Basically what we wanted them to do was just to pave the road and just make it to have a better place to live, more organized, and more developed. They just wanted to take the oil. We weren't pleased with that, so we said no.

What ensued was a bloody civil uprising between the leaders of Wisdom's village and Nigerian government officials. During the month-long conflict, Wisdom, his mother, and some of his siblings escaped. Wisdom's father, one of the leaders in the village, stayed behind to defend the village. As Wisdom reported, "He was more in danger than most other people. They caught most of the leaders and what happened was that they hung him. They killed him."

Wisdom and two of his older siblings were smuggled across the border to a refugee camp in Benin. Wisdom's mother and seven other siblings were not able to make the journey. They remain in Nigeria. At the time of this study, Wisdom had not seen his mother in over 8 years and commented candidly that he doubted he would ever see her again.

Wisdom's schooling in Nigeria began at a young age with preschool and kindergarten programs. The schools were public, but according to Wisdom, families had to pay for "everything"—textbooks, uniforms, exams, paper. Many families could not afford to send their children to schools, and even more children who started school were unable to finish due to financial constraints. Wisdom explained:

> It was very hard to pay the school fees. The thing is that the political leaders that were there—they were greedy people. That is the problem I have, that there are some greedy people that are not . . . that do not look to the future for the kids, for the next generation. They just look after themselves right now. And that was part of the problem. It was very hard for children to finish school because you had to pay for everything.

The difficulty of making those payments meant that most of Wisdom's siblings did not finish their education.

In some ways, Wisdom did not fit the profile of an English language learner. As a Nigerian, English was his national language. But throughout the country, more than 50 languages are spoken in various villages and communities. In Wisdom's village alone, there were four languages aside from English that were spoken. He spoke Gukana with his family and considered it his first language. Although he studied English during his kindergarten and elementary school years, he reported using a mix of English and Gukana in the classroom. Although Gukana was his spoken language, he learned to read and write in English first. Wisdom's literacy education in both languages was interrupted by the conflict in Nigeria, and for 3 years, he lived in a refugee camp in Benin with only limited opportunities to continue his studies. Unlike the other participants in this study, Wisdom felt a strong sense of ownership of the English language. He was also the student participant who had been in the United States the longest at the start of this study—5 years.

When he arrived in Mill River, he was placed in a magnet ELL program at the elementary school with other second language learners from throughout the city. In middle school, he was placed in a pull-out ELL program, an indication of his strides toward proficiency in English, and by 8th grade, he was in all mainstream classes and only saw his ELL teacher on rare occasions.

Wisdom was one of the most tenacious and resolute participants in this study. He was deeply concerned with doing well in school and determined to go to college. He put tremendous amounts of pressure on himself to do well in school, reviewing each of his progress reports and grade sheets and scrutinizing his teachers' comments meticulously. Although his brothers and sister did not track his every test score or grade report, he felt that there was a level of expectation that has been placed on him by his family. As he explained, "I don't take any opportunity I have for granted." He continued, "There is a lot of pressure because they [his family] want me to get a better education, especially my mom would be very happy when I finish college and everything. She just wants me to be educated." For Wisdom, achievement in school was not only about hard work and good grades; it was a matter of honor and obligation to his family and to his father's legacy.

Meet Vildana

> I don't care if I have to go to college for 4 or 5 years. If that is something I like, I'll go for it, and become what I always dream about. I would be proud of myself because I'll be the first one who graduates from college in my family.
>
> —Vildana

Vildana carried herself, in her words, as a "modern Muslim woman." In her classes at the local university's bridge program, she wore woolen slacks and crisp, white linen tops—always with coordinating heels. Her light brown hair fell to her shoulders, and in class, she often wrapped it in a tight bun as she concentrated on a classroom reading or lecture. She was born in Bosnia-Herzegovina, and she arrived in Mill River when she was 14 years old. When I met Vildana, she was 17 years old and completing her junior year of high school. She had enrolled in a local high school–to–college bridge program for ESL students.

She had to come to the United States 5 years after the siege of Sarajevo ended, but she had childhood memories of the city's bombings. Her parents joined extended family in the United States after the war ended, and they hoped to secure a better education for their children and a better-paying job for her father. Vildana's connections to the city, her extended family, and the Bosnian community were well established when she arrived. Refugees from Bosnia had created in the community a strong network of support for newcomers.

Her high school teachers described her as an "enthusiastic learner" who was goal-oriented in her academic pursuits. She liked reading novels and magazines. She often read books in her native language, noting her fluidity in her native language in contrast to her slower English reading, which often required her to stop and look up words in a dictionary. Her favorite book in English was *The Catcher in the Rye*. In our interviews, Vildana revealed that her "life dream" was to become a pharmacist or a physician's assistant. When she talked about her future goals, she noted, "Everything I did in math class here was nothing for me. I knew it since 7th or 6th grade [in Sarajevo]. Biology class, too. I knew a lot of stuff." But she was less confident when it came to her language arts classes. In a recommendation, her health and science teacher described her as a positive role model for her peers and a "young woman of excellent character." Her ELL teachers described her as an intermediate-level student in terms of her written and spoken English. Vildana was an A/B student, enrolled in mainstream Level 2 classes. Her goal was to attend college in

Boston or New York City because some of the best colleges and universities were in those cities.

Vildana described her classes in Bosnia as strict, with challenging and interesting work. She saw American classes as much easier, pointing to multiple-choice exercises and tests and noting that she didn't have to read or write much. "I don't read too much. I'm not a good one honestly. I would rather spend time online or drawing. I even prefer writing to reading." She was taking Latin courses in order to prepare herself for the medical terms that she would encounter in college. In discussing her move to U.S. schools, she commented:

> Honestly, I never study a lot. That is a boring thing for me. But I'm an A/B student. When I was in my country, I used to study a lot. I had to. The first year I came to high school here, I had all the easy subjects. I never had any homework. So I didn't study anything. I didn't have anything to study.

Vildana reported that she had done the most writing in her junior year of high school. Prior to that, she was only asked to write grammar lessons and short 1- to 3-paragraph papers or long-answer questions.

Vildana felt underprepared to write for upper-level coursework and college: "I never liked language, and the rest of my life, I'll spend in a field with a lot of science in it." As a high school junior, she had found that the workload was increasing, but despite her concerns, she was getting good grades in her classes. But she was concerned that the courses she had taken in high school wouldn't prepare her for college. During the summer before her senior year, she chose to attend a summer bridge program at a local college in order to learn more about getting into an American college and develop her college writing skills. This program was one way in which she was hoping to test the waters, to learn more about college professors' expectations, and to learn about entrance requirements. She considered it a privilege to attend, particularly since she had won a scholarship for the program. She noted that the opportunity to learn about college expectations was important; as she explained, "I take school seriously."

CHAPTER 5

Survival, Writing, and Cycles of Inopportunity

English learners often find themselves on the periphery, physically and pedagogically outside of the richest academic discourse.

—Rebecca Callahan, 2005, p. 309

Near the end of March, I met with Paul. He had grown at least 4 inches since the summer, and as he sat across the table from me, he rummaged through his backpack, looking through his binder. We were talking about his favorite writing experiences so far that year.

> *Paul:* I have this essay. I wrote it 2 weeks ago. For English. It was a compare-and-contrast essay. We could write about anything. I didn't know what to do. But the day before, I'd seen *Freddy vs. Jason.* You know that movie?
> *Christina:* Freddy Krueger?
> *Paul:* Yeah, she [the English teacher] said mine was one of the most creative. Here it is.
> *Christina:* Tell me what you wrote about.

As Paul described his essay (Figure 5.1), he didn't talk much about the characters or the details of the film, though in a later conversation, he provided many vivid details about the nature of these characters, their gruesome origins, the audiences that see the films, and the use of camera shots to capture the more ghastly moments of the film. On this day, though, Paul would share his view on the success of this assignment, focusing only on the essay's form, paragraph by paragraph:

> At first I compared how they died. In the second paragraph I wrote on how they were killed. [pause] And then in the next [paragraph] how are they strong. [pause] It was four, almost five paragraphs long. I got an A-.

FIGURE 5.1. Paul's Compare-and-Contrast Essay

Freddy Krueger and Jason
Compare/Contrast Essay

Freddy and Jason: two of the most famous horror-movie characters. They both kill people, but there are some differences between them.

Freddy kidnapped and killed little children, building up his own kingdom of terror, when he was alive. The parents of his victims killed him by setting his home, along with him, on fire. They took justice on their own hands. Then he began appearing in children's dreams, so that he wasn't forgotten in children's minds. Filling them with fear, obtaining his powers to hurt more children.

Jason on the other hand, died when he was eleven years old. He was drowned in Crystal Lake at Summer Camp. His mother, who is in hell, won't let him die. That's why he's invincible.

Freddy appears in children's dreams turning them into nightmares, but he can also appear in real life; that's how he begins killing more children. He can also use his victim's bodies and use them by just appearing in their dreams and making an illusion he's being swallowed by them. That's one way he can appear in real life. It's so weird...

Jason and Freddy have their own powers and killing instruments. Jason uses a machete, but I've also seen him using a chain saw. Freddy uses razor blades attached to a glove that he wears. In the movie "Freddy vs. Jason" you can tell the difference between their powers and how they give an advantage. In the movie, when Freddy appears in one of Jason's dreams, Freddy has so much advantage. He can use about anything that comes to his mind as a weapon. Unfortunately for Freddy, Jason doesn't seem to get hurt at all and he just won't die. Jason chops off one of Freddy's arms but he just regenerates. It's ridiculous.

When Freddy appears right in front of Jason in real life, Jason has a major advantage. Jason's stronger and Freddy cannot regenerate himself when his arm is chopped off. In the end both of them seem to be immortal.

In conclusion I think that although both of them having different powers and disadvantages Freddy wins psychologically because he can easily manipulate Jason, who I think wins physically.

He wrote the essay in one draft, turned it in to his teacher, got it back with her marks, fixed two spelling words, and turned it back in for the final grade. It was the lengthiest writing assignment that he had to complete for his ELA class.

In this chapter, I share the experiences of Paul, Wisdom, and Vildana to highlight the struggles of ELL students who have been exited from ELL programs, but despite their academic prowess, intelligence, and determination, can remain on the outer edges of college preparatory coursework and writing instruction. Over time, these students began to believe that they weren't intellectually capable of reaching higher. Their loftier academic goals seemed impossible to reach.

SURVIVAL GENRES

Paul's compare-and-contrast essay on Freddy Krueger and Jason was a piece of writing that he was particularly proud of, but his discussion of the piece focused almost exclusively on the structure of the essay—five paragraphs. The number of lengthier writing assignments (anything beyond a single page) was limited, and often nonexistent. Across four different ELA and ELL classrooms, the following activities represented the students' main opportunities for putting pen to paper:

- Fill-in-the-blank exercises used to demonstrate understanding of literature or grammar lessons
- Vocabulary sentences in which students generated sentences that showed their understanding of new terms
- Notes taken verbatim from teacher's writing on the whiteboard
- Brief letters and notes to parents or teachers (often completed in ESL classes) that informed parents, guardians, and other teachers of ESL-sponsored activities in the school or community
- Responses to prompts, generated from stories that they had read
- One- to two-paragraph entries in ungraded home writing journals
- Five-paragraph essays
- Copying down information for projects or assignments, as dictated by their teachers

In short, what the ELL students practiced and learned the most were survival genres.

Survival genres are those genres that secondary school students learn in order to pass high school classes and demonstrate a level of proficiency on high-stakes testing. Instructionally, they are often the very basics that students need in order to complete homework assignments and tests and to take notes.

But as writing goes, they are predominantly audience-less. Their purpose is to demonstrate understanding, to scan and report back information (often verbatim) from textbooks, or to memorize material for future tests. They teach students how to handle writing a response to a 45-minute testing prompt. These genres are rarely seen beyond the classroom or the assessment test.

The lengthiest of these survival genres is the ubiquitous five-paragraph essay. In practice, it is the ultimate survival genre taught to second language learners and many of their native-English-speaking peers. In the eyes of many teachers, government officials, and administrators, mastery of the five-paragraph essay remains the key to opening the gates set up by state-mandated testing, college entrance exams, and college placement tests. The five-paragraph essay, with its standardized and predictable form, is easily read and scored by machines and outside raters. As a result, it has become the genre for demonstrating what is often called "writing competence" on state-mandated exams, on the SAT, and even on college placement tests.

But the five-paragraph essay doesn't really exist in the world beyond K–12 schools, and teachers know that. We teach it as a training ground for our students, starting in the elementary school grades. We know it is a somewhat diluted form, often *arhetorical*—without any sense of a real audience and purpose—and more focused on its form than its content. In my study, it became very obvious that the five-paragraph essay was the default form for all the ELL students whenever they were asked to write a page or more. Posters in the ELL classrooms of Therese and Ken-zhi depicted the five-paragraph structure in large letters, using colored sentences to show how paragraphs matched to the opening and closing sentences. Notes from their ELA classrooms featured similar rules and instructions about how the form should work.

But the five-paragraph essay, as a default form, masks important distinctions between descriptive, narrative, personal, argumentative, and even compare-and-contrast essays. For example, successful narratives and nonfiction essays often invoke characteristics of fiction writing using scenes and character development to "show" the story. But for the ELL writers in my study, all these five-paragraph assignments—from narrative to argument—looked and sounded the same. George Hillocks, Jr. (2002) has called this trend the "homogenization" of the five-paragraph form (p. 110). He notes that this homogenization has been encouraged by standardized, mass-produced rubrics that do not distinguish between various genres, the intentions of the text, or the author's audience. Paul, like many ELL writers, quickly learned that mastery of the structure led to good marks.

But—and here is the worrisome part—in most classrooms, ELL writers are rarely encouraged to move beyond this survival form to develop content, detail, and language, or to expand their repertoire. This is often true in English Language Arts classes, but also in other content-area classes across the curriculum. Enright and Gilliland (2011) examined the writing curricula of ELL students in high school science classes, finding that ELL students were overwhelmingly placed in a lower-track earth science, instead of higher-track biology, which included honors students and only fluent English speakers. The writing that was required of students in the lower-level course perpetuated this division. Both the biology and earth science classes had standardized assignment types across the two "tracks," and superficially, there appeared to be parity between the two levels. But—and here is the major concern—the biology class offered more opportunities and more time for students to learn to write as scientists, to stretch their thinking and writing abilities, and to grapple with extended explanations. In contrast, writing assignments in earth science were noticeably less involved and less frequent. Students composed only rote answers, often copying word for word from the pages of their books. The lower-track students, according to the teacher, struggled more with the "technical aspects" of science writing, and they tended to only summarize procedures in their writing, rather than offer explanations for their lab observations. In response, the teacher turned to graphic organizers and fill-in-the-blank worksheets. Graphic organizers and other scaffolding techniques are proven ways to help ELL students understand and develop their ideas about content-area material (Vogt, Short, & Echevarria, 2008). But the ELL students in earth science never got to move beyond the scaffolding. Their experiences with science writing were ultimately watered down, requiring "very little elaboration or explanation" (Enright & Gilliland, 2011, p. 189).

The lack of advanced writing opportunities and instruction leaves even the most proficient and talented of these ELL students underprepared and ill-equipped for upper-level coursework. And the "triumph of form over substance" does not help academically talented students like Wisdom or Paul to improve as writers (Harklau, 2011, p. 228).

AT ODDS: CONCERNS ABOUT OVER-SCAFFOLDING AND LOWERING WRITING EXPECTATIONS

It is a tricky balance. We want our ELL students to do well and to stay current with the content in our classrooms. So we build bridges to previous information; we scaffold; we use graphic organizers to help students demonstrate their understanding of chapters and plot lines. But what happens when writing is the content?

By secondary school, writing is not often treated as its own content area. It is seen as a skill, not a performance. For many ELL writers, writing opportunities are replaced by visual activities, graphic organizers, and teaching tools that help ELL students demonstrate content knowledge and build new understanding. Don't get me wrong. I do find this type of scaffolding to be valuable on many fronts. I even advocate for its use in much of my work with ELL students and their teachers. However, when it comes to writing, I've grown concerned in recent years for two reasons: (1) the scaffolds, designed to assist students toward more language, can end up replacing opportunities for students to engage with writing and revision and (2) some teachers and administrators don't see writing as its own content area, which means teachers are not trained or given the time to teach students how language facilitates understandings between readers and writers in their writing. There are reasons why this happens in our schools. For one thing, writing is transparent. The writing itself, and how the authors make that writing function for readers, fades into the background as the information it conveys comes into focus. That level of transparency can mean that we miss opportunities to teach writing and writing strategies as an act of craft and performance. By making writing either formulaic or invisible, we do a great disservice to English language learners. Many of them end up having only limited opportunities to experiment with advanced genres or to develop a meta-cognitive awareness of the decisions that writers make.

When I think of students like Paul, Wisdom, and Vildana, I can't help but question how often promising ELL writers get stuck in the very scaffolds that we create. The metaphor of scaffolding suggests that, at some point, the scaffold will be taken down and the new building will stand on its own. When does that happen for ELL writers? If the five-paragraph essay is indeed a scaffold to help inexperienced writers, when do writers like Wisdom and Paul move beyond this structure? When do we allow these writers the opportunity to grow in their writing by developing critical thinking strategies for their writing tasks and encouraging them to venture into more advanced genres and more rhetorically complex writing situations?

Is it possible that students who still struggle with thesis-driven arguments may, at the same time, be ready to experiment and venture into creative writing, argumentative writing, workplace writing, and multigenre writing? Is it possible that ELL writers could draw upon strengths in other areas of rhetorical analysis or creative prose that may strengthen their confidence and surprise their teachers?

And what happens if we fail to provide these experiences for them?

"I USED TO BE AN HONORS STUDENT"

Paul and Wisdom had been in U.S. schools for a number of years. Paul, for his part, was exited from the ELL program by the beginning of 8th grade and was formally placed on "monitor" status as he entered high school. His middle school teachers described him as "an excellent student," "a hard worker," and "motivated." Paul purposefully explained to me, "I used to be an honors student in El Salvador," where his school was considered elite. In Mill River, his middle school teachers noted how well prepared he was in terms of content-area knowledge in science, math, and geography. His Spanish language skills, in both reading and writing, were impeccable. His English teacher in the summer ESL program commented, "Paul's writing skills are strong. His voice comes through in his writing. He just needs to focus on developing more detail in his descriptions."

Wisdom was as talented and ambitious as Paul. He had been in the United States even longer. For over 5 years, he had been in U.S. schools, and in 7th grade, he was placed in all mainstream classes. Wisdom, despite his years in a refugee camp, voraciously embraced his academic abilities in U.S. schools, getting good grades and impressing his teachers throughout middle school. In 8th grade, he kept a writing portfolio that showcased his teacher's praise for his written work and demonstrated the care that he used in his writing. He often spoke of himself as a writer, and referenced the speeches of Martin Luther King, Jr. as inspiration for his writing.

Even as first-year students, Paul and Wisdom knew that success in high school would determine their college choices. At the end of 8th grade, Paul and Wisdom were disappointed when guidance counselors in the district told him that they would only be taking Level 2 courses, the lower mid-level academic track, at the high school. Teachers were cautious, unsure of how Paul and Wisdom might do in the new, larger environment of high school. Knowing the students' disappointment, their teachers encouraged the young men to work hard, explaining that they would be moved up the academic tracks shortly.

But throughout the fall and winter, Paul and Wisdom were convinced that there had been a mistake in their placement, especially when it came to their English classes. They expressed frustration, noting that the work seemed "easy," the class conversations were often about note-taking, and the teacher didn't seem to ask much of them. Their native-English-speaking peers were often uninterested in the classroom activities, and Paul and Wisdom weren't sure how to react to their peers' complacency. As adolescents, they were torn between following the "norm" set by their peer group and their own ambitions to achieve more. The reality was that Level 2 courses were a kind of "catch-all" academic track that included both students who thought about going to college and others who had the potential but not always the motivation. They were large classes, often overcrowded, and in stark contrast to the more seminar-style courses and the advanced genres of the higher-level tracks and AP courses. Paul and Wisdom complained that many of their Level 2 English-speaking peers fell asleep in class or failed to do their assignments. For his part, Paul wasn't sure how to prove to his teachers that he wanted to do more, socially or academically, in these classroom environments. So he did what he was asked to do, assuming that it was enough.

Over their first year, Paul and Wisdom began to learn what they were missing in upper-level English classes. In middle school, they had worked side-by-side with many of these honors students, and in study hall, they regularly borrowed assignment sheets from them to see what honors students were doing. Writing assignments looked more involved and required more in-depth drafting, discussion of the writers' goals, and revision, as well as the integration of research, evidence, and opinion. It was no coincidence that most native-English-speaking parents in the district talked about the necessity of getting their children into these upper-level tracks, especially if they were college-bound. Wisdom and Paul's parents knew very little about this strategy to success, but Paul and Wisdom quickly deduced the long-term advantages of these upper-level classes, and they wanted in.

They followed the advice of their middle school teachers and worked hard, hoping to convince guidance counselors and their teachers to let them "jump" the track and enter honors classrooms. Wisdom continually heard from his ELA teacher that his writing was "fine." As she explained to him and to me on various occasions, Wisdom's writing was good and she ranked him "right in the upper-middle of the pack," when she compared him to his Level 2 peers. According to the teacher, his papers still betrayed "an accent," even though the content, organization, and sentences were cohesive and developed. Wisdom complained that he received very little feedback on his written work and almost no teacher comments that might help him improve. There were few, if any, opportunities for explicit instruction on how to advance his work beyond formulas. Like Paul, he was passing the course with A-'s and B's. No one was concerned. He was surviving.

CYCLES OF INOPPORTUNITY

In many American schools, ELL students are "remarkably absent from many academically advanced classes" (Ortmeier-Hooper & Enright, 2011, p. 173). Even if they gain higher levels of English proficiency, they move only horizontally out of ELL classrooms and into mainstream ones. It is rare for them to move vertically up the academic track (Valenzuela, 1999).

When Paul and Wisdom approached their respective English teachers and guidance counselors about moving into the next tier of ELA courses (Level 3) for their sophomore year, they were encouraged to remain where they were. As I've reported elsewhere, Wisdom commented:

In English, I was going to take Level 3, because I know it is something I could have done. I have a strong B in English. . . . I could have signed up for Level 3, but [the teacher] and [the guidance counselor] suggested Level 2. (Ortmeier-Hooper, 2010, p. 14)

Subtly, Wisdom and Paul were cautioned by their guidance counselors that taking a chance on Level 3 classes could endanger their school records. They were told that once they signed up for the higher-level classes, there would be (ironically) less support, and if they failed, the repercussions on their grade point averages would be dire. Paul and Wisdom became scared of the risks. There was no mention of mentoring and pathways that might build support into those upper-level courses and help them meet their academic aspirations.

Notably, the students' writing was often held up as a gatekeeping measure to informally, and sometimes formally, assess their ability to succeed in upper-level courses. Wisdom and Paul found that their lack of experience with more advanced writing genres and instruction was often pointed to as a sign that they were not prepared for honors and advanced coursework. The very work that they completed for their Level 2 ELA courses did not satisfy those expectations nor did it provide them with the instructional opportunities they needed to advance, despite their cognitive abilities and their willingness to work hard.

By mid-sophomore year, Wisdom and Paul became discouraged. They began to question the system and their own academic abilities. Like many of their Level 2 peers, they began to purposefully look for opportunities to avoid writing. They finished assignments as quickly as possible, following the rote procedures that their teachers expected and rarely engaging in any sense of craft when it came to their writing assignments. They felt locked into their tracking groups—both academically and socially. (Davidson [1996] has written about the ways academic tracking can influence social circles and student identity.) By the end of his sophomore year, Paul acknowledged that he had pretty much given up on moving up the track in English Language Arts. He would sign up for whatever the teacher told him to (Ortmeier-Hooper, 2010). The cycle of inopportunity was simply his reality. English wasn't his language, you know, he confided to me. Maybe he wasn't an honors kid after all.

FROM HIGH SCHOOL TO COLLEGE: MORE RAMIFICATIONS

Vildana Tests the Waters

In high school, Vildana had taken 2 years of advanced ESL courses, which often focused on grammar exercises and "coming up with ideas" for writing.

What are Advanced and High-Status Genres?

The work of genre is to mediate between social situations and the texts that respond strategically to the exigencies of these situations.

—John Swales, 2009, p. 14

Advanced and high-status genres vary across courses and content areas, but in general, they share a level of involvement and critical thinking that requires students to consider the content and purpose of their writing. Widening students' understanding of advanced genres encourages students to see writing, and the genres that we use in various situations, as "frames for social action" and performance (Bazerman, Bonini, & Fieguerido, 2009, p. 6). High-status genres offer student writers more complex rhetorical situations and allow them more creative possibilities, more decision making, and more development as writers. Advanced genres for students can include some of the following:

- Arguments
- Closing arguments (legal)
- Eulogies
- Mission statements
- Political leaflets
- Workplace genres (reports, memos, formal letters, white papers, usability reports)
- Fiction writing
- Memoirs
- Research essays (based on the synthesis of outside sources)
- Formal proposals (for grant money, school initiatives, and so forth)
- Historical narratives
- Comedy writing
- Genre fiction (horror/crime/sci-fi/fantasy)
- Case studies
- Profiles
- Screenplays
- Satire
- Ethnographic writing (nonfiction essays on place, community group, and subculture based on student field research)
- Shorts (nonfiction or fiction)
- College admission essays
- Web-based writing (blogs, websites)
- Reviews (movies, music, and so on)
- Creative nonfiction
- Inquiry-based writing
- Personal statements
- Multigenre essays
- Journalism (feature stories, sports columns, and so forth)

In her 3 years of mainstream English, she was taught to outline, brainstorm, and write a first draft. She also learned to write an essay. She explains that the amount of writing she did varied greatly: "It all depends on what kind of teacher you got."

In the summer before her senior year, Vildana enrolled in a full-day, high school–to–college bridge program to learn more about the expectations of college professors and to improve her academic writing skills. The course was taught by a college English and ESL instructor, who had regularly taught first-year college composition to native and non-native speakers for over 20 years. The course covered a number of college academic skills, but here, I want to look exclusively at Vildana's struggles with writing and her professor's concerns.

The overarching writing assignment for the course was a multipage essay profiling an important person in the students' lives. The final draft would be due at the end of the 5-week term. A well-constructed assignment included an array of prompts to help students generate ideas and material. The professor emphasized a process approach, and explained that college writing professors often wanted to see students' notes and drafts as evidence of their learning and thinking.

In the computer lab, a day after the assignment was presented, Vildana was the first one to finish her draft, which was four paragraphs in length. As the rest of the class continued to work on their essays, she spellchecked her draft. She looked at the punctuation, added a comma or two, and then printed out the essay and placed it in her instructor's folder. "Done," she whispered to me, confidently. In an interview, Vildana explained that she was pleased with the essay. She wrote about a cousin whom she cared for "like a sister." She had written an assignment like this one in the past and got a high grade from her teacher. The next day, during peer review, she listened to her peers—some of whom were older, nontraditional students. They raised questions about her narrative and asked for more details, and after the session, she returned to the computer. Again, she was the first one done, having added one more paragraph to increase the length, but she had not adjusted her content to any great extent despite some good questions and suggestions from her peers.

Later, when her instructor and I discussed her essay, he expressed concern. Vildana seemed overly concerned with form. Her instructor had seen many essays by other ESL writers, so he could work through the sentence-level errors. But what concerned him most was the lack of development in her piece and his sense that she lacked any sense of how to think critically about her text. Her revisions were only additive and she didn't seem to be thinking about her purpose or her readers, even when those readers were her peers. She didn't seem to know how to respond to feedback, even though she was a conscientious student.

The instructor was also confused because Vildana's daily journal writings in response to the professor's prompts had been much more thoughtful, focused, and engaged. They were first draft pieces, often without paragraphs and with errors, but they revealed an engaged, interesting, and thoughtful mind. For example, in a journal entry on religious freedom, she tackled difficult questions of Christianity and Islamic conflicts, referencing material from class and drawing connections between her school and home life. The journal entries, though unpolished, demonstrated that she had the potential to write with more cohesion, richness, detail, and depth. Her instructor wondered aloud why she didn't bring those same qualities to her more formal essays.

When I spoke with her about her essay, Vildana was convinced that form, spelling, complete sentences, and error-free punctuation would matter most. When she received her essay back at the end of the term, she was genuinely surprised by her low grade and the instructor's comments. She worried aloud about doing well at a 4-year college. She wondered if her high school experiences had prepared her enough to get into pharmaceutical colleges after she graduated. She wasn't sure.

Voices from Other Studies

Many adolescent ELL writers who gain access to U.S. colleges and universities are surprised by how little experience they have actually have as writers. Studies on the transition of ELL writers to college demonstrate these concerns in powerful ways.

For example, Harklau (2000) found that ELL adolescents were often seen by high school teachers as hardworking and determined, but these descriptions of the students tended to highlight them only in terms of their behavior and not their academic potential. Although most of them were in mainstream classes, the students had few opportunities for more advanced writing instruction. When Harklau followed the students from high school into their community college classrooms, the students were surprised and angered to find themselves suddenly placed back into remedial writing courses and repositioned as ELL students, a label they thought they had long left behind. In another example, Leki (2007) shared the case study of Jan, a college student who had immigrated from Poland as a teenager. His written work in high school had focused only on short-answer questions and multiple-choice exams. In college, he felt unprepared to write and develop lengthier pieces that required more depth and elaboration. He expressed frustration when college teachers asked him to revise and develop his ideas on the page. As Jan explained, "Pretty much when I finish my paper it's pretty much like five lines long. I can't express for longer. You know, write about blah, blah, blah, blah, blah. I write short." (p. 142). The rote patterns he had learned in high school had not prepared him for the critical thinking and development that college teachers now wanted to see in his written work.

As these studies suggest, the result of teaching only "survival writing" practices to ELL students is that they can enter college classrooms underprepared for the range and depth of writing and thinking that will be asked of them. They are not used to the idea that writing is a thinking tool. They are confused when the forms and formulaic patterns that garnered praise and encouragement from their high school teachers no longer work. The discovery that they lack strategies and writing experience can torpedo much of the confidence that they established in their high school classrooms.

MOVING BEYOND SURVIVAL: SOME IDEAS

So how do we begin to move beyond "survival" in our work with ELL writers? The remainder of this book takes up this question in greater detail, considering the strengths of these writers, developing inclusive writing curricula with these writers in mind, and establishing effective methods of responding to their writing. But here are some initial ideas on how we might encourage and help students like Wisdom, Paul, and Vildana to unlock their potential and find passageways into more advanced academic opportunities:

- Limit ELL students' options for opting out of writing.

ELL writers want to be successful in school and often identify writing in English as a minefield that can further inhibit their progress and lower their grades. They learn from many native-English-speaking peers that there are ways to navigate through school without writing. For example, in one class, the teacher offers all her students, including her ELL students, the following options: (1) Storyboard a scene from the novel; (2) compile a yearbook/scrapbook for a character in the novel; and (3) write a 2- to 3-page paper analyzing a character.

Even her most academically and English proficient ELL students quickly realize that there are ways to get out of writing and rule out option 3. They notice that no amount of writing is explicitly required for options 1 and 2. In theory, they won't have to write much, so these are safer options.

But these wonderfully creative project options could also be served with a side order of mandatory writing. For example, students might be asked to write a business letter to potential yearbook customers encouraging them to buy the yearbook, or they could write a sales pitch to sell their storyboard to a local TV producer.

- Introduce ELL writers to upper-level courses by initiating some of the following ideas:

» In mid- and lower-level tracks, include explicit and supportive opportunities for writing assignments that are typical in upper-level courses. Provide students with samples of early and later drafts.

» Develop bridge writing courses/writing electives that purposefully and explicitly prepare ELL students in 8th, 9th, and 10th grades for the writing and norms of upper-level ELA and AP courses.

» Create pathways of mentoring to help ELL writers move up the academic track. For many ELL writers, who are hoping to go to college, jumping the academic track seems like a dangerous proposition. But it doesn't have to be that way. We can create individual mentoring opportunities for ELL writers and build small initiatives that make the systems in our schools more transparent and less intimidating for ELL students.

• Some ideas for providing ELL writers with advanced academic preparation include establishing:

» *Academic Buddy Programs.* Young ELL students aspiring to join honors-level courses work with and are mentored by older, upper-level peers on collaborative research and writing projects. These peer-based academic mentorships could also be established with college-age students through local college and university writing centers.

» *Teacher Mentors from AP and Honors-Level Courses.* ELL writers often comment that they feel almost invisible to teachers who teach upper-level courses in their schools. Without any personal connection to these teachers, the students are intimidated and feel that these teachers, and the courses that they teach, are out of reach. One option to change this dynamic is to create small cohorts of ELL writers who are mentored, advised, and encouraged by supportive teachers who regularly teach upper-level courses.

» *High School Research Programs.* Such programs provide mentoring and advanced academic preparation for ELL writers through research and inquiry-based opportunities. At the college level, the McNair Scholars Program, sponsored by the U.S. Department of Education, provides a possible model. In the McNair program, students with academic potential from traditionally underrepresented groups are identified. The program prepares them, as undergraduates, for advanced graduate studies through involvement in research, mentorships and other scholarly activities. Students are given individual mentoring by faculty and graduate students and they also have opportunities to present their work to public audiences. Although various summer programs exist at the high school level, it is rare to find a school-based program, like McNair, that is part of the regular extracurricular offerings.

CONCLUSION

At the end of the day, the expectations of their teachers will often dictate how ELL writers perceive their own abilities and aspirations. If we teach them to survive, they will indeed survive. By raising our expectations and aiming for them to thrive, we may be surprised by the writing and thinking strengths that they can bring to the written page and to the writing classroom. It is this belief in identifying and building on ELL writers' strengths that I'll take up in the next chapter.

ADDITIONAL RESOURCES

The following resources offer some creative ways to expand the repertoire of writing and research that we offer to ELL writers in our schools:

The McNair Scholars Program. For more information on the McNair program, visit their website at http://mcnairscholars.com/.

Cox, M., Ortmeier-Hooper, C., & Tirabassi, K. (2009). Teaching writing for the real world. *English Journal, 98*(5), 72–80.

Romano, T. (2002). *Blending genres, alternating styles: Writing the multigenre paper.* Portsmouth, NH: Heinemann.

In addition, I recommend the following two books for teachers interested in learning more about the experiences of ELL writers as they transition out of high school and into college composition courses:

Harklau, L., Losey, K., & Siegal, M. (Eds.). (1999). Generation 1.5 meets college composition: Issues in the teaching of writing to U.S.-educated learners of ESL. Mahwah, NJ: Erlbaum.

Roberge, M., Harklau, L., & Siegal, M. (Eds.). (2009). Generation 1.5 in college composition: Teaching ESL to US-educated learners of ESL. New York, NY: Routledge.

CHAPTER 6

Identifying the Strengths and Resources of ELL Writers

A bilingual personal has special linguistic resources, resources beyond what a monolingual person in either of the languages has.

—Carmen Martínez-Roldán & Maria Fránquiz (2009), p. 327

In their book *Making Content Comprehensible for English Language Learners: The SIOP Model* (2008), authors Jane Echevarria, Mary Ellen Vogt, and Deborah Short encourage content-area teachers to incorporate *Building Background* activities into their instruction and lesson planning. Specifically, they suggest these kinds of teaching activities are ones in which "(1) concepts should be directly linked to students' background experience. This experience can be personal, cultural or academic," and "(2) links should be explicitly made between past learning and new concepts" (p. 41).

In teaching writing, however, we often think that the background knowledge and writing experiences that students bring from their first language (L1) are inaccessible to us as their teachers, especially if we don't share the same language. As one of my native-English-speaking teaching students once noted, "I know that he was an excellent student in Korea, but I don't speak, read, or understand Korean. I don't know how to help him. I don't know how to connect what he learned there to what I'm teaching here. What can I do?"

In this chapter, I'll take up that question, and look at how we can identify the diverse writing strengths, literacy resources, and language competencies that ELL writers bring with them.

A MULTICULTURAL VIEW IN THE ELA CLASSROOM

Most teachers will acknowledge that diversity in the classroom is a good thing. We encourage multicultural perspectives in our book selections and readings, and we value the cultural contributions that many English language learners bring to our schools in terms of language, customs, music, poetry, and experiences. They reflect a vibrant weaving of the American cultural fabric.

But sometimes that cultural fabric can feel like it only has aesthetic merit, like a beautiful tapestry that hangs on a museum wall. In the museum, we often admire the weaving of the cloth and the images, but we fail to remember that the tapestry served another functional purpose: warming and insulating the cold interior walls of ancient stone castles. In a similar fashion, we tend to admire the multicultural backgrounds that our students bring to the classroom but we do not always see the functional aspects of their backgrounds, particularly in terms of writing.

In recent years, researchers in the fields of second language writing and emergent bilingual education have made persuasive arguments about the limiting ways in which we define these students and their strengths. Our perspective on L2 writers is limited by a tendency to look for deficits, focusing almost exclusively on concerns and challenges in teaching them (Canagarajah, 2002). The glass always seems to be half-empty, and students get trapped in what I've called a "deficit model" (Ortmeier-Hooper, 2008, p. 392). ELL writers internalize this perception of their skills, especially when teachers and monolingual peers don't expect them to contribute much in English or English writing. For example, Chiang and Schmida (2006) found that teachers often expected minority students to "stumble over the English language" and students internalized that assumption, even when English was their primary language (p. 106). As one student in the Chiang and Schmida study commented,

> I think I will never be a good writer because I am Asian. It is excusable for me to not be good at writing. I am not supposed to [be] good anyway. . . . This expectation gives me an excuse to avoid writing. "People don't expect me to do well anyway," or "why bother? I will never learn to speak or write like natives," I always say to myself. (p. 100)

Internal doubts, like these, cause ELL writers to distance themselves from writing tasks, shying away from those activities that make them feel academically weak and vulnerable (Chiang, Perez, Wong, Nguyen, & Hernandez, 2009). Many ELL writers assume that they have only weaknesses, and they (and their teachers) are unsure what strengths they can bring to their writing tasks.

But in recent years, writing and literacy scholars like Canagarajah (2002), Jordan (2009, 2012), and Valdés (2003) have sought to upend this assumption. Canagarajah (2002) and Jordan (2009) point out that in an increasingly global world, many ELL writers are not strangers to English. They often have a rich understanding of the "hybridity" of language and language use from experiences in their first language, knowledge of the international uses of English, and experiences with translation and technology. (Canagarajah, 2002; Jordan, 2009; Valdés, 2003).

Canagarajah (2002) reminds us that "multilingual students do—and can—use their background as a stepping-stone to master academic discourses" (p. 13). But teachers need to look beyond the deficit model and actively seek out the writing competencies that ELL writers bring with them into classrooms and lessons. Canagarajah (2002) has called this shift in perspectives a move from "difference-as-deficit" to "difference-as-resource" (pp. 12–13).

Literacy specialists Bill Cope and Mary Kalantzis (1999) suggest that the demands of the 21st century require teachers to adopt a "multiliteracies" perspective—one that broadens standard definitions of literacy development and takes into account the increasingly interconnected and globalized world that we live in. This perspective encourages us to unearth the other types of literacy and rhetorical expertise that ELL writers often use outside of our classrooms. They suggest that students can and do use analytical insights from other literacy experiences to help them develop stronger cognitive understandings of academic writing. If we can identify ELL students' experiences in digital literacies, creative writing, computers, video games, social networking tools, extracurricular activities, workplace writing, home language use, out-of-school literacy practices, negotiations across languages and dialects, and so on, we can use these competencies and resources—these *sites of validation*, as I call them—as empowering touchstones for our ELL writers to draw upon as they encounter new writing tasks and expectations.

Second language writers have a great deal to teach teachers and native-English-speaking peers about the globalized world in which we live and how we can communicate and negotiate—across language, across dialects, across differing expectations, across genres, across cultures (Jordan, 2012). These are the language skills that English language learners use every day. When we add a globalized and rhetorical perspective to teaching students, the experiences and analytical skills of our ELL writers as multilingual individuals can become active and advantageous resources for them as writers and for us as their teachers.

IDENTIFYING THE RHETORICAL AND LITERACY STRENGTHS OF ELL WRITERS

Many young ELL writers aren't sure how to share (or define) these kinds of strengths and competencies for their teachers. These are skills that they know are useful in daily life, but it may seem like they are of little use in the classroom. One solution for teachers, then, is to create activities that encourage ELL writers to share their literacy worlds and experiences with us and open up conversations about the ways writers use language to connect and influence readers.

One of my goals in this project was to learn more about the writerly strengths of the ELL writers and to put names to the abilities and resources they brought to their writing and academic pursuits. In sorting through pages and pages of interviews, field notes, and writing samples, I began to see glimpses of their special linguistic and rhetorical resources—ones that could yield powerful contributions to a classroom of student writers. I also listened to Wisdom, Therese, Miguel, Paul, and Ken-zhi as they told me about reading, writing, and social and academic resources that played a role in how they used language and how they wrote. But when I tried to probe more deeply into those resources and strengths, our conversations often ran into a roadblock. I'd asked questions, but the students often weren't sure why or how to respond. They weren't sure if what I termed a resource could be considered school-related or writing-related.

To help me expand that conversation with the students, I developed a mapping activity that provided a tactile way for them to articulate the experiences, people, literacy events (Heath, 1983), places, and items that impacted their writing. Using visual icons, students demonstrated and discussed the literary and academic influences in their lives. The tangibility of this mapping exercise was particularly important because the students often felt that they were unable to express the depth of their thoughts in English. (For interpreting the maps, readers can turn to Figure C.1 in Appendix C for a key to icons and mapping activity.)

The posters that the students created highlighted their wide range of individual experiences, competencies, and literacies, revealing what I came to call their *sites of validation*. Sites of validation are places—physical, virtual, and/or emotional—where the students can derive confidence and demonstrate their competencies as language users. Their posters and accompanying conversations revealed incredible variations, motivations, and influences, reemphasizing how unique each second language writer is, and the distinctive gifts, backgrounds, and lenses that these writers bring with them into their texts and their classrooms. I read these maps against the backdrop of my interviews with the students, my field notes, and the students' own writing to show the range of literacy and rhetorical competencies that English language learners bring into our English Language Arts classrooms. The mapping activity led to new conversations between me and the students about the ways in which they drew upon other literacy activities and sites of validation to develop and gain confidence in their academic abilities. Through the mapping exercise and the conversations that followed, students revealed their intelligence and savvy by conducting genre analyses of models and mimicking other writers' strategies. They explained how they drew inspiration from reading activities and language interactions at home and in their communities. They shared how they experimented and played with their writing, drawing on their cultural affiliations. They revealed how their sites of validation, as well as the literacy experiences that the students derived from them, helped them see themselves as competent readers and writers in a variety of multimodal contexts. These sites were used by students to create compelling and rich identities for themselves, helping them uphold their sense of themselves as competent writers, even when certain school situations made them feel incompetent and unintelligent. In all the cases, these sites helped students move beyond institutional—and often remedial—labels and position themselves in more positive social identities, providing them with resiliency to face the other challenges in their academic lives.

In the following pages, I'll share these maps and discuss some of the strengths that emerged from my work with these students. These discussions of Wisdom, Ken-zhi, and Therese illustrate what we might learn about the competencies, linguistic abilities, language strengths, and academic experiences of other ELL writers.

LEARNING FROM WISDOM

Understanding English as a Global Language and Writing as Social Responsibility

As I've noted earlier, Wisdom was the most experienced English writer and longest U.S. resident in this study. He knew a great deal about American schools and culture. Plus, his prior experience with Nigerian English meant that he came to his writing with a strong sense of English ownership. But Wisdom also brought with him a rich understanding and ongoing interest in world politics and social activism that often spurred his readings and his writing.

Wisdom's map (Figure 6.1) illustrated these interests and showed a strong sense of social responsibility, driven by a deep connection to his mother, who remained in Nigeria, and to his father, who was killed for his political activism. The symbols for his mother and father figured prominently in his map, positioned next to his own name, where he placed those elements in his life that most inspired his writing and aided him in his academic achievement. As we talked about his map, he explained that watching "[his] father getting to pay a lot of money for education [and] helping younger ones" was an influential moment in his life. His father's dedication to securing an education for his children remained an important touchstone for Wisdom's own academic ambitions. He wanted to build on his father's legacy and felt a sense of social responsibility to help provide an education for his nieces and nephews, as well as his family members who remained in Nigeria.

Wisdom's sense of social responsibility also contributed to his awareness that writing could be persuasive, political, and profoundly influential in causing social change. In the map, Wisdom identified Mahatma Gandhi and

FIGURE 6.1. Wisdom's Map (See Appendix C, Figure C.1 for a key of icons and mapping activity)

Martin Luther King, Jr. as two important historical figures that figured prominently in his own writing ambitions. He explained that he had read multiple versions of their biographies, watched film versions of their lives, and read excerpts of their letters and autobiographies. He was inspired by their political activism and sense of social responsibility.

He explained to me that both men used writing as a tool to persuade their audiences and that their writings had convinced him of the power of the written word. Wisdom wanted to develop a similar sense of mastery and persuasion in his own writing. This interest fit with Wisdom's reading choices as well. Often, I would often enter the city library for our interviews and find him reading the international news section of the local paper, scanning for stories on Africa or the war in Iraq, eager to discuss the latest international current events. In other conversations, he compared the nature of racism and oppression in the United States and in his native Africa. On occasion, he would articulate how two treatments of the same news event from an African online newspaper and *USA Today* reflected a certain political stance or spin, depending on the writer, the audience, or the publisher.

Understanding the Power of Writing as a Creative Act

Outside of school, Wisdom poured his passion for written language into poetry and music. Wisdom embraced an image of himself as a writer. He was the only student I worked with who did so. He loved language and words. Writing was a way to express himself. In 8th grade, he had kept a journal and writer's portfolio. In 9th grade, he poured that creative energy into writing lyrics and composing music to accompany his words. (See an example of his musical composition, titled "Let it Go," in Figure 6.2.) Wisdom experimented with songwriting, learning to use digital recording software like the program Fruity Loops (included as a literacy influence on his map) to lay down tracks and beats. After school, he'd work in a friend's studio, putting down beats and playing with vocals, which contributed to his identity as an artist and a writer. His lyrics and poetry, written in English, also served to reinforce his identity as an authentic owner (and competent user) of the English language.

Wisdom's work on lyrics, music compositions, and poetry sustained his passion for writing, even when he felt that his opportunities for classroom writing were limited, when he got limited feedback from his teacher, and when the overall lack of classroom discourse on writing disappointed him. His English notebooks were interspersed with pages upon pages of poetry, multiple drafts and revisions, lyrics, notations about beats, and possible bridges to a chorus.

In the final month of his freshman English class, the teacher introduced a unit on poetry. Wisdom was thrilled. All his energy and writing that had been building up outside the school curriculum found a home in the classroom. He excelled throughout the poetry unit. In one of our last interviews, he proudly declared that the poetry unit was his best academic writing of the year, while sliding a copy of his recently completed music CD across the table for my listening pleasure.

Naming Wisdom's Writing Resources

Many second language writers have a rich sense and understanding of world events and their own home language communities. They are aware of how different communities and news organizations depict certain arguments,

FIGURE 6.2. Excerpt from Wisdom's Song

choose perspectives, and target certain kinds of readers. Given the opportunity to explore the linguistic and rhetorical strategies designed to achieve these goals in a written text, these students may surprise us with what they have to contribute. Wisdom's experiences as a political refugee and the son of a political activist provided him with political and social awareness. His interest in politics helped him see how a writer could use certain themes or devices to persuade, and he could identify the use of these strategies in a particular essay or letter. Although he wasn't eager to share his traumatic personal past in Nigeria with his classmates, he was eager to talk about language, politics, Africa, journalism, and economics. For example, he compared how news was covered in Nigerian papers versus U.S. ones and European ones, examining these papers in their online formats and regularly visiting their sites. He was also interested in news about his community (both locally defined and more internationally defined through the Internet). He eagerly approached and interviewed individuals whom he saw as stakeholders in issues that concerned him, like the funding of a local Boys and Girls Club. In these ways, his ability to research and find sources of information was far broader and richer than that of his monolingual peers, but he didn't initially realize that these competences and experiences had value in his ELA classroom or in the development of his writing. In his other classes, like economics, civics, and even art class, Wisdom enjoyed sharing his knowledge of foreign events and politics, but he found it difficult to make similar connections to his work in the English classroom. Guidance from a writing teacher could have helped him see these connections.

For example, he could have developed writing and inquiry-based writing projects (arguments, research papers, and so forth) that helped him find research questions and topics related to his political or musical interests, allowed him to display his investment in community concerns, or encouraged him to draw on a wider array of research sources. The mapping activity, along with the conversations between Wisdom and me that the activity prompted, helped me see these resources and better understand Wisdom's literacy competencies. As teachers, we need to be invested in developing a deeper rapport with and knowledge of our ELL writers and their language/literacy experiences if we hope to guide ELL writers toward functionalizing these resources in the classroom and in their writing.

Wisdom's story also reminds us about the value of the creative writing and exploration that can prove to be a validating outlet for ELL writers. His love of poetry, songwriting, and creative verse were all important outlets that made him feel like he owned the English language. These creative outlets, when acknowledged by teachers, can play important roles in the literacy development of second language writers, nourishing their need for language and expression in ways that academic language and writing cannot. Severino, Gilchrist, and Rainey (2010) have noted that academic settings like school tend to assign L2 writers to certain roles and allow for only academic writing experiences, "[limiting] their identity explorations and identity options" (p. 174). In many schools, creative writing often occupies an ambiguous role, particularly in those classrooms with high numbers of ELL writers. We need to find moments in our writing classrooms to celebrate and acknowledge the creative ways that our students use writing outside of the academic setting. Creative literacy activities, including informal publication and public reading events, can build resiliency and positive identity associations for writers like Wisdom, helping them gain confidence and feel pride in themselves as writers even if they struggle on other fronts.

LEARNING FROM KEN-ZHI

Thinking Critically as a Writer

Part of Ken-zhi's frustration with English writing was grounded in his almost innate understanding of how certain texts should appeal to readers. Though Ken-zhi sometimes struggled to find the right words to express himself, he could identify how writers constructed texts in order to impact their readers. It was a rhetorical competency that Ken-zhi drew upon in his own writing practices.

When faced with a new writing assignment or challenge, Ken-zhi would analyze and investigate similar texts. His strength was a well-developed sense of *genre awareness* (Devitt, 2004). He would study and mimic writing styles and techniques that he found in books, the occasional teacher's model, and his peers' writing, particularly with tasks that he saw as fun, risk-taking experiments with English writing. For example, when his English teacher introduced a writing assignment mimicking excerpts from Robert Fulghum's *All I Needed to Know I Learned in Kindergarten*, Ken-zhi discovered that he could use a diary format in his writing. He spent time and purposefully studied the excerpts that the teacher had given him, underlining and highlighting sections of the text, to think about the ways that he might mimic Fulghum's style to achieve his own goals and meet the teacher's expectations. In Ken-zhi's final draft of the assignment, he mimicked the diary format, a technique that was not required for the assignment, but one that he thought was "cool." In addition, his voice evoked that same quality of playfulness and informality as Fulghum's, using multiple exclamation points and capital letters to express his shock or enthusiasm as the days unfolded. His ability to note the conventions of the genre and mimic them in order to achieve his own objectives spoke to his keen ability to analyze texts from the standpoint of a writer. These skills also helped him figure out the expectations of his teacher and his American audience.

He drew upon these skills often, sometimes extracting writing ideas from native language texts in order to aid his English academic writing. As illustrated in his map, Ken-zhi was an avid reader of Chinese-language books, including Chinese translations of the Harry Potter series and other adventure novels (as shown in his map, Figure 6.3). He would borrow rhetorical strategies from these books when he grew discouraged. For example, Ken-zhi was frustrated by topic sentences. Although he understood his teacher's lesson on topic sentences and took many notes on their function and their value, he found them difficult to write. As Ken-zhi explained, "You use some topic sentence. If you write the [topic] sentence that represents every idea up, then you have nothing left to write." He argued that the problem with topic sentences, and thesis statements for that matter, was that they told the reader everything. And then, he, as the writer, had nothing left to say.

Ken-zhi's solution to this problem was to start using questions as his topic sentences. He determined that if he began the paragraph with a question, then he could "answer the question" without having to give away all of his details and ideas in the opening sentence. When I asked Ken-zhi about the inspiration for this strategy, he told me:

FIGURE 6.3. Ken-zhi's Map (See Appendix C, Figure C.1 for a key of icons and mapping activity)

I just started doing it earlier this year. I read some types of these books. And I just like copy the books' ideas. I discover some books that wrote like this, and then I like, I really like this [writing technique].

Ken-zhi went on to explain that whenever he had a writing assignment for English or ELL class, he often thought about the books he had read earlier and "[would] use the book idea" in his writing. He would study the style of the authors that he read, noting their storytelling techniques, their use of time and characters, and even their stylistic strategies at the paragraph and sentence levels. In our interview, when I asked Ken-zhi which books he had used to develop his strategies as a writer, he noted with pride: "Most of the books were Chinese. They are different from English."

Invoking Culture as a Resource

It wasn't the first time that Ken-zhi had drawn upon the rich literature of his native culture. In other instances, he invoked his native culture, literature, and language to build a positive, rich identity as a bilingual and biliterate writer. One example of this practice was illustrated in a ghost story that Ken-zhi wrote. In the narrative, written for his ELL class, Ken-zhi set the story at his grandmother's house in Taiwan. He then described how his family is haunted by a floating head and the ghost of a girl. As the narrative came to a close, he revealed that the grandmother's home was once the site of a girl's murder and "her oul was left in that house" (Ken-zhi's narrative). In one of our interviews, Ken-zhi told me that his narrative was indeed "a real story." He explained to me with great dramatic flair and in hushed tones, "It really happened." But he also admitted that he was influenced by the ghost stories and other folktales that he often heard from family and friends when he lived in Taiwan. His narrative was one of his favorites and one of his most accomplished writing samples from the year. In her written feedback on the piece, his ELL teacher commented, "This 'reads' like a mystery story. I can't wait to find out what happens. Excellent description!! Is this a true story? I believe it is. You are a really good storyteller." In fact, during one of my observations, his teacher pulled me aside after class and commented on how impressed she was by Ken-zhi's narrative skills. Ken-zhi's efforts to weave his cultural literacy into his academic English writing received a positive response from his teacher and validated his abilities as a storyteller and writer.

Writing in a Digital, Transcultural World

Outside of school, Ken-zhi worked diligently to craft a bicultural and bilingual identity for himself using his prowess with technology. After school,

Ken-zhi quickly discovered that the Internet opened venues for writing in both Chinese and English to him. In email correspondence, even to English speakers like me, he used both Chinese and English. For example, quotations written in Chinese characters often served as a tagline at the bottom of his messages and his moniker as a sender was always in Chinese characters. Ken-zhi actively emailed friends and music teachers back in Taiwan, asking questions and seeking advice when needed.

At the end of his freshman year, Ken-zhi took these exchanges to a new level by creating his own weblog. While blogging, he often wrote in Chinese, in an effort "to keep up my Chinese." Online, he found a circle of friends like him—adolescent Chinese immigrants attending high schools across the United States. They visited one another's blogs frequently, sharing stories about their experiences in high school. Sometimes they chose to write in Chinese and other times in English. They used the blogs to provide constructive comments to one another as a way of improving their writing in both languages. These friends inspired Ken-zhi to achieve a higher level of artistry and proficiency in both Chinese and English in his own blog, which he saw as a place to demonstrate his competencies in writing across languages and modalities. Ken-zhi's online literacy circles created venues for him to have writing experiences that proved powerful in *validating* his identity as a bicultural, bilingual individual with talents in both English and Chinese.

Naming Ken-zhi's Writing Resources

Ken-zhi's ability to read rhetorically and to learn from new genres showcased his abilities as a critical thinker and an intellectually engaged student. He also knew how useful these abilities could be, and when encouraged, he could articulate his writing approaches, processes, and challenges. He brought sophistication to his reading of his own texts and the texts of others. But even though he found these strategies personally useful, he had no idea that they might be of value to others or of interest to his English teachers.

One of Ken-zhi's goals as a writer was to remain, in his words, "true to [his] Chinese roots." His map and accompanying interview illustrated the importance of his ties to his native country and language. He visually represented friends in Taiwan, Chinese texts, and a music teacher in Taiwan with whom he corresponded over the Internet. These values also led him to explore new technology and writing venues in order to remain connected to his language and his identity as a transcultural writer.

Ken-zhi also demonstrated competence in rhetoric and writing when it came to his Internet practices. In ways that would have surprised his teachers and many of his peers, Ken-zhi explored various languages and discourses as he wrote in online environments. He mastered the modalities and symbols needed to write in these environments, and he also established a strong understanding of the conventions and communicative norms of these spaces, particularly when it came to writers' and readers' roles. For example, he explained at length the ways in which he used the comment features on a friend's blog, negotiating his goal of leaving constructive feedback for an individual writer, while at the same time helping the writer "save face" with the larger public audience that would also see Ken-zhi's comments on her blog.

His digital writing projects also required Ken-zhi to develop expertise in using various symbol systems, software applications, data resources, online networks, and other digital modes for communicative and research purposes. Yi (2010b) documented similar findings in her study of a Korean student and her use of online spaces in her extracurricular writing. As Yi reported, the student's "choice of languages (Korean, English, and Chinese characters) for writing across contexts shows that her multiliterate practice is a reality and an asset" (p. 28). Yi argued that this engagement of both L1 and L2 in digital contexts showed the student engaged in the "*joint development* of L1 and L2 literacy" (p. 28). For his part, Ken-zhi's digital writing experiences also paralleled ongoing discussions in English education about what it means to be literate in the 21st century (Miller & Fox, 2006). Teachers and literacy specialists continue to identify ways in which teachers can bridge out-of-school literacy practices and classroom practices (Yi, 2010b). Given the chance (and the invitation to do so), Ken-zhi might have offered his peers and teachers insights into how he made choices and negotiated his purposes in writing for these digital environments. Outside of school, he was successful at explaining new online applications and programs to new users, and he was willing to introduce peers and teachers to new resources on the digital frontier of literacy.

LEARNING FROM THERESE

"Being Bilingual" as a Demonstration of Competency

Therese was often hesitant to draw upon her Spanish language and literacy skills when it came to her writing assignments in English and ELL classes. But her competencies in Spanish served other important functions that helped her hold onto a sense of confidence and her identity as an intelligent, talented, and valuable student.

While Therese often felt "bad" and frustrated when it came to writing in English, she felt far more confident when it came to her Spanish-for-heritage-speakers class. This Spanish course, designed for native speakers of Spanish, was a place where Therese felt successful in her encounters with literature and writing. In that classroom, she could fluently and intellectually talk about her readings, her opinions, and her ideas. She could write about literary conventions, respond to readings, and analyze texts with prowess and confidence. She felt, in her own words, "intelligent," academically challenged, and "like one of the best in the class." As Therese told me in an interview: "I think I [do] well. . . . I am the newest one here. I know almost everything about Spanish. So the teacher always tells me to read and to read aloud to the class." On another occasion, she confidently told me about an exam she had taken in her Spanish class, saying, "It was easy. Because I'm intelligent. That's why."

The contrast between her sense of certainty in her Spanish class and her lack of confidence in English class was palpable. In her Spanish class, she felt a sense of authority and ownership that translated into her writing. In this setting, she knew that she was intelligent and was not hampered by language in her efforts to express her intelligence, her thoughts, and her opinions. In comparing it to her English class, Therese explained, "It is different [in Spanish class]. When I have to say something, it comes out easily than when I am in my English class."

Being Bilingual as a Workplace Strength

In the 21st-century workplace, bilingualism is not a trait that is treated lightly or dismissed. In one Canadian study, researchers found that bilingual employees earned more than their monolingual counterparts even if they weren't using their language skills on the job (Christofides & Swidinsky, 2010). In the United States, corporations and small businesses have found that employing bilingual employees can increase their domestic and international markets. Therese did not receive validation for being a bilingual speaker and writer until she enrolled in a school-to-work program at her school. This federally funded program, in which a small group of students was selected to participate, set up internships for students and provided instruction twice a week on professional writing, interviewing, workplace etiquette, job searches, and so forth. The program tutored students, took them on field trips, created opportunities for mock interviews and conference presentations, and worked with them to create resumes, job applications, cover letters, and memos. Therese was recruited into the program because her brother had been a prior participant; her status as an English language learner had nothing to do with her acceptance. In fact, in my observations and conversations with Therese's school-to-work teacher, Karen, she made no reference to Therese's status as an English language learner or her English language proficiency. Karen encouraged Therese to use her Spanish abilities to help fellow Spanish-speaking students, and during Therese's summer internship, one part of her job description was to serve as an interpreter for Spanish-speaking customers and as a bilingual intermediary between management and the Spanish-speaking clients. In my observations, I witnessed Therese's fluidity as she code-switched between Spanish and English with ease, adjusting her tone and even her physi-

cal stance as she helped navigate the communicative goals of various stakeholders.

Naming Therese's Writing Resources

Therese's Spanish-for-heritage-speakers class served as an important site
of validation for her during some very difficult days in her other classrooms.
It was a place where she could identify herself as a strong student and showcase her intellectual abilities, reaffirming a positive identity that enabled her
to maintain her confidence when she struggled in tasks like academic English
writing. Heritage language classes offer an opportunity to build the academic
resiliency and writing prowess of English language learners.

In recent years, the political climate for bilingual education in the United
States has been difficult, even impossible; many states and school districts
have effectively shut down bilingual education. In doing so, the value of "being bilingual" in school contexts has also been diminished. But Therese's successful use of her Spanish-for-heritage-speakers provides a strong example of
how these kinds of classes can build students' biliterate capabilities. Heritage-
language courses emphasize literary texts, conventions, and culture and provide opportunities for students to engage in academic writing in their native
language—skills that might serve as valuable bridges to the writing curriculum in English classes.

Therese's use of her Spanish in the school-to-work program was also
striking. During the other parts of her school day, Therese saw Spanish strictly
as a social language, one that she used with her friends. It was a language that,
perhaps with the exception of her Spanish class, was not part of her academic
life or her academic writing. In fact, she often felt that her Spanish abilities
were either a nonfactor or a deficit when it came to her day-to-day school life.
But the school-to-work program gave her a site of validation where her bilingual abilities benefited her in the program and the workplace, where she was
regularly seen as a valued expert in Spanish and English.

In her study of young bilingual students, Valdés (2003) noted their exceptional competencies as language interpreters. She argues that young bilinguals
have high degrees of competency to "selectively encode communications" and
can "carry out selected combinations of abstracting, synthesizing and reor-
ganizing messages," depending on the dynamics of a communicative act and
the audience that they were attempting to reach (p. 168). Bilingual students
had excellent listening skills, patience, and a strong sense of tact when it came
to language use. They were able to interpret and respond to the feelings and
emotions of others as they communicated their needs, made arguments, and
solicited information. These gifts that came from working across languages
and with various stakeholders had led young bilinguals, like Therese, to have

a strong memory for and sensitivity to the nuance of language, to think across multiple languages and registers, and to do abstract thinking. Therese also regularly demonstrated strong decision-making skills about how to read a situation and position herself appropriately. Knowledge of these language negotiation skills could help Therese and her teachers design powerful bridges into her work as writer in ELA classrooms.

Let me highlight one other aspect of the school-to-work course in terms of Therese's identity as a competent writer. Throughout the course, Therese worked on a range of writing assignments in various professional and workplace genres. These assignments—all professional genres, like cover letters, memos, resumes, proposals, and job applications—were all discussed with a clear sense of their rhetorical purpose. Consistent with the program's objective to train students to consider employers' needs and goals, interactive conversations in the small class regularly discussed the expectations of employers and how the employee/student might meet those expectations, both in workplace performance and in workplace writing. The program often brought in business owners to help students with their resumes or interview skills, providing authentic audiences for these genres. Therese was encouraged to use writing to construct a bilingual identity for herself, one that also validated her identity as an English language *user* as well as her knowledge and intelligence in both English and Spanish.

Indeed, all her professional writing for the course—a resume (Figure 6.4), cover letters, and memos—reflect her sense that her bilingualism was a strength that gave her an edge over her classmates, most of whom spoke only English.

Her experiences convince me that there are important bridges between these other sites of literacy and her English academic writing that should be built upon instead of ignored. For example, Therese's experiences with professional writing offer insight into how to better teach writing to second language students. Courses on professional and community writing at the secondary level could provide valuable places for students to explore and build upon their rhetorical understanding of how writing works across contexts (Cox, Ortmeier-Hooper, & Tirabassi, 2009). Second language writers, like Therese, often find that working with professional writing genres creates literacy experiences in which bilingualism is valued and acknowledged as an asset instead of an academic negative.

Therese's role as a valued member of the school-to-work program and an intelligent member of her Spanish literature class mitigated those moments when she felt unsuccessful and frustrated in her English class. In Spanish and workplace writing, she felt competent and confident; in turn these experiences provided Therese with sustenance when she felt frustrated and insecure in her other academic writing pursuits.

FIGURE 6.4. Therese's Resume, an Example of Professional Writing Completed for Her School-to-Work Program

Therese Rodriquez

XX XXXXX St.

Mill River, XX XXXXX

Objective:

    To obtain a part-time job in order to learn and utilize new employment skills, as well as to use my time in a productive manner.

Employment;

    Summer July 2004 - Dec. 2004

    -Salvation Army, Mill River

- Maintaining order in the clothing closet
- Supervised the filling and distribution of back to school backpacks

Volunteer Experience;

    Salvation Army, Mill River

    9-04-Present

- Translator for Spanish speakers utilizing Salvation Army Services

Community Affiliations;

    -SchoolWork Inc. Mill River North High School, Mill River

        -In school employability, career and training program

Certifications;

- Red Cross CPR Certified
- Red Cross First Aid Certified

Strengths;

- Motivated to learn new things
- Friendly, helpful person
- Patient
- Bilingual

Education;

    Mill River North High School – 104 Main Street, Mill River

    Class of 2008

References;

    Available upon request

BRINGING ELL WRITERS' COMPETENCIES INTO THE CLASSROOM

ELL writers come into our classrooms with a range of literacy experiences, and more important, they come with competencies. I have illustrated the resources of Wisdom, Ken-zhi, and Therese in this chapter, and in the chart on the following page (Figure 6.5), I summarize them for readers in order to highlight the range of competencies evident in even this small group of writers.

More often than not, though, teachers do not learn about these competencies, and ELL writers are uncertain about sharing them. They don't know if their L1 (native language) or out-of-school language experiences matter to their English teachers. And they can't always demonstrate those experiences and their knowledge in their in-class writing. Without invitations and prompts from their teachers, many ELL writers won't disclose what they know or have learned from those experiences.

Paul, for example, drew upon his fascination with video games to help him create moments of suspense in his narratives, to scaffold degrees of tension in his action sequences, and to build ongoing storylines in his fiction writing. It was a strategy that many of his peers might have found helpful as well. Miguel's teachers never knew that his notebooks included pages upon pages of passages from the books they read in class that Miguel diligently copied out word for word. This wasn't a mindless activity. He explained to me that he copied the texts in an effort to remember certain scenes since his class wasn't allowed to bring the book home. He reread the notebook passages at night. He explained that writing out the passages helped him to understand English better; it was almost as if he were trying to get inside the texts, trying to understand how they worked. According to Miguel, the "copying" helped him understand and mimic how writers made "English words go together."

My conversations with students, particularly those that emerged from the mapping activity and the resulting discussion of their extracurricular literacies, demonstrated the students' aptitude in writing skills that move far beyond the five-paragraph essay. These students' experiences with professional writing, blogging, music software, and digital literacy demonstrate that ELL writers who are depicted as vulnerable and "needing the basics" often have a deeper understanding of the multimodality of texts, text forms, and audiences that are increasingly part of the work and "life-worlds that they engage with now and will continue to engage with in the future" (Cope & Kalantzis, 1999, p. 4).

As multilingual learners of language and new cultures, these students are also incredibly savvy about the cultural and linguistic diversity that is becoming a more prevalent fact of life in multiple social, workplace, and academic situations. As Jordan (2009) has noted, in the 21st century, "more and more 'English' interactions will involve words, phrases, tones, rhythms, gestures, references, routines, and other characteristics that reflect diverse symbolic repertoires. Multilingual English users frequently and actively negotiate situations using strategies that native English users cannot detect" or imagine (p. W314). The multinational nature of our economy and the globalized world that exists through the Internet means that monolingual Americans will find themselves writing for readers across national boundaries; our students will encounter English readers from a range of international perspectives. The emerging term *English as an International Language* (EIL) underscores a view of the English language that is not strictly owned or governed by monolingual English speakers in the Western world. A case in point is that there are currently more Eng-

FIGURE 6.5. Summary of Competencies, Resources, and Sites of Validation

Wisdom	Ken-zhi	Therese
Naming Rhetorical and Literacy Competencies		
A rhetorical knowledge of how certain writing and language can move people toward social action and social change A knowledge of multiple international media outlets through consistent reading of international publications An understanding of broader world perspectives An interest in community issues and interviewing stakeholders on issues Experiences with English as a world language (Nigerian English) A competence in creative language, sensory imagery, performance, and artful phrasing (in music and poetry)	A competence in digital literacy practices that require the ability to negotiate across "multiple registers, discourses, and languages, in addition to different modalities of communication (sound, speech, video, photographs) and different symbol systems (icons, images, and spatial organization)" (Canagarajah, 2002, p. 612) An innate knowledge of how to "read," study, and analyze texts as models in order to learn how they work, how they impact readers, and how authors use language A savvy sense of how to use his culture and his language in ways to engage readers and express his own voice	An ability to code-switch and shuttle between languages Her experiences in reading and writing in Spanish A knowledge of which language was most effective for the audience that she was trying to reach or the response that she hoped to receive An understanding of various workplace and community genres, coupled with a knowledge that writing is a fundamental tool of communication for people in the workplace An engagement in analyses of texts written by others, including published authors and historical texts from other cultures (Caribbean, Spain, Central America, etc.)
Identifying sites of validation:		
Middle school portfolio and writing experiences Poetry journals Music writing and experiences with digital songwriting software Inspirational texts and authors (King, Gandhi) Family legacy	His blog Chinese books, stories, and oral traditions Chinese translation of English books, such as Harry Potter His music and his instruments	School-to-work classes (on campus) Summer internship/job Spanish-for-heritage-speakers class

lish language users in China than in the United States. But our monolingual students are not aware of this new reality in their worlds, and they are not prepared for this shift. And our ELL writers have no sense of the strengths they bring to these new communicative realities.

As teachers, we need to think deeply about how we can teach writing in ways that help students connect their existing competencies back to their writing. At the end of the day, if our goal is to raise the writing levels of our L2 students, we must begin by providing opportunities for these students to realize and share what they know about language, about readers and writers, about genres, and about communication.

CONCLUSION

There are still many questions about how to foster L2 students' competencies. For instance, even if we do begin to map these, even if we become more aware of the literacy activities that give these writers confidence, how do we create curriculum and writing assignments that build upon these strengths?

In the next chapter, I take up that question and explore a range of lesson planning techniques and approaches to teaching writing that have benefits for all students in our ELA classrooms.

ADDITIONAL RESOURCES

I recommend the following articles and books for readers seeking to learn more about identifying the strengths and competencies of their ELL writers.

Canagarajah, A. S. (2002). *Critical academic writing and multilingual students*. Ann Arbor: University of Michigan Press.

Jordan, J. (2012). *Redesigning composition for multilingual realities*. Urbana, IL: Southern Illinois UP/NCTE.

Valdes, G. (2003). *Expanding definitions of giftedness: Young interpreters of immigrant backgrounds*. Mahwah, NJ: Erlbaum.

Yi, Y. (2007). Engaging literacy: A biliterate student's composing practices beyond school. *Journal of Second Language Writing, 16*(1), 23–39.

CHAPTER 7

Specific Teaching Strategies for Working with ELL Writers

My friend Claire and I are sitting at a local café, drinking coffee, and she is generously reading chapter drafts for this book. Claire teaches 9th grade; she has up to 26 students in a single ELA period. In one class, she has four kids on Individual Education Plans (IEPs), another six who are non-native English speakers, and another 16 students with a range of interests and abilities. She wonders aloud how she will ever be able to meet the needs of her ELL students, with all the other student demands in her classroom. She points to the clock on the café wall to emphasize her concerns: There are only 52 minutes of class time. As she reads the stories and experiences of Miguel, Wisdom, Ken-zhi, Paul, Vildana, and Therese, she asks me what all this means for her classroom, her teaching, her lessons on writing. She finds the stories compelling, and her own experiences with ELL students have been positive. But how will she meet the writing needs of these students, as well as every other student in the room? How can teachers begin to approach writing instruction with a more inclusive approach?

Claire keeps me honest by reminding me that research on the writing of adolescent ELLs needs to yield practical strategies for the classroom and curriculum.

TOWARD AN INCLUSIVE WRITING CLASSROOM: THREE IMPORTANT QUALITIES

This chapter is all about creating writing lessons, assignments, and classrooms that support ELL writers, as well as the other student writers in the room. Some suggestions will help teachers to retrofit their current curriculum, but other strategies ask us to reassess how we design our writing curricula from the ground up. The strategies that I share here are informed by second language writing pedagogy, systemic functional linguistics, and rhetorical genre theories. Even more important, they are informed by my experiences with young writers and their teachers. On the whole, these activities and strategies embrace the following three qualities: They are inclusive, they are inquiry-based, and they aim to create rhetorically savvy writers.

- *Inclusive:* The strategies that I advocate for are universal in approach. These ideas for writing instruction are informed by second language writing research and teaching practices, but they hold benefits and value for all the student writers in our classrooms. In embracing an inclusive writing curriculum, teachers do not just create separate assignments for their ELL writers. Instead, the goal is to design assignments that meet the needs of ELL writers, but also create writing experiences that are advantageous and instructive for all students. For example, ELL writers often need guided instruction in academic English and revision, but these are crucial learning objectives for all students, not just ELLs.

  Likewise, an inclusive approach aims to bring the resources and voices of all students into the classroom. In the previous chapter, I illustrated the strengths and resources that ELL writers bring to their writing and other academic pursuits. Inclusive writing instruction builds upon those findings by providing opportunities for ELL writers to share their knowledge as language users and informants with their peers. The goal is to help all students achieve a broader sense of their communicative goals as writers in an increasingly diverse and globally connected world.

- *Inquiry-based:* The writing assignments and activities in this chapter are student-centered and teacher-guided. They aim to engage students in real-world questions about writing and the rhetorical situations that writers encounter. Inquiry-based approaches to writing instruction promote drafting, writing, and revision as problem-solving acts. These approaches encourage student writers to ask questions and reflect on their purposes, their readers, and the genres that they are using. Inquiry-based writing assignments and activities encourage students' critical thinking skills. They help students gain meta-cognitive understandings of their writing decisions and learn how writing decisions for one project can inform future decisions for new projects, genres, and writing opportunities. Many of the inquiry-based strategies discussed in this chapter are derived from systemic functional linguistics (SFL) approaches to writing. Functional approaches use highly interactive and collaborative classroom activities that aim to make our implicit understandings about how texts work *explicit* for our students.

- *Rhetorically savvy:* Throughout this book, I've been drawing on social and rhetorical models of writing. Rhetorically situated writing instruction and assignments, like those introduced in this chapter, aim to create rhetorically savvy writers—that is, writers who can analyze the stakeholders (readers, writers) in a given text, the purpose of that text, and the language and genre conventions that are most appropriate for a given situation.

Writing scholars like Amy Devitt (2004) have suggested that 21st-century writing instruction needs to embrace rhetorical and genre theories as a more overt way of teaching students to understand writing as a series of interactions and transactions between readers and writers. This approach encourages writers to analyze the ways texts work and to consider how audiences, writers, genres, and purposes (i.e., the rhetorical situation) impact a writer's choices. In this model, students learn that writing is always socially situated. They learn to see writing as a communicative act between writers and readers, much like speaking. For ELL writers, this communicative framework for thinking about writing is accessible and corresponds well with many of their other language experiences.

I believe that rhetorical models of writing need to be taught explicitly to young writers. We need to share the concepts, but also the terminology. We need to give ELL writers, in particular, a vocabulary to talk about their work and their choices as writers. By providing students with a vocabulary to talk about texts as communicative events, this rhetorically savvy approach gives ELL writers opportunities to make connections between their own expertise in negotiating across language and cultural situations and the negotiations that occur between writers and readers on the written page. Similarly, rhetorically savvy instruction embraces writing for academic and literary purposes, but it also considers the writing that students will (and often already) do in a variety of settings, content areas, digital spaces, workplaces, and civil interactions.

In the pages ahead, I'll draw upon these three qualities of inclusive, inquiry-based, and rhetorically savvy instruction. The first part of the chapter will explore how we can design rhetorically situated writing assignments for our students and why approaching writing curriculum in such a way matters. The second part of the chapter will focus on specific writing activities and instructional practices that help teachers promote inquiry-based, functional understandings of language, genre, and writing in our students.

DESIGNING INCLUSIVE WRITING ASSIGNMENTS

The Importance of Fingerholds

Fifteen years ago, I took part in an experiential education program for teachers. For 6 days, we headed deep into the White Mountains of New Hampshire

---

Learning Objectives for Rhetorically Savvy Writing Instruction

The following learning objectives are useful in guiding the creation of rhetorically savvy writing curricula:

- Students will see writing, of all genres, as socially situated, always influenced by the reader, the writer's purpose, and the rhetorical situation.
- Students will learn to see that writing is highly contextualized, shifting its demands across various readers, purposes, genres, and cultures.
- Students will know what genre is and understand that writing exists in a wide variety of in-school and out-of-school contexts and traditions. Students will identify and analyze various genres, their conventions, and how they respond to rhetorical situations. Genre study will not be limited to literary texts, but will also include nonfiction texts, workplace writing, and community writing.
- Students will experience writing in various genres (both formal and informal), including high-status genres.
- Students will consider and share their thoughts on how a writer's use of language, tone, and genre may shift across various rhetorical situations, depending on the writer's goals. As writers, students will see and learn to articulate how word choice, language usage, and grammar are, in many ways, rhetorical in nature, aiming to draw certain responses from readers.

---

to challenge our notions of learning and school. One of the most terrifying and truthful moments of that journey came on the day when we climbed the face of a nearby granite peak. I had never gone rock climbing, and as I fastened my harness and donned the helmet, I was shaking. They say that on the side of the mountain is where you face the same thrills and fears that come with teaching, including the emotion, the adrenaline, the victories, the doubts, the flexibility to shift plans, the need to see and plan two steps ahead of yourself. From the bottom and the top of the peak, the coaches shouted to me, explaining what to look for, encouraging me, and helping me recognize what I sometimes already knew but couldn't remember in the moment. It was the fingerholds—the triumph of finding one and then recognizing the next one—that helped move me and motivate me to continue up the side. Those spaces in the rock were the fingerholds—small ledges and crevices—that my chalked fingers dug into as I swung my weight against the rock—sometimes moving up, sometimes moving laterally to a better position—but always inching higher to the top, fingerhold by fingerhold.

I share this story because the act of writing for our students can feel a bit like climbing up that granite cliff. As their teachers, though, we can plan our writing assignments by identifying and creating fingerholds for student writers to grab onto in order to propel themselves upward toward completion and success. Joy Reid and Barbara Kroll (1995) remind us that our writing assignments should "offer student-writers, whether NES [native English speakers] or ESL, the best possible opportunity to demonstrate their strengths and to learn from their writing" (p. 268). Building writing assignments with *rhetorical fingerholds* relies heavily on thinking about how we, as teachers, position our writing assignments in social contexts and rhetorical situations. We begin to do that when we discriminate between low- and high-context prompts.

Defining Low- and High-Context Writing Prompts

Writing prompts can be *low-context* or *high-context*. *Low-context writing prompts* are isolated exercises that present writing as a mere set of exercises, meant to satisfy a teacher or testing requirement. These assignments provide student writers with limited social or rhetorical context or lack it altogether; in such assignments, students gain little sense of purpose, audience, or authenticity. They produce a given text for its own sake (e.g., to demonstrate their awareness of a certain form). Paul's compare-and-contrast essay shown in Chapter 5 is one such example.

Low-context assignments tend to water down the communicative and socially situated nature of writing. Watering down the communicative situations surrounding a writing task can eliminate the very "fingerholds" that ELL writers can use to develop and strengthen their confidence and their texts.

In contrast, *high-context writing prompts* place a writing task within a believable and authentic social and rhetorical context, including the position of the writer, the subject, the audience, and the genre. High-context writing assignments also need to be engaging for both teacher and student (Reid & Kroll, 1995, p. 269). Students need to feel a level of personal investment in the writing task, and for ELL writers, it is beneficial to consider how such writing assignments might allow them to draw upon their past literacies and rhetorical experiences.

Students themselves can play a role in creating the high-context rhetorical situations for their writing tasks. In these instances, teachers can guide (and coach) students to set their own terms for writing tasks, coaching student writers to establish their own subjects, identify audiences, and think critically about the most appropriate genres for their purposes.

FIGURE 7.1. Low- and High-Context Assignments

Sample Low-Context Assignment	Sample High-Context Assignment
Write about what your plans are for this coming summer.	Write a letter (genre) to a friend (audience, writer) to provide information about possible summer activities that you two might do together (subject, purpose).
Should the U.S. government provide quality health care, free of charge, to all children (ages 0–18)?	Produce a trifold brochure (genre) explaining (purpose) to the voting public (audience) why the U.S. government should or should not provide health care to children (subject).

As the examples in Figure 7.1 illustrate, high-context writing prompts provide ELL writers and their peers with more "fingerholds" for their writing. Students can bring more of their background and rhetorical knowledge (e.g., seeing their cousins as readers, sharing their local summer activities, and so on) to these kinds of prompts. Certainly, some high-context assignments will require more stretching, moving ELL writers beyond "safe harbor" contexts, but overall, high-context prompts provide valuable learning opportunities for all students to analyze and assess the audience and genre of a given writing task. For example, drawing on the example above, teachers and students can have valuable whole-class discussions about "which people make up the voting public" or analyze the features (e.g., contents, text placement, use of visuals, and so forth) of a convincing "trifold brochure." ELL writers *can* tackle and discuss controversial and cultural topics, but ultimately, they need to feel as though they have some authority and investment in their subjects.

Maria Fránquiz and Cinthia Salinas (2011) provide a valuable example of writing assignments that invest students in their futures and their communities. The newcomer ELL students in their study used digital historical archives to read and write about the 1957 integration crisis in Little Rock, Arkansas. After working with the materials, students wrote telegrams and letters in which they positioned themselves in relation to the historical events, at one point writing to President Eisenhower as concerned citizens.

Optimally, high-context writing assignments, like the one discussed by Fránquiz and Salinas, are embedded into a larger writing project that provides explicit opportunities for students to:

• Analyze the assignment and assess the rhetorical context of the writing task

- Inquire, problem-solve, and research (through text- and field-based sources)
- Use a process approach with opportunities for multiple drafts, active revision, feedback, and reflection
- Implement revision strategies that encourage them to think critically about their texts and their rhetorical goals as writers
- Reflect upon their decisions, challenges, and actions as writers
- Self-assess their texts

As we approach writing curricula in linguistically diverse classrooms, we need to consider not only the backgrounds of our students, but also their futures, including their goals and aspirations. Our goal, then, is to create assignments that provide "fingerholds" that are safe harbors for student writers and also to create moments that move students toward more advanced genres and opportunities.

Balancing Opportunity and Safe Harbors in Our Assignments

One benefit of designing from a rhetorical perspective is that it provides multiple fingerholds not only for students, but also for teachers.

Inclusive writing assignments begin with teachers creating writing-prompts and projects that are socially and rhetorically situated. Such assignments have (or mention) four identifiable rhetorical factors: readers, writers, purposes, and genres. The assignments give a situation, a problem to solve, and an audience to write to. The assignments help students (implicitly or explicitly) to figure out what stance they need to take as writers in a given situation. When we plan such assignments, we need to begin by considering the rhetorical possibilities we'd like to see students consider (see Appendix E). By adjusting and experimenting with the four rhetorical factors, we can open a range of possibilities and scenarios for young writers. As we design assignments, we can think about building prompts on a kind of sliding scale in which we adjust the difficulty level of these rhetorical factors in accordance with the experience and confidence levels of our student writers.

In Figure 7.2, I've included a chart that serves as a problem-solving device for teachers to use as they think through their objectives for a given assignment and the needs of their students. In the chart, I've provided three descriptors, ENTERING, BRIDGING, and ADVANCING, that outline the levels of difficulty that students might be working from as they encounter the rhetorical factors of a given assignment.

ENTERING factors would include familiar topics, tasks, readers, and roles that students feel comfortable with and understand from previous life experiences. BRIDGING describes more school-based situations. ADVANCING de-

FIGURE 7.2. Building Rhetorical Fingerholds into Our Assignments

WRITER'S POSITION (Choose one from Entering/Bridging/Advanced)	AUDIENCE (PRIMARY, SECONDARY) (Choose one from Entering/Bridging/Advanced)	TOPIC/INQUIRY QUESTIONS (Choose one from Entering/Bridging/Advanced)	GENRES (Choose one from Entering/Bridging/Advanced)
Overlaps in this category are intentional. Some students may feel that certain kinds of roles are more routine to their identities than others, depending on their past experiences in these roles.	**Entering/Incoming** Parents, Family/siblings/cousins, Friends, Home language communities, Class community, Fellow teenagers (in school, in community, in digital spheres)	**Entering/Incoming** Choose topics/questions that: Draw on student's current reading interests, Draw on student's current activities (in-school and after-school), Draw Personal experiences, Choose community-based topics/inquiry questions, Use community-based resources for field research (interviews, observations, surveys, etc.)	**Entering/Incoming** Postcard, Email/Tweet, Personal letter, Journal entry, Shorter personal story
Entering/incoming Son/daughter, Brother/sister/cousin, Sibling, Grandchild, Student, Athlete, Musician/dancer/gamer, Friend	**Bridging** Teachers (outside of a given class), School principal/administrator, Larger school community, School board, Mayor/town officials, Potential community employers, Scholarship givers Local community leaders, Home community (letters to individuals, groups), New friends/peers in an organization or new peer group	**Bridging** Choose topics/questions that: Draw on student's expressed interests or new interests, Draw on questions they want to answer, Draw on problems they wish to solve, Employ a more expansive list of field-based research and resources, Add library-based resources/databases to research process, Use new community-based resources for field research (interviews, observations, surveys, etc.)	**Bridging** Brochure (for school/peers/family), Short story, Researched report/essay, Personal narrative, Resume for after-school job, Business letter (*to local employer or community member*), Proposal for class research project, Book/movie/music review to share with peers, How-to directions for community members/peers, Lab report for science class, Profile of community member (from local community/home language community), Formal letter/persuasive letter to parents/school officials
Bridging Student, Team member, Gamer Club member, Captain of team, Dancer/musician, Athlete, Babysitter/mentor, Sports fan, Volunteer, Employee Advocate, Interpreter			
Advancing Future college student Future community leader Future parent Future entrepreneur Future worker/job applicant Future scientist/journalist/historian Future web blogger Future Informational Technology (IT) assistant	**Advancing** Potential employer, Home language community (*to be shared through more formal venues like newspapers/ newsletters/ speeches*), Monolingual English community (*through newspapers/newsletters/speeches*), State/federal politicians, Law enforcement, Scholarship committees, College admissions committee	**Advancing** Choose topics/questions that: Aid students in learning about a new issue/problem in the community/country, Aid students in learning about a new process related to college/workplace/community interaction, Employ new kinds of reading/research materials, Employ new technology or other resources that the student wants to learn to use, Develop a response or position on an issue.	**Advancing** Formal letter/business letter, Resume/cover letter, College application essay, Formal proposal for funding a community project, Science/medical informative report for local community members, Op/ed essay for local newspaper, AP exam practice essay question, Scholarship application essay, Multigenre memoir, Personal essay, Podcast, Screenplay, Political/persuasive speech, Closing argument, Mission statement.

scribes those rhetorical factors and scenarios that may feel more distant and unfamiliar to students. ADVANCING might include rhetorical situations that speak to where ELL students hope to be in the future.

For ELL writers, the ENTERING category will be those rhetorical situations and genres where they have the most confidence. Students know the readers personally and the context or problem is one that is familiar. It is the "safe harbor" of the rhetorical variables in a writing assignment and draws closely upon experiences and interactions that are already familiar to them.

When teachers bring in BRIDGING rhetorical factors and scenarios, they aim to connect students' comfort zones to their academic worlds. In these kinds of writing assignments, students are asked to transfer understandings from out-of-school literacies/experiences and make connections to academic learning. Contexts will include school-based situations, school-based readers, and academic genres.

ADVANCING rhetorical factors provides students with an opportunity to consider writing tasks and readers beyond school, such as in professional workplace settings, higher education, and community writing activities. These factors also include more advanced and higher-status genres.

Teachers can mix and match across ENTERING, BRIDGING, and ADVANCING categories as they brainstorm new writing prompts and projects. The teacher can create prompts that have more challenging rhetorical factors, like more complex genres, but that also include "sheltered" rhetorical factors, like a known audience. This mixing-and-matching approach to designing writing prompts and projects can enable writers to work from comfortable, safe harbor positions in some aspects of their writing, while at the same time stretching their work as writers in other critical areas. ELL writers can then use their confidence in one area (like genre) to help boost their writerly confidence and knowledge in another area (like purpose). As teachers, planning writing assignments in this way allows us to raise and lower the challenge of various aspects of the writing task, depending on the student writers and their needs.

For students, an understanding of how to analyze and interpret these rhetorical factors helps them to develop thinking "tools" that they can transfer across writing tasks inside and outside of the classroom. Learning to move across different writing tasks and genres is an important skill for all writers (Johns, 1999). Teachers can guide student writers to question how their strategies might change as the rhetorical factors change. How might their texts look if they were writing to their grandmother? How might that same topic look if they were writing to the governor? What strategies would be the same? What genres and language choices might be different?

Over time, teachers can add more ADVANCING factors into writing assignments with an eye toward helping ELL writers achieve specific goals, like moving up the academic track, applying to college, writing for the workplace, writing in a digital environment, or writing to advocate for a community.

TEACHING WRITING EXPLICITLY:
FUNCTIONAL AND SEQUENCED APPROACHES

The use of writing and critical thinking activities to promote learning does not happen through serendipity. Teachers must plan for it and foster it throughout the course.

—John Bean, 2001, p. 1

In the classroom where I am guest-teaching, four groups of middle school students sit at their clusters of desks with a stack of texts in front of them. In one group, Ahmed picks up a brochure from the local school bus company and asks his peers, "Who do you think this one is for?"

He reads aloud passages from the brochure, which explain bus safety and schedules for different neighborhoods. His peers point out a red stop sign on the back cover and the big letters that read "Stop for the School Bus!" Ahmed passes around the brochure, and one student comments that it is a good size, easy to pick up and put in a purse or something. Another student comments on the bright yellow paper, noticing that the writer of the brochure really wants to get people's attention. Lidia, from Mexico, quietly reaches out for the brochure and says, "I think it's for grownups, moms . . . parents . . . people who drive." The other kids around the table start to nod, and then they begin to discuss the formality of the language in the brochure and what kinds of decisions the writer had to make in terms of format, design, and word choices. In their discussions, I hear words like *audience, readers' use,* and *writer's purpose.* Then Ahmed picks up a copy of the school newspaper and says, "What about this one?"

In our English Language Arts classrooms, we often speak about the genres of literature—poetry, novel, short story, biography, and more. Often, we teach the various traits of these genres and the literary conventions that help shape them in order to help students analyze these texts. But we don't often teach explicitly about other written genres (from science lab reports to brochures to business proposals) and the ways those genres act as communicative tools in social contexts. Functional approaches to writing instruction offer teachers innovative ways to teach student writers to think critically about the decisions writers make as they construct texts, the conventions of particular genres, and the ways writers' decisions are informed by the function that the text performs for both reader and writer. These approaches emphasize not only the process and product, but also the classroom discourse that students need to have as an integral part of writing instruction.

Functional approaches to language and writing (Christie & Derewianka, 2008; Gebhard & Martin, 2010; Halliday, 1985; Schleppegrell, 2004) have their roots in Australian educational theories of language and genre. Systemic functional linguistics (SFL) approaches to language learning stress language as a communicative and social tool—between real people and real situations. As Derewianka (1990) explains, "We develop language to satisfy our needs in society. Language is functional when it fulfills those needs effectively" (p. 4). In a functional approach to writing, students are taught that writing is always for a specific purpose with a particular audience in mind. It considers how language works at the text level. Words and sentences are considered as part of the whole, not as isolated, stand-alone entities. In the classroom, functional approaches emphasize to student writers that their texts will vary and shift, depending on (1) their audience, (2) how near or far that audience is from their social/rhetorical position as a writer, and (3) the purpose of the text and the writer.

Developing Students' Genre Awareness

The Genre Awareness activity, described in the opening of this section, is one example of a hands-on group activity that gets students talking and thinking critically about the audiences and purposes of texts. When I lead students in this activity, we begin with a class discussion on a writer's purpose and sense of her audience when she writes. I introduce terms like *purpose, audience, readers, formality* and *informality of language*, and *genre*. We talk about how a letter might switch in tone, language, and even form, depending on the anticipated audience. For example, I ask: How might you write a letter telling your grandmother about your soccer team's victory? And then, how might you write a letter to a buddy in Colombia about the very same win? Inevitably, we talk about the formality and conventions of the letter form. But students also suggest that the letter to the friend in Colombia might actually be more effective as an email or a text message. We talk about how the genres, and then the readers, impact our decisions as writers.

We also talk about how real-world texts are used by readers. For example, why might a landscaper want to have a laminated copy of directions for installing a new mailbox post? Why might instructions for a senior citizen be available in a larger print size or font? We consider how writers make design decisions like these based upon the readers' needs.

Students are then put into groups of three to four and given a stack of texts. The stacks purposefully represent a wide array of genres—from a novel or children's book to stock announcements; from teacher's journal to bike magazines; from local newspapers to school newspapers; from brochures to flyers/announcements, and more. The stacks of texts can be tailored to the age group, and I often include college application materials and job application materials, along with reports to stockholders or business memos when I work with older high school students. For younger students, I try to bring in text materials that are directly related to the communities in which they live and organizations with which they have contact (e.g., the Boys and Girls Club, local animal shelters, local school correspondence, the police or fire department, public library, children's books for preschoolers, children's books for new readers or older children, and so forth).

During class time, students work in groups, discussing and analyzing these texts from a rhetorical and functional perspective. They consider form, audience, purpose, and the author's language choices. Groups fill out a Genre Tag (shared in Appendix D) for each text with this information to complete their analysis.

After they've completed their analysis of the texts, groups create large genre posters with samples from their pile of texts. Each one is labeled with the tags that they have created. Groups then present their findings to the class. The posters are hung around the room so that we can refer to them in further conversations on writers and readers throughout the term.

The Genre Awareness activity is one example of the ways in which teachers can help students see the inner workings of texts and familiarize them with the concepts of genre, audience, and purpose.

Modeling Texts, Joint Deconstruction, and Joint Reconstruction

At the heart of an SFL approach is the focus on genre and language use, but it also emphasizes class discussion.

SFL approaches help us pull back the curtain for student writers, and let them look behind the stage. When teachers first turned to writing process approaches in the 1980s, we did just that. We showed students that writing didn't just come out as polished, perfect products. Sloppy copies, crummy first drafts (Lamott, 1995), getting feedback, revision—they all became part of our vocabulary for talking about writing. We learned from Graves (1983), Murray (1990), and others to let kids "in" on the truths of how writers work. In many ways, SFL approaches encourage us to pull back that curtain again and, this time, to reveal to students how *texts* work.

SFL approaches recommend that teachers help their students see their language, style, and genre choices in a very nuanced manner by considering how writers determine their *linguistic register* for a given piece of writing. Brisk, Hodgson-Drysdale, and O'Connor (2011) explain:

Different situational contexts require different language choices based on the topic discussed (*field*), the relationship between the writer and audience (*tenor*), and the channel of communication: written, oral, or multimodal (*mode*). Together these elements constitute the *linguistic register*. (p. 2)

Everything from the content to the audience for whom a writer is writing to the mode that is being used to communicate the message (the genre, the technology, and so on)—all of these play a role in the vocabulary, the kinds of sentence structures, and the kind of formality that a writer uses. In SFL approaches, these decisions and discussions about these decisions take center stage in the classroom.

SFL instruction is always inquiry-based and discussion-driven. It is often collaborative and highly interactive—students working with students, teacher working with students, and entire classes engaging in writing tasks together. There are many opportunities for students to volunteer and clarify orally their knowledge and insights about writing. The sequence of instructional activities, which I'll describe below, begins with whole-class inquiries into a model text.

Sample Texts. Modeling sample texts is not a new idea for teaching writing. But in a functional approach to models, using a sample text becomes the first step in a larger sequence of lessons. Even more important, models are not simply handed out or briefly glossed over. Instead, the model texts become vital centerpieces to extended classroom conversations about writing, readers, and writers' intentions. In short, they assist teachers in putting the discussion of writing at the forefront of any writing project.

In the activity, as described by Brisk, Hodgson-Drysdale, and O'Connor (2011) and Derewianka (1990), teachers introduce a model to the class as part of a writing project on a given genre. The model texts are enlarged and displayed on overhead projectors or Smartboards, and teachers are able to mark them up, based on students' comments and insights. The teacher engages the class in a discussion of the purposes of the genre in the wider world. Drawing on features from the sample text, students then work together, as a class and with the teacher, to deconstruct the text, using questions like those supplied by Derewianka (1990) and shown in Figure 7.3.

Brisk, Hodgson-Drysdale, and O'Connor (2011) describe the use of this technique at length by sharing the case of Cheryl, a teacher in a mixed classroom, working with her students on report writing. Through class discussion, Cheryl asked students about the kinds of research that they saw represented in a sample report that she projects onto a wall. Guided by questions from Cheryl, students chimed into the conversation, noting that the report featured a variety of sources. One by one, they speculated on the kinds of research that

FIGURE 7.3. Derewianka's (1990, pp. 5–6) Sample Questions to Guide Discussion

- What do you think we might use this sort of a text for in our society?
- What could we call it?
- Remember when we were writing Explanations? Why is this text different from an Explanation
- Look at the beginning of the text. What do you think the writer is doing here? What does the beginning tell the reader?
- What name could we give this sort of a beginning? What about a term like "orientation" to remind us that is setting a scene?
- Which words link up the text and show us when the action took place? We could call these "linking words."

must have taken place, the sources the author turned to, and the notes that were probably taken by the writer in preparation. These moments provided the teacher with repeated opportunities to stress "the need for students to educate themselves before writing about a topic and informing their audience" (p. 4). In subsequent discussions, Cheryl asked students to look more closely at the wording of the report and to consider the kinds of language and word choices that the author used. As a class, they asked: What is appropriate for this audience? They discussed the audience that would read the report, how those readers might use it, and what their expectations might be—in terms of content, tone, openings, and form. To help students see how language choices and detail might make a difference for readers, Cheryl shared an example with the author's descriptive language and then an example without it. She then asked students to share "which piece was more informative and why" (p. 4).

One particularly powerful aspect of discussions like these is that they encourage students to put themselves in the position of readers and writers, as they think critically about how the text is constructed. The ability to move back and forth between the roles of reader and writer helps students become both better writers and responders to their own texts and others'. They begin to realize the importance of considering readers when they write, and they also realize the power of detail and description in their texts.

Throughout these discussions, genres are not held up as static fill-in-the-blank forms, but rather are presented as dynamic and socially situated in real communicative moments. As students and teachers examine a model of a given genre, they discuss at length the context of culture, the relationships between writer and reader that may be in play, and the context of the situation at hand. The Profiling Our Readers activity, which I shared in Chapter 4 (pp. 107–109), complements these discussions nicely.

For teachers, the end goal of using these kinds of strategies is to help students make explicit what they may already know about texts and writing. Class discussion allows students, particularly ELL writers, to share and build on one another's knowledge. Teachers help bridge this knowledge by adding new terminology and insights in order to build students' resources for discussing their own writing and for articulating the ways that writers make decisions about text construction. The deconstruction of the sample text, which can take place over an entire class period, sets the stage for the next writing activity in the sequence: Joint Construction.

Joint Construction. In Joint Construction of a text, the entire class participates in writing a text collaboratively. Again, the teacher works from large pieces of newspaper print displayed on an overhead projector or a Smartboard. Students brainstorm together, identifying a topic and even delving into research on the subject matter. Teachers facilitate the conversation, encouraging students to contribute and pool their knowledge as writers to make decisions about what words, sentences, paragraphs, and sections of the text need to be included and how they should be phrased. As the teacher guides them, students contribute information and ideas, asking questions and making suggestions along the way. The teacher serves as a scribe for their ideas and insights, and encourages students to see the act of composing a text as a series of decisions that they must make as writers.

As Schleppegrell and Go (2007) explain, "This approach offers ways of linking meaning and structure that help students write in fuller and more effective ways" (p. 529). The goal is to make every writing assignment an opportunity to add to students' understanding of writing and to fuel their language resources.

Teachers can use joint reconstruction activities to demonstrate revision strategies, too. For example, a teacher might ask a willing student to volunteer to share an early draft with the class. This text then becomes the centerpiece of the joint construction and the student gets input and suggestions from other class members. In this instance, teachers can use joint reconstruction to demonstrate how writers decide what and how to revise. As a whole, students and teachers can model how to interrogate their first drafts in order to set goals for the next round of revision. Teachers might complement these discussions by sharing revision strategies, like the ones I shared in Chapter 4.

Obviously, a sense of community is essential when asking students to share their work in such a public way. Teachers can foster this kind of classroom climate by emphasizing the importance of community for writers and acknowledging that sharing writing always feels a bit risky. Students need to feel comfortable enough to take suggestions on their work, and their classmates need to feel comfortable enough to offer their opinions and suggestions.

For that reason, joint construction that features a single student's draft as the example is best used after all the students have gained some experience and familiarity with this kind of writing instruction.

Independent Construction. The final activity in this SFL sequence moves students toward independent construction of their own texts. These individual constructions then become part of the larger writing process in which students are encouraged to develop and share drafts, teachers provide a response to these drafts (an issue I address in the next chapter), and students revise further. They come to these steps in the process with more vocabulary and confidence to discuss their own writing and the writing of their peers. This sequence of activities can be particularly empowering for ELL writers, who are often unsure of how to talk about their writing, and sometimes equally uncertain about whether their insights into texts and rhetorical situations are worth sharing. The earlier sessions on mentor texts and joint construction also provide them with concrete models and explanations on why these models work as they begin to construct their own texts. The mentor texts, provided by the class joint constructions, provide them with textual examples for their own writing. At the same time, they provide ELL writers with examples of how to think critically about their writing and make decisions about how to piece together ideas, organize a text, and appeal to their readers.

Teachers can also encourage students to demonstrate their knowledge of the genre and the context by providing more precise feedback to one another. Brisk et al. (2010/2011) advise teachers to prohibit students from responding with, "This is very good. I like it" (p. 5). Instead, teachers should encourage students to use the vocabulary and insights they gained through the model text deconstruction and joint reconstruction to offer more specific comments on one another's projects. Teacher need to instruct students to respond to their peers' specific word choices and explain how they, as readers, picked up on the writer's intent. One student mentioned in Brisk et al.'s study (2010) captured this kind of specificity well by commenting to a peer: "Your word choices, 'the slithery, sneaky, venomous cobra' captured my attention and showed me that you were thinking about word choice" (p. 5).

Finally, for teachers working with ELL writers, functional approaches provide us with many opportunities to see what our ELL students know and understand about language, rhetorical situations, and writing. These instructional activities give us insights into their competencies and their critical thinking skills. They help us to see ELL students as true writers, because they are able to share their insights from writing not only in English, but also in their home languages or in their other extracurricular activities. SFL approaches can help teachers see what may not always be apparent on the written page. According to Derewianka (1990), "The knowledge of language provided by a functional model helps us to identify what children's strengths are and to make clear and positive suggestions as to how they might make their texts more effective, instead of vague, superficial comments or mere corrections of spelling and punctuation." (p. 5).

Sequenced and Linked Writing Assignments

In earlier chapters, I shared Therese's experience of "getting stuck" in language and Miguel's Sisyphus moment. Both stories shared the challenge that ELL writers face and the time they often need to locate content and vocabulary for their essays. And just when they have located that language and content, it is often time for the class to move on to the next topic and a new set of demands for vocabulary and content.

Let me add a codicil here: I acknowledge that working with a new topic can be valuable as a vocabulary-building skill; it can expose students to new vocabulary and help them use that vocabulary in their own texts. But the downside is that exploring new topics in a short time frame often means that ELL writers are consistently frontloading their writing experiences, spending most of their time generating material, learning new words, attempting new spelling, and building their content. Opportunities to think critically about the desired impact on readers and time spent on thoughtful revision get shortchanged. The next writing topic becomes a new hurdle of invention, and ELL writers remain in a phase of writing where they are constantly trying to generate new language for their writing tasks, rather than engaging with other writing skills.

Ilona Leki (1991/1992) offers an alternative: sequenced and linked writing assignments. In suggesting an alternative to the start-and-stop scenario of continually starting over with new topics, Leki suggests a more advantageous strategy in which students can link topics across different writing assignments and projects. As Leki explains,

> In this way, the work done for each assignment services as the basis for the next assignment, building students' skills (including vocabulary and editing since the same terms and structure are likely to appear in subsequent papers). More importantly, such an approach permits the content of the students' writing to build. (pp. 19–20)

Sequenced writing assignments address the issues of language concerns, encourage high expectations of L2 writers, and aid L2 writers in learning how a topic can change across genres and audiences. Leki begins by having students brainstorm a topic that they find thought-provoking and interesting, a topic in which they can maintain and sustain their interests for a full semester. It must also be a topic with which they have some personal experience. Students then consult with Leki, who helps guide them through their possible topics, advising them on the likelihood of finding information about these topics. Students then embark on a series of writing assignments, five in all, "all done within the context of a process-approach in workshop-style class" (p. 21).

In the first essay of the sequence, students write about their personal involvement with the chosen topic. They share everything that they currently know about the topic and explore the significance of the topic to their own lives. The next writing assignment is a summary that has students find three informative sources (e.g., published articles, documentaries, public announcement pamphlets on the topic, and so on) and then summarize them in an essay. In the summary essay, the writer introduces each source, summarizes the main points and conclusions of each piece, and describes links across the three sources. The third and fourth assignments introduce students to field research. In the third installment, students write and design surveys and use them to learn about others' opinions and experiences with the topic. Students write a report of their findings, based on the survey data. The fourth paper requires them to identify and interview an expert on their topic. They create the interview questions, set up the interview session, and write up the information from the interview. Often, students are intimidated by this kind of field research that actually takes them out into the community. For ELL writers, they may worry about whether their English is good enough, and other student writers may be uncomfortable with talking to community members and other authority figures. Despite these concerns, the interviews are usually very successful and students are surprised by their success. Leki (1991/1992) explains,

> This [interview] assignment allows students to confront problems affecting them and to realize that they are capable of investigating solutions and entitled to look to others for help. ESL students and underprepared native students need exactly this kind of empowerment. (p. 21)

In my own modifications of Leki's sequenced approach, I link together three of the essays that I want my students to work on. For example, I start with a personal essay on a significant experience or relationship, which usually leads students to inquiry questions for their research papers. After students complete an exploratory research paper, I then ask them to take an argumentative stance on some aspect of their research topic, which may result in an op/ed piece or a persuasive letter.

Here are two examples of how my students approach these sequenced and linked papers. One student, Brian, explored his love of playing baseball in a personal essay, in which he retold the story of his first ballgame. For his second piece, he wrote a compare-and-contrast piece on Red Sox and Yankee fans. His final essay, a research paper, investigated the tradition of baseball in his native Dominican Republic.

Another student, Maite, began by writing about her mother's battle with breast cancer for her initial personal essay. She then decided to explore breast cancer as her topic for her research question. Together, we worked to narrow her focus on that topic, which she agreed was quite large. Through our conversations, she decided to research and write about treatment options for breast cancer. Her research included library-based sources, web sources, and also field research. Drawing on her community connections, she interviewed her mother and also her mother's physician, who spoke Spanish. She wrote the exploratory research essay on her findings, including recent budget cuts at the federal level that threatened research monies for the treatment and prevention programs she had studied. For her final persuasive writing assignment, she decided to write a formal letter to her local congressperson, advocating for an increase in federal funding for research on breast cancer treatment. Her final argumentative piece, which she did indeed send to the congressperson, incorporated persuasive and narrative elements from her personal narrative and her research paper.

As these two examples suggest, my goal is for ELL students to gain a sense of what Leki (1991/1992) has called "authorial expertise." To become empowered and invested in their writing, ELL writers need to feel that they have some ownership of their topics. Often, as teachers, we see our ELL students produce their strongest work when they write about their personal experiences as immigrants (Campano, 2007). They *own* these stories, and they pull their readers into them with powerful and moving narratives of immigration and language learning. Leki's sequenced writing assignment offers teachers a way to expand upon that sense of authorial expertise and lead ELL writers more confidently into new topics and other academic genres. Along the way, ELL writers build new areas of expertise and a broader repertoire of genres, expanded notions of audience, and a strengthened sense of academic and other formal discourses.

From a rhetorical perspective, sequenced writing assignments encourage students to see how writers have to shift and change their voices, language, and styles across a variety of genres and audiences. They become more aware of the rhetorical shifts and decisions that writers must make. Consider how a paper's content and tone shifts as it moves from personal narrative to research paper. Students, with the help of their teachers and peers, have to decide who they see as the readers for a particular piece, analyze the readers' stance and expectations, and consider what their purposes are as writers. For example, a writing class might discuss what a formal letter to a congressperson would look like in terms of form, language use, and tone. In this way, sequenced writing assignments complement many of the activities used in functional approaches to writing instruction, such as the Genre Awareness, Model Texts, and Joint Construction activities discussed earlier.

CONCLUSION

Second language writing specialist Barbara Kroll writes,

> The goals of every course should be individual student progress in writing proficiency, and the goals of the total curriculum should be that all student writers learn to become informed and independent readers of their own texts with the ability to create, revise, and reshape papers to meet the needs of whatever writing tasks they are assigned. (quoted in Ferris & Hedgcock, 2005, p. 73)

These days, our student writers are encountering texts at every turn. Writing is everywhere—in the workplace, in schools, in their communities, in their digital lives, and in their personal interactions. To help prepare all of our students to be writers in the text-rich world, our teaching needs to be guided by what John Bean (2001) calls the "new rhetorical" writing process. Like the approaches discussed in this chapter, the "new rhetorical" model encourages teachers and students to see writing as a series of decisions and foster a "problem-driven model of the process" (p. 33). Bean advises teachers that "instead of asking students to choose 'topics' and narrow them, we need to encourage students to pose questions or problems and explore them. Show how inquiry and writing are related" (p. 33). Twenty-first-century writing instruction needs to nurture active problem solving and embrace "talk time" and writing as part of those problem-solving efforts. The new rhetorical and functional approaches to writing instruction have advantages for our ELL writers, as well. The methods offered here help teachers accord ELL student writers the vocabulary and the invitation to enter these conversations, so that they can share their insights as language users, too.

ADDITIONAL RESOURCES

For further reading on developing inclusive writing curriculum, I recommend the following articles and books. I've starred sources that provide additional insights into systemic functional linguistics (SFL) and the use of this approach and genre studies in teaching writing to ELL writers.

*Christie, F., & Derewianka, B. (2008). *School discourse: Learning to write across the years of schooling.* New York, NY: Continuum International Publishing Group.

*De la Paz, S., & Graham, S. (2002). Explicitly teaching strategies, skills, and knowledge in writing instruction in middle school classrooms. *Journal of Educational Psychology, 94*(4), 687–698.

*Derewianka, B. (1990). *Exploring how texts work.* Rozelle, Australia: Primary English Teaching Association.

Fránquiz, M. E., & Salinas, C. S. (2011). Newcomers developing English literacy through historical thinking and digitized primary sources. *Journal of Second Language Writing, 20*(3), 196–210.

Kroll, B. (1990). *Second language writing: Research insights for the classroom.* New York, NY: Cambridge University Press.

Leki, I. (1991/1992). Building expertise through sequenced writing assignments. *TESOL Journal, 1*(2), 19–23.

CHAPTER 8

Responding to ELL Writers and Their Texts

Issues of Response, Error Correction, and Grading

> When I tried to write commentary on the example of L2 student work, I found that I had a really hard time knowing where to start. I felt like the easiest thing to do was just to correct all the spelling and grammar mistakes. But they didn't make much of a difference to the development of the piece overall. Also, I began to worry about just circling and crossing out mistakes that the student made. I wanted to be sure that they understood what was wrong with what they wrote.
>
> —Kelsey, student teacher

Response to any student writer is always fraught with some tension. We strive to meet their needs, provide timely feedback, and get through the stack of papers on the desk. We're not sure if our comments matter to students; we may have standardized rubrics that make us pause and debate between a 3 or a 4 on a given scale. Often, the standardized rubrics don't seem to respond to the actual students writing in our classrooms, or to the assignments that we give. We struggle with how much student effort should matter. Sometimes the students don't seem engaged in their writing, and the efforts to provide a response feel meaningless. In some districts, our writing curriculum may have become so compressed that students have little time to work with our comments. Similarly, our responses are sometimes linked solely to evaluation and assessment and we find ourselves commenting, not to provide feedback and nurture our student writers, but to justify and make sense of grades for them—and for us. These concerns over responding to student writing are not new, but they do become more complicated when the student writer is a non-native speaker of English.

As my student teacher, Kelsey, noted in the opening quote to this chapter, the texts of adolescent L2 writers can catch us off guard, particularly when we have not read many papers by non-native English speakers. For native English speakers, particularly those of us who thrived as college English majors, errors in verb tense, incorrect spelling, and missing articles can disturb our expectations of style and usage; our reading is interrupted by the accents of ELL students' texts. In my teacher education classes, I often share sample L2 papers with my student teachers in the middle of the semester, after we've learned a great deal about ELL writers and the process of writing in a second language. As the teachers read the samples, the silence is palpable. There are generally two reactions—some reach almost instinctively for a pen and begin editing the texts one line at a time. Others become almost paralyzed, unsure how to respond, what to write, or where to begin.

In this chapter, I'll consider the question of response from three different angles—response, error correction, and evaluation—separating and defining them in order to clarify feedback procedures for ELL writers. For some teachers, establishing a response system for ELL writers may mean developing strategies that are different from those they use with native-English-speaking students. For others, it may mean enhancing response procedures that are already in place.

VOICES FROM THE CLASSROOM

In late October, Ken-zhi received a copy of a teacher's code with the standard explanation for editorial marks, like ¶ for starting a new paragraph (see Figure 8.1). Over the course of the school year, all the students were regularly handed back first drafts with responses like this one.

In this sample, Ken-zhi's teacher has crossed out entire sentences and sections, added new phrases and conjunctions, and made notations for new paragraphs. On the written page, the error corrections are given with no explanation of why these changes are necessary. The feedback is concerned solely with error correction. There are no comments on the content of the essay or Ken-zhi's efforts as writer.

For his part, Ken-zhi had deliberately incorporated elements of the actual interview into his writing—a method he purposefully used in order to, in his words, "add the person's voice" into his writing. He had hoped for comments from his teacher on the effectiveness of that strategy. He was also particularly proud of his use of the word *nourish* in the sentence: "She doesn't nourish hatred." That word choice was crossed out with no explanation. Ken-zhi was confused and uncertain about his progress as a writer. There was no note to him personally explaining what did work and what didn't in this piece.

The teacher did spend a moment or two with each student to discuss their drafts, but those brief moments couldn't lead to engaged conversations between teacher and students about the writing. There were no opportunities or invitations for one-on-one conferences to talk further. Since he had

FIGURE 8.1. Ken-zhi's First Draft of His Interview Essay with His English Teacher's Response

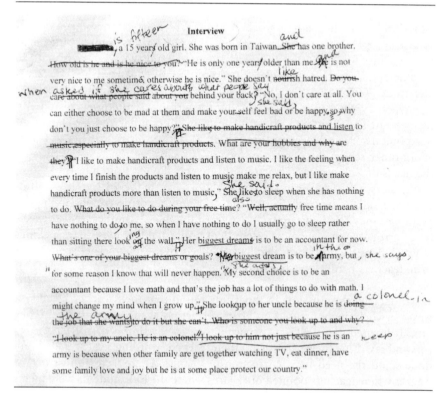

no additional guidance, Ken-zhi simply rewrote the essay with the teacher's changes and turned in the "revised" version. He got a good grade, a B+, but in interviews, he expressed frustration because he said that he felt like "she [his teacher] wasn't really reading" his work.

In the end, seeing our responses to ELL writers as solely editorial endeavors involves two hazardous misconceptions: (1) that ELL students are not capable of engaging and talking with their teachers about their writing, and (2) that error correction is the *only* response that they need in order to improve as writers.

DISTINGUISHING AMONG TEACHER RESPONSE, ERROR CORRECTION, AND EVALUATION

In the field of second language writing, these three concepts—teacher response, error correction, and evaluation—are often discussed as three distinct areas. Of course, there is a connection between error and content; errors in verb tense can cause difficulties and confusion for readers about the time frame of a given event or a particular action (Ferris & Hedgcock, 2005). But L2 writing researchers advise teachers to see error correction and content response as separate issues when working with ELL writers. Simply put, teachers' strategies for "detecting and marking lexical and syntactic errors tend to be different from their strategies for responding to content issues" (Ferris & Hedgcock, 2005, p. 200).

When I've spoken to teachers about the writing of multilingual students, many point first and foremost to concerns over grammar and mechanics. At one point, I surveyed teachers throughout Mill River district, as well as teachers in other school districts, in order to get a sense of their perspectives on the needs of ELL writers. Their responses echoed what I often heard at local conferences. One teacher in Ken-zhi's school wrote in the survey: "Many multilingual students are easily frustrated by the number of 'exceptions' in English grammar; they often give up trying to learn the rules." Another teacher gave a list of errors that he saw most often: "Not understanding tense, odd spellings of word, slang we use, words that have a variety of meaning." These comments from teachers paralleled what students experienced in terms of teacher feedback.

In fact, all the students in this study found that their teachers' feedback was overwhelmingly focused on error correction at the sentence level. They quickly learned that they were expected to revise by simply correcting the errors and rewriting their papers with their teachers' wording, even if they didn't understand the need for a correction or change. There were almost no instances where teachers pointed out places where the ELL students were meeting writing objectives or excelling as writers.

Teachers' singular focus on error correction reaffirmed these students' self-image as individuals incapable of engaging in reflective, critical discussion on writing and other intellectual activities. The students found the marks confusing, and although they could make the changes that the teacher had indicated, they often couldn't explain the reasons beyond them.

Craving Teacher Response

At the heart of our response procedures for ELL writers, we need to understand that learning to write in a second language is a lifelong process. Even with mastery, the English writing of an ELL writer may never fully mimic the writing of native English speakers. But that does not mean that our responses to ELL writers' work are insignificant or disregarded. Indeed, our ELL writers are often eager for our response and eager to implement our requests for revision, especially if they understand why those revisions are needed. In her essay, "One Size Does Not Fit All: Response and Revision Issues for Immigrant Student Writers," Dana Ferris (1999) argued that "immigrant student writers take teacher feedback very seriously and value it highly" (p. 151). Based on her research, Ferris noted that "immigrant student writers are capable of utilizing teacher feedback to improve their papers during revision" (p. 151). Indeed, even when they struggled, every single one of the students I worked with took their teacher's comments to heart, especially when they were delivered by a constructive and kind hand. They willingly made all changes, but they also wanted to learn more about what their teachers thought about their ideas, their voices, and their development as writers.

ESTABLISHING APPROACHES TO TEACHER RESPONSE

Transmitting Teacher Response to ELL Writers: Initial Thoughts

In one of my focus group meetings with Ken-zhi, Paul, Therese, and Wisdom, I asked the students about teacher feedback. They all agreed that they had three concerns as writers. First, they often had difficulty reading teachers' handwriting or understanding cryptic comments/symbols. Teachers' comments were often too implicit or offered little explanation or suggestion about how to address the problem. Therefore, one way of improving feedback to ELL writers is to reflect on how comprehensible and clear our responses are to our linguistically diverse students. Second, the students reported that teachers overwhelmingly marked their papers in such a way that they could not prioritize which concerns were most pressing or where they should start revising. Third, and one of the most important problems from their perspective, teachers did not tend to praise or identify places where students were doing well in their written texts. The students had difficulty telling if there was anything of value in their writing. These concerns impacted the level of investment that the students brought to their drafts and revisions.

To address these concerns, Dana Ferris, the foremost expert on response to L2 student writing, recommends that one of teachers' first priorities should be to read through ELL students' texts without making any comments or marks. If the impulse to correct and edit is strong, then the teacher can jot down on a separate piece of paper the concerns and questions that emerge as she reads. Another way to reconcile this impulse is to make two copies of ELL student papers, marking one to aid the teacher's understanding of the text and using the second copy for selective comments to the student.

As teachers read and consider the students' writing, the goal is to prioritize feedback, ascertaining the major points that we want students to consider (Ferris & Hedgcock, 2005). Teachers of ELL writers don't need to correct and address every issue and problem that is present in a student paper. For many ELL students, the over-marking of their texts feels overwhelming and counterproductive; they aren't sure where to begin. The result is that some students disengage with their writing, much as Ken-zhi did above, and others simply give up. To counter these reactions, teachers need to be selective and prioritize when they respond to ELL writers and their texts.

Ferris (2002) recommends that teachers who are faced with deciding whether to be clear or brief in their comments should aim for clarity over brevity. If ELL writers can't understand comments or suggestions, they cannot improve their texts. Ferris (2003) also makes the following recommendations for teachers:

- Try to give personalized feedback that includes the student's name, and try to include praise in the margins, as well as noting concerns.
- Show interest in the students' ideas, and note progress from previous writing assignments and drafts.
- Be sure that ELL writers understand the vocabulary of writing (thesis, transitions, purpose, writer's intent, expand, and so forth) and provide examples when possible.

Comments given in a combination of endnotes and marginalia are often the most effective for ELL writers. As teachers, we should try to write notes at the end of a paper that include moments of praise, refer back to margin comments (if used), and summarize the issues that we'd like to see ELL students address in their next drafts.

Many L2 writing specialists also like to use one-on-one conferences with students because it gives students a chance to clarify their ideas orally. Teachers can also check for understanding. In these conferences, ELL writers should leave the session with a written set of notes about what was discussed. Often, the cognitive overload of engaging orally while simultaneously listening, reading, and critically thinking about a text can make it difficult for students to remember the details of the session after they finish talking to the teacher. The notes serve as tangible written artifacts that help ELL writers remember the comments and suggestions that were discussed. Teachers can act as notetakers, including the students' comments along with their own, during the session. Another option is to take the final moments of the session to have the students jot down a summary of points discussed and possibilities for revision, while the teacher listens and clarifies.

As new technology emerges, tools for responding to student writing are continuously improving. Beyond the paper and pen, teachers can now offer feedback in a number of ways that will benefit ELL writers. For example, teachers can (1) use audio recordings of their responses so that ELL writers can listen to teacher feedback and suggestions, or (2) have students hand in drafts via emailed attachment and use electronic feedback (Ware & Warschauer, 2006). For example, Microsoft Word has an "Add comments" feature that allows writing teachers to embed typed comments into the margins of students' texts. This technology allows teachers to make sure that their comments are legible and provide additional explanations or clarifications. Teachers can also use the comment feature to include hyperlinks to websites that may provide additional instruction for students.

Developing a Two-Stage Response Process for ELL Writers

Many L2 writing specialists, including Leki (1992), suggest a two-stage process for responding to ELL writers. She recommends concentrating first on global and then on local concerns. In some classrooms, teachers have ELL writers submit two subsequent drafts as part of the feedback cycle.

When teachers respond to the first draft, their goal is to help the student writer address "global" issues or higher-order concerns (HOC) and content development. This first level of response engages teachers in conversation with an ELL writer in order to consider the overall structure of the student's argument, description, or narrative. Teachers actively and supportively encourage ELL writers to develop their writing further. Teachers can ask students to consider their intent and purpose as authors. They point to places where writers might expand, build a better opening or ending, consider a question, write with more detail, strengthen a claim with evidence, embark on a new line of argument, and so on (see Figure 8.2 for Leki's suggested questions). In this first stage of response, teachers address only those errors that severely interrupt the writer's ability to communicate meaning and intent to the reader.

ELL writers then revise their drafts to develop their papers further and to address these global concerns. In the second round of feedback, the writer turns in the revised draft and the teacher offers feedback on more "local" errors (see guiding questions in Figure 8.3). Here, teachers concentrate more closely on mechanical errors in grammar, punctuation, paragraphing, and other sentence-level concerns (spelling, use of conjunctions, verb tenses, word order, and so forth). I discuss strategies for error correction in more detail shortly.

For ELL writers, this two-stage response practice can be particularly effective. Adolescent ELL writers are often hesitant to change their writing in any drastic fashion once they have corrected sentence-level problems. That isn't surprising, when we consider the time and energy that went into writing the text in a second language, as well as mastering and correcting those sentence-level concerns. For them, the paper is now perfect. But an error-free essay can continue to have issues with meaning, development, and substance.

FIGURE 8.2. Questions to Guide Teachers' Global Response

Ilona Leki (1992) has recommended that teachers of ELL writers begin globally with the following questions in mind:

- Does the writer's draft respond to the demands of the assignment?
- Does the writer articulate a good understanding of the readings (data, field observations, lab experiment, and so forth) that s/he is writing about?
- Are the writer's main points clear to readers?
- Does the draft fulfill the writer's intentions? Are the writer's ideas communicated effectively to his/her readers?
- Has the writer found an effective way to organize the draft (based on the genre, the purpose, and the audience)?
- Are there places where the writer might develop or write with more detail? Does the writer use appropriate and sufficient evidence?
- Is the writer's introduction to the draft effective?
- Are the writer's paragraphs well developed? Are the paragraphs unified?

FIGURE 8.3. Questions to Guide Teachers' Local Responses

Ilona Leki (1992) has recommended questions to guide teachers' responses at the local level:

- Where do sentence or word-choice problems interfere with the writer's communicating clearly with readers? Are there any confusing sentences?
- Are there any grammatical errors?
- How could the writer improve his/her word choice?
- Are there punctuation errors? Are there proofreading mistakes?

Our goal as teachers should be to encourage ELL writers to stretch, to engage in more advanced revisions, and to think critically about their writing and its impact on readers. But the students' hesitancy to change anything in their "now-perfected" texts makes it difficult for them to engage in any substantive revision. In addition, if entire sections of the student's text might change in the process of revision, addressing sentence-level concerns in the initial response can seem almost irrelevant.

With the most advanced adolescent ELL writers, teachers can consider responding to content and language accuracy in one draft, particularly as the students become more experienced with a given genre. The main concern, which may manifest itself in some assignments but not others, is that ELL writers, due to the unique challenges of writing in a second language, will shortchange their revisions by prioritizing "error correction" at the expense of content. Overall, research suggests that teacher response needs to be personalized to the individual ELL writer. As Ferris (1999) has noted, there is no one-size-fits-all, and for each new assignment, every ELL writer will have somewhat different needs at different moments in the year.

SO WHAT DO WE DO ABOUT ERROR CORRECTION?

Researchers from the field of second language writing continue to investigate what actually works and helps to improve the written accuracy of ELL writers. My experience suggests that the students in my study did not often know what to do with the teachers' corrections when they received them. They weren't always sure what the marks meant or why certain changes were necessary, even when teachers handed out code sheets with a list of markings and phrases that were supposed to help students understand. ELL writers often found these lists confusing and they weren't sure what made a sentence "awkward." Even questions in the margins could seem cryptic.

Although the students made changes because the teacher had marked them, they did not always understand why the corrections were necessary. They often couldn't hear "the error" in their written work in the same way that their native-English-speaking peers could. In these instances, the students knew that they had made an error, and they appreciated that the teacher had written in "the correct way" for phrasing or grammar. But they were never quite sure what rule they had violated or why a certain phrasing might be a better choice. When I asked the students about how they used teachers' marks to improve their writing, their responses echoed this sense that they were not necessarily internalizing changes for their future writing. Miguel told me: "I change the spelling." Paul noted that, "I went back to the writing and make some changes so that it looked and sounded better." Ken-zhi commented, "I just correct it."

The Importance of Follow-through

Helping ELL students understand the rules of language usage is an important part of their development as writers. Any level of error correction that occurs on the students' written work should be accompanied by companion strategies that help students understand how to improve their language accuracy. Worksheets and grammar drills don't often help ELL writers to internalize these usage rules. In fact, many students excel at the worksheets but continually make the same errors when they write. The problem is that there is a sense of disconnect between the grammar rule and the actual writing.

Teachers can resolve this sense of disconnect by teaching grammar as a set of rhetorical choices, directly tied to the perceptions of readers and the intent of the writer. Rhetorical and functional approaches to grammar complement the curricular and writing instruction strategies discussed in Chapter 7. For example, teachers can engage with joint deconstruction and construction of sentences, phrases, and paragraphs in order to prompt students to engage in discussions about why certain choices are more accurate or appropriate than others. Mini-lessons on certain errors in accuracy can be particularly effective when they are tied to a particular genre of writing (for example, memoir essay and past tense). Teachers can also use models from actual student writing or their own writing to demonstrate a certain usage or to explain an error that is prevalent in students' texts.

Using Error Logs

ELL writers do need to develop strategies for correcting their own work, in order to help them move toward independence and awareness. One strategy to help build this skill is to start an error log for each student (Ferris, 2003, pp. 154–156). For the younger or less experienced writer, the teacher would begin the log and identify one or two local errors that the student should concentrate on. An older or more experienced writer could work with the teacher to identify challenges and keep his/her own logs. In both cases, the teacher explains the error type, writes down an example of the error, and writes out a possible correction (see Figure 8.4).

After the teacher reviews the error and the possible correction with the student orally, students scan their written work with an eye toward identifying and correcting these errors in their writing. Then, with each new assignment or as students master an error, the teacher can add another local concern that the student should learn to scan for and correct in his or her writing. Error logs also encourage ELL writers to become more active, independent, and engaged readers of their own texts.

SUMMARIZING SUGGESTIONS FOR RESPONSE AND CORRECTION

Most of the suggestions for responding to multilingual student writing are good teaching ideas for all students. For example, balancing praise, critique, and suggestions is an approach that most teachers try to remember as they comment on student writing. We also know that it is good practice to explain the reason that students should consider certain changes or additions, so that they can understand and internalize these questions and reasons in their next drafts. The following recommendations highlight the strategies that I emphasize in my own work with ELL writers.

FIGURE 8.4. Sample Error Log

Date/ Assignment	Error Type (with Example from Student's Paper)	Possible Correction	Checked by Student (Y/N)
Jan. 2011	Inconsistent use of verb tenses (tense shift). In this journal entry about your previous schools, the past tense is a good choice, but you need to be consistent. Ex. First, I attend school in Bosnia when I was six years old.	First, I attended school in Bosnia when I was six years old.	Yes, I checked the essay for consistent verb tenses. – Samira (student)

When Reading a Student's Paper

- Skim the paper in its entirety before making any written comments on the draft. Provide comments on the strength of a paper, in order to indicate areas in which the student is meeting expectations. Try to have students clarify confusing points orally, if possible.
- Offer a few possible solutions or suggestions for a given concern. Providing options helps ELL students to engage more with their own writing by making choices. Such strategies promote critical decision making and steer ELL students away from the "teacher-says-I-fix" model.
- Be aware that it can be quite easy for ELL writers to feel overwhelmed by excessive correction. Try to identify three major concerns to work on with each paper. Also, assure ELL students that some errors are common among many students, even native speakers of English (e.g., transitions from one idea to the next). In other words, it's not just that student.
- Prioritize issues and help students focus on the global issues in their writing first (i.e., finding a strong topic, developing the language to talk about the topic, ideas, organization, and so on). Sentence-level concerns and grammar can be an issue for ELL students, but often adolescent ELL writers will focus only on these concerns and neglect to build and strengthen their writing skills in other areas (topic development, invention, expansion, use of evidence, drawing connections, writing with detail, and so forth). Many sentence-level concerns can be dealt with at a later stage in the paper's development.

In the Classroom

- Before and even during the drafting stage, provide models of student papers that are glossed with comments pointing to specific features that exhibit how their authors have met expectations. Discuss these models and the comments as a class or in small groups so that students can orally raise questions and comment on the writers' strategies, use of language, and purpose.
- Train and engage students in learning good strategies for peer response. (See ELL Writers and Peer Response section below.)
- Explain the need for citations. Rules about citation and plagiarism are cultural constructs, very much based in American traditions of individuality and entrepreneurship. For many ELL students, the idea of owning a text may be a new concept, and others may have no experience working on academic papers that require citations. Still others may use what Currie (1998) has called "textual borrowing" and mimicking to help them become more confident in certain genres or conventions (p. 7).

ELL WRITERS AND PEER RESPONSE

Peer response is another important way for students to gain feedback on their writing, but there are unique challenges in using peer response with L2 student writers (Carson & Nelson, 1996; Zhu, 2001). In some peer response activities, ELL students are asked to write and formulate a response in the very language they are still learning to master. Studies have found that ELL writers can be at a disadvantage with native English speakers in peer response sessions. For example, Zhu (2001) found that L2 writers often had their voices silenced, interrupted, and generally pushed to the outskirts of the peer response conversation. Sometimes ELL writers are hesitant to contribute, feeling like they have limited authority. When interrupted, ELL writers often give up their turns and do not finish making their comments, even when they were about to make a good point. Some ELL writers may also be less direct in their feedback, often clarifying what they have read or asking questions. They imply or suggest changes rather than insisting upon them.

ELL writers are also navigating across different communicative expectations and figuring out different attitudes about group work in the classroom. In my study, Miguel, Wisdom, and Therese saw some benefits from peer review and enjoyed the social aspects of those classroom interactions. But Kenzhi hated peer review sessions in his ELA class, often "forgetting" copies of his papers for those sessions, even when they were tucked neatly away in his binder. Ken-zhi did not like to share his writing with his native-English-speaking peers. On one level, he was nervous and self-conscious about his English writing. On the other hand, he was anxious and unsure about the social norms involved. Would his new American friends become angry if he critiqued their writing? What if his comments were dumb? What if he seemed too smart? Ken-zhi wanted the approval of his teacher, but he was also worried about risking the approval of his friends. Ironically, Ken-zhi loved peer review in his ESL classroom, where he felt like his voice and his knowledge as a writer were valued by his peers. Despite these challenges, studies on peer review sessions have consistently found that ELL writers can gain a great deal from peer response and can be just as accomplished in helping their native-English speaking peers to strengthen their papers.

So how can a teacher navigate peer review in a mixed class? Evidence suggests that preparing all students for peer review is a necessary component of building a productive peer review model in the writing classroom. As Zhu (2001) contends, there is a need to "prepare all students with guidance and instruction so that they can become equal participants when engaged in oral response" (p. 211). Liu and Hansen (2002), in their book *Peer Response in Second Language Writing Classrooms,* offer a number of strategies for teaching and directing students toward more productive peer review sessions. Their suggestions, which I summarize and expand upon below, provide some examples of how teachers can work "behind the scenes" in order to lead our classes toward more productive peer response sessions.

1. Create student groups. Keep each group limited to three to four students and strategically bring together students with different strengths and mutually beneficial styles of response.
2. Openly discuss turn-taking strategies with the whole class, and suggest procedures in order to level the playing field for all student reviewers.
3. Use a "fish-bowl" technique to let the class watch as fellow students act out a good example of a peer response session and a poor example. Then discuss as a class what worked and what didn't. Use the demonstration as a way to set classroom goals/guidelines for peer review. Videos of such sessions are also useful, and many examples from college writing centers can now be found online through YouTube.
4. Have a class discussion in which the teacher and students discuss useful vocabulary for participating in peer response. Create a word wall with those cues posted for all students to refer to.
5. Provide clear guidelines (i.e., a handout with guiding questions). Include rules for time, roles, and comments. Assign roles to each student in a peer review group in order to ensure that everyone is participating and to provide a clear structure for the group work.

6. Allow students to read the papers the day before so that the time in class can be used solely for responding.
7. Allow ELL writers to use their first language to help with note-taking during the sessions.

For ELL writers still struggling with listening, reading, or speaking, Liu and Hansen offer the following ideas:

- For students who have difficulty understanding their peers, consider using a written mode of peer response first and then allow students to use the filled-out response sheets when discussing. Allow students to record the oral discussion, or choose a person to be the note-taker for the group.
- For students having difficulty with content-area vocabulary, group students together by the content area or by similar subjects. Then allow students to meet before composing their first drafts in order to share background information on their topics. This technique helps all participants develop schemata for the following session.

Finally, I suggest that teachers avoid relying on a single mode of peer response. Although many L2 writers are comfortable with the oral aspects of peer response, it is useful to create opportunities for written feedback as well. After students have had experience with traditional small-group peer response, other alternatives may prove successful. For example, a colleague of mine, Michelle Cox, uses a paper-swap peer review process in which the entire class, including the teacher, participates in a silent review session of one another's papers. Students create two piles of their papers on her desk, and Michelle attaches a sheet of questions to guide responses to each paper. Then students take a paper, read silently, and respond in writing. After they finish with one paper, they return to her desk to choose a second one. The goal is for all students to receive at least two sets of responses from their peers. Michelle participates, too, often choosing the papers of students she knows may be struggling with the assignment.

Training all students for peer response has many benefits in the writing classroom. It provides teachers with opportunities to share and it invites students to use meta-language about writing, language, and rhetoric. Interactive discussions between the class and the teacher on good response techniques and language can create opportunities for the whole class to engage in discussions about writing. The interactive discussions also open new avenues for ELL writers to join in, to find their voices as fellow writers, and to gain experience in thinking critically about their own written work and the work of others.

EVALUATING ELL WRITERS AND THEIR TEXTS

When I speak with ELA and ESL teachers about their students, grading is always a top concern. Teachers often acknowledge that the written product did not always reflect the cognitive abilities of the students, but they weren't sure what was fair, equitable, and instructive for students in terms of grading. The following two responses offer a sampling of the viewpoints from the surveyed teachers from districts in and around Mill River:

- "Grading and assessment are tricky because their language barrier does not reflect their effort." (9th grade English Language Arts teacher)
- "I am also concerned about how to grade them. How do you distinguish between an 'A' [for NES students] and an 'A' [for ELL students] for a particular student?" I think language barriers present problems with expression for the kids as well." (11th grade English Language Arts teacher)

These comments reflect teachers' concerns about the progress of their ELL students. They acknowledge the difficulty of language learning, express empathy for the students' struggles to learn English, and respect the efforts of these students. Other teachers worried that when they gave ELL writers grades based only on their ideas, students walked away with a false sense of their English improvement and needs. Overall, their comments reflect teachers' uncertainty, as well as their questions: How do I balance fairness and standards? How do I acknowledge the efforts of writing in a second language? Did the rubrics from my textbook even consider L2 writers when they were written?

The remainder of this chapter takes up the question of evaluation and grades. My goal here is to raise some questions about the grading tools and practices that often penalize those writing in a second language for not achieving native-like fluency in their texts. But I'll also make suggestions for ways to value ELL writers' texts and their contributions in the writing classroom. I advocate for a balanced approach to grading ELL writers, one that begins with implementing more inclusive writing assignments and instructional activities and considers not only where ELL writers need improvement, but also where they show strengths. (I share additional information on large-scale assessment practices and computer-assisted scoring in Appendix F.)

Mastering writing in a second language is a lifelong process. We need to acknowledge this reality in our assessment standards and tools. At the same time, we need to weigh the realities of writing in a second language with our goal of providing ELL writers with a fair assessment of their improvement and achievement. We can begin by thinking more critically about how L2 writing and writers factor into the evaluation tools we already use.

Rubrics and Second Language Writers

Most mainstream ELA rubrics don't take L2 writers into account, reflecting standards that were set with only native English speakers in mind, particularly in terms of organization patterns and conventions. Like so many English textbooks and curriculum, these tools are normed solely on native English speakers (Matsuda, 2006), and as a result, they require L2 writers to write exactly like native monolingual English speakers in order to achieve the highest scores. Often, rubrics do not acknowledge that there are multiple definitions of "good writing" or that these definitions may be culturally defined (as discussed on pp. 25–26, "The Study of Contrastive Rhetoric"). Rubrics help teachers make judgments based on "clarity" or "organization of ideas," but they don't offer flexibility or advice on how teachers might interpret those standards when it comes to their non-native English writers. The assessment tools rely on a "one-size-fits-all" model that may not reflect the diverse student writers in our classrooms. In the current educational climate of efficiency, testing, assessment, and other pressures, it is often easy to forget that ELL students' texts will almost always reflect some characteristics of writing in a second language, even when they achieve near-perfection in other aspects of their writing.

I should add here that I actually find rubrics to be helpful for ELL writers. I'm aware of the criticism of rubrics articulated by Maja Wilson (2006) and others. Their arguments are important for writing teachers to keep in mind. But for ELL writers, a rubric can be a useful, tangible tool for helping to understand the criteria and expectations of an assignment, especially when it is created with care and shared before the final draft is due. Yet we do have to ask: Is it fair and ethical to assess second language writers in ways that do not account for the difficulty or differences of learning to write in a second language? Are there ways to acknowledge the areas where ELL writers still need to improve, while at the same time more actively valuing the risks they are taking and the innovations they are bringing to their texts and the writing classroom?

Seeing Rubrics from an L2 Writing Perspective

Mass-produced mainstream rubrics often fail to account for the writing strengths that many multilingual writers bring to the text. There are no categories for innovations or phrasings that bring new meaning and new perspectives to an idea or subject. There are no categories for multilingual perspectives or rhetorical decisions that consider a more international or culturally diverse readership. Currently, the only place where ELL writers may receive benefits on a rubric is in sections that emphasize "voice."

In addition, the top tiers of some writing rubrics do not allow much, if any, room for ELL writers' inaccuracies. Teachers, using these tools, are not asked to consider how much those inaccuracies actually impact the reader's understanding or distract the reader from the paper's goals. Spelling and punctuation must be 100% accurate, as must all verb tenses, pronouns, antecedents, and so on. For many L2 writers, this means that the paper has been essentially "scrubbed free" of all L2 writing characteristics. No, it is not impossible to do this, but often this "all or nothing" expectation can lead ELL writers to compose "clean papers" that don't say much or that take few risks in content, as well as sentence variety, style, and vocabulary. Our grading criteria can send unintended messages to our ELL students that impact their overall motivation to write, as well as their decisions about what aspects of the writing process and product they should value most.

Creating More Inclusive Assessment Strategies

How can we account for ELL writers' non-native writing characteristics, while at the same time encouraging them to reach high expectations and be competitive with native-English-speaking peers? The process begins with critically examining the rubrics we already use, and becoming aware of the wording and language that may ignore the ELL writers in our classroom. Take a look at one rubric that you regularly use in your writing assignments. Interrogate it with an eye toward your ELL writers. What do you notice? How do the criteria and the categories of assessment take into account those students working in their second languages? Are other aspects of writing—rhetorical analysis, insights given to peers and classroom discussions, attempts at revision or risk—rewarded or considered? Do length requirements take into account the amount of time that it often takes ELL writers to compose and generate material in a second language? Are there "no error" policies that suggest that all writers have a native-like "eye" or "ear" for seeing and hearing grammatical mistakes in English? Are the advantageous resources of ELL writers acknowledged and identified in any of the grading criteria or standards?

Rubrics and scoring criteria designed with L2 writers in mind often acknowledge that minor or infrequent grammatical errors may still occur. The criteria consider the writer's intent and the evaluation is based on how much the inaccuracies distract the reader from meaning and intent. Teachers start by asking: Do the inaccuracies disrupt readers' understanding, and to what degree? In other words, the impact of an error is measured in terms of the text's rhetorical efficacy. In rubrics that are inclusively tailored, spelling and punctuation criteria, at the highest level of achievement, are described as "*generally* accurate" (Ferris & Hedgcock, 2005, p. 317, my emphasis), allowing some leeway for those writing in a second language. There is an acknowledgment that some level of error may still be present for second language writers, but the majority of the rubric is built around the texts' "*effectiveness for readers, acknowledging that as purposes vary, criteria will as well"* (CCCC Statement on Second Language Writers, 2009, para. 10, emphasis added). Similarly, rubrics with L2 writers in mind provide high points for students' choice of vocabulary, knowing that such criteria provide incentive for L2 writers to expand or take risks with their vocabulary. These more inclusive grading approaches encourage what Sara Weigle (2002) has called "positive washback," meaning that the assessment tool encourages positive changes in the curriculum and in the writing that students produce (p. 54).

Writing assessment specialists continue to agree that the best scoring guides and grading criteria are those that are created locally (Crusan, 2010; Huot & O'Neil, 2008; Reynolds, 2010). Such assessments are designed with the students of a particular classroom or a particular school in mind, and in response to our goals in the classroom and the goals of our students. For teachers working with ELL writers, this often means designing their own rubrics or making adjustments within a given rubric to create a more inclusive and accurate measure of student written work and rhetorical savviness.

Establishing Multiple Measures for Evaluation

In the same way that I've suggested our writing assignments need to be more fully contextualized with rhetorical "fingerholds" for ELL writers, our grading tools should take into account how well ELL writers respond to the contexts and rhetorical situations in their written texts. In grading, our goal is to provide an accurate portrait of student mastery in writing. The best kinds of assessment strategies for measuring the success and progress of ELL writers are ones in which teachers and teams of teachers use the grades on assignments/projects, but also examine growth over time and across assignments, along with meta-cognitive development, through the use of portfolios and self-assessment. A multiple measures approach helps teachers gather the best information on the needs and progress of ELL student writers in order to make better decisions about final grades, placement, future assignments, and future writing instruction.

We must also begin to look for mastery in student writers' contributions as readers and discussants, particularly in those aspects of writing where they can demonstrate rhetorical understandings of how texts work and their own innovations. Below, I offer ten additional suggestions for valuing the work of ELL writers and providing fair assessments that open doors for our ELL writers, rather than closing them.

1. *Build rubrics that are directly aligned with the writing assignment at hand.* Before beginning, think about the goals of the assignment and

what you hope for the students to accomplish. Create rubric categories, criteria, and descriptions that reflect the rhetorical and contextual "fingerholds" that you included in your writing prompt.

2. *Design and build rubrics for an assignment with your class.* Part of the goal of more-inclusive writing instruction is to include ELL writers in more conversation about writing. When teachers work with their classes to discuss and decide on the important qualities and expectations in a given writing assignment, students develop deeper analytical understandings of a given genre, the importance of language choices, and readers' expectations. Class discussions on what matters and what gets graded on a given assignment are important opportunities for ELL writers to add their voices and to hear why certain criteria are important to other readers.

3. *Provide checkpoints and formative feedback along the way.* Teacher response and peer response are two ways to build formative feedback into your assessment strategy. Students should also have benchmarks and checklists en route to the end product. Design your summative assessment criteria first, and then go back and build checkpoints and objectives that you'd like to see students meet at various points in the schedule leading up to the final product. These checkpoints can include quickwrites on students' meta-cognitive understanding of writing, their questions and challenges with a given assignment, and their triumphs as they successfully complete aspects of the assignment. For younger writers, you might frame this as a "Mad, Sad, Glad" writing prompt, in which they identify aspects of their writing that make them "mad" (or frustrated), ones that make them "sad" (or feeling lost or challenged), and others that make them "glad" (feeling triumphant and successful) at a given point in the assignment.

4. *Offer credit for innovative types of research (field-based, interviews, observations, community-situated, and so on).* Encourage ELL writers to use their access to their home communities and their bilingual language abilities to develop innovative research sources for projects and papers. These innovative sources can include field-based research—interviews, observations, local community focus groups, and more—or text-based sources that include newspapers or reputable websites based in other regions of the world.

5. *Grade for rhetorical skills, as well as product or process.* Provide a category in the rubric that focuses on students' ability to interpret and show awareness of the rhetorical situation in their writing. Provide ELL writers with an opportunity to explain the decisions they made

in their written texts in order to meet the goals of the genre and the rhetorical situation.

6. *Provide credit for oral contributions in small groups, large class discussions, and peer response activities.* Increasing the amount of time that we engage our students in talking about their decisions as writers is an important component of building a more inclusive and explicit focus on writing into our curriculum. Consider ways to demonstrate the value you place on ELL writers' oral participation and insights in peer response groups or whole-class discussions on writing. For example, students might receive credit for their roles in class participation during joint deconstruction and reconstruction writing activities, like those discussed in Chapter 7.

7. *Use student self-assessment as part of an overall assessment strategy.* It can be difficult for ELL writers to assess their own work. Consider some of the difficulties that come from writing in a second language. Couple that with the fact that many ELL writers struggle to feel that they "own" English as their own language. But the act of reflection and learning how to assess their own written work is an important aspect of writing instruction for ELL writers. One of my favorite ways of helping students to initiate that level of introspection and meta-awareness comes from Linda Rief, a middle school teacher and author of many books, including *Seeking Diversity* (1991). Rief has her students complete a "history of the paper" handout, in which students answer a prompt about the history of the paper and their process in writing it. Though Rief (1991) is not discussing ELL writers, her strategy can be a useful way to gain insight into how ELL writers developed and considered their writing tasks. Students attach the completed "history of the paper" handout, included in Rief's book, to the final draft. Students provide both a narrative and two grades for their text—one based on content and the second based on language/presentation. Self-assessment tools can also include checklists or brief questionnaires about students' process and decisions as writers. Tools like these can increase ELL writers' roles as stakeholders, moving them away from simply being bystanders in their writing.

8. *Create a category and criteria for innovations.* Consider creating a rubric that has an open category for students that allows them (or you) to consider innovations in student writing that may not be predictable but add value to the reader's experiences with a given text. These innovations might include new levels of creativity in word choices (including uses of L1 phrases or descriptors that add flavor or potency to the writing), original and inventive narrative structures, and advanced multilingual/cross-cultural insights and understandings.

They can also include alternative ways to look at or define a problem or a student's ability to find novel implications or solutions to a challenge (Wiggins & McTighe, 2005, p. 82).

9. *Consult ESL standards and rubrics.* ELA teachers may find it useful to examine rubrics and standards developed specifically for ESL writers. Descriptions and criteria from these tools can help inform the development of scoring guides and other assessment tools for evaluating ELL writers' texts in the context of mainstream classrooms. The WIDA Consortium, part of the Wisconsin Center for Education Research, promotes the academic achievement of linguistically diverse students. Their standards have been adopted by more than 23 states, and the group has created an extensive set of standards for ELL writers across the various grade levels. These rubrics offer helpful starting points for thinking about ELL students' writing progress and our expectations as teachers. (See www.wida.us for more information.)

10. *Increase the role of portfolio assessment in your writing classroom.* Portfolios allow teachers to see the development of ELL student writers over time and across various genres. They allow us and our students to track their writing progress and to consider their development in a contextualized way. They reveal much more about ELL writers' development and progress than many other standardized assessment procedures. O'Malley and Valdez-Pierce (1996) describe portfolios as systematic collections that include the following essential elements: samples of student work, student self-assessment, and clearly stated criteria. For ELL writers, "the use of portfolios encourages students to reflect on their work, to analyze their progress, and to set improvement goals" (O'Malley & Valdez-Pierce, p. 35). Portfolios provide a multidimensional portrait and assessment of ELL writers' comprehension, language use, rhetorical awareness, critical thinking skills, and written product.

I encourage students to include samples of their writing from other classes (science labs, history reports, art reviews, language heritage classes, and so on) in their portfolios. I also ask ELL writers to include writing from workplace settings, extracurricular activities, and online activities (blogs, web pages, fan fiction sites, and so forth). I gain a sense of writing tasks in other settings, my students' achievements, and their writing development in different genres. Recently, the emergence of electronic portfolios has offered us new ways to administrate portfolio assessments, letting teachers digitally archive and share students' writing portfolios (for example, from ELL teacher to ELA teacher, or from 8th grade to 9th grade) in an effort to track the growth and efforts of ELL writers across grade levels.

Finally, we need to embrace multiple measures for assessment and grading when it comes to ELL writers. By assessing our ELL writers in more than one way, we can discover different sides of their understanding and their development as writers. Our goal, in the end, is to have an accurate portrait of their mastery and their progress. Accurate portraits of ELL student mastery do not come from one-shot writing tests. As the CCCC Statement on Writing Assessment (2009) reminds us,

> One piece of writing—even if it is generated under the most desirable conditions—can never serve as an indicator of overall writing ability, particularly for high-stakes decisions. Ideally, writing ability must be assessed by more than one piece of writing, in more than one genre, written on different occasions, for different audiences, and responded to and evaluated by multiple readers as part of a substantial and sustained writing process. (para.10)

ADDITIONAL RESOURCES

Dana Ferris's books on response and error correction are some of the most comprehensive texts available on these topics.

Ferris, D. (2002). *Treatment of error in second language student writing.* Ann Arbor: University of Michigan Press.

Ferris, D. (2003). *Response to student writing: Implications for second-language students.* Mahwah, NJ: Lawrence Erlbam Associates.

I also recommend the following articles and books on peer response and second language writers:

Liu, J., & Hansen, J. (2002). *Peer response in second language writing classrooms.* Ann Arbor: University of Michigan Press.

Nelson, G., & Carson, J. (2006). Cultural issues in peer response: Revisiting "culture." In K. Hyland & F. Hyland (Eds.), *Feedback in second language writing: Contexts and issues* (pp. 42–59). Cambridge, United Kingdom: Cambridge University Press.

Ware, P. D., & Warschauer, M. (2006). Electronic feedback and second language writing. In K. Hyland & F. Hyland (Eds.), *Feedback in second language writing: Contexts and issues* (pp. 105–122). Cambridge, United Kingdom: Cambridge University Press.

For more on portfolio and other measures of authentic assessment for ESL writers, I recommend the following volumes. In particular, O'Malley and Valdez-Pierce have an array of tools and handouts that help teachers and students implement these assessment strategies in the classroom.

Hamp-Lyons, L., & Condon, W. (2000). *Assessing the portfolio: Principles for practice, theory and research.* New York, NY: Hampton Press.

O'Malley, J. M., & Valdez-Pierce, L. (1996) *Authentic assessments for English language learners.* Reading, MA: Addison-Wesley.

Finally, the CCCC Position Statement on Writing Assessment, written by some of the best researchers on writing assessment, offers thoughtful guidelines for approaches to large-scale and small-scale assessment practices. It can be found at: http://www.ncte.org/cccc/resources/positions/writingassessment.

CHAPTER 9

Conclusion

Looking Beyond the ELA Classroom

Some of my most enthusiastic readers have raised questions about how to build and advocate for broader networks of support for ELL writers within their schools. As I've mentioned before, learning to write in a second language is a lifelong process. It doesn't just happen in a single semester or school year. The reality is that we don't just need individual English teachers to nurture and expand the writing experiences of these students; we need schools that do. Our work with these multilingual student writers cannot just happen in ELA or ELL classrooms. But, as ELA and ELL writing teachers, we often still lead the way; our students and colleagues turn *to us* for guidance when it comes to matters of writing.

Throughout the previous chapters, I've offered insights into the process of writing in a second language, shared some principles and strategies for curriculum design, and offered activities to aid teachers working with ELL writers in their classrooms. In these final pages, I suggest ideas and directions for broader institutional encouragement for ELL writers and their teachers. In particular, I'll focus on the following three questions teachers and administrators might ask to bring about innovative school-wide responses to the writing needs of their students:

- What school-wide writing programs for students and faculty can be established to help these student writers beyond ELA and ELL classrooms?
- How might some traditional extracurricular activities and initiatives be transformed to help ELL writers find their voices and celebrate their successes?
- How do these kinds of initiatives impact ELL writers? Why does it matter?

As I share these questions as a framework, I know that they hardly exhaust the array of possible concerns about our work with ELL writers. But I do believe that to embrace ELL students as writers, we need to investigate school-wide responses that foster writing, writers, and talk about writing as part of a larger institutional goal for *all* students and faculty. Tirabassi (2007) has defined this goal as creating an "institutional writing culture," one that reverberates across different content areas, across creative and informational genres, and across the extra-curriculum (p. 123). It is a vision of literacy that embraces the writing and writing practices of its members as a vital part of a vibrant learning community. In doing so, it broadens the scope of whom students see as writers—teachers, students, administrators, business owners, community leaders, parents, and so on. It also emphasizes writing as integral to critical thinking. We begin to build that kind of cultural appreciation and awareness for writing into our schools when we begin to consider the following section.

SCHOOL-WIDE WRITING PROGRAMS FOR STUDENTS AND FACULTY

Writing centers and Writing-Across-the Curriculum (WAC) programs are two school-wide initiatives that can help schools expand the conversations on writing and the teaching of writing. Such programs create alternative and supplemental spaces for supporting students in their work as writers.

Writing Centers

Pam Childers (1989), a secondary school writing center pioneer, once wrote:

> When I started to dream of creating a writing center for the students I saw five days per week each year, I knew that the most advanced, the least skilled, and the highly creative writers all need a place for their writing, a community of writers, an ear to listen, and a voice to respond. So did I. (p. ix)

Writing centers, long a staple of colleges and universities, are a growing phenomenon in secondary schools. Writing centers provide alternative, supplemental spaces for students to get feedback on their writing from trained tutors and teachers who can provide them with the kind of feedback they need to become more effective writers and thinkers. They serve an important need as schools become more invested in the writing work of their students and their faculty. For English language learners, writing centers are important spaces, outside of ELA and ELL classrooms, where student writers gain supplemental support for planning, organizing, and carrying out a writing task. Since writing center tutoring often emphasizes a conversation-based approach to writing, these sessions can be particularly fruitful for ELL writers who are learning to articulate their ideas and goals about their written work.

But writing centers don't just serve ELL writers. In fact, the best writing centers emerge as a writing space for all writers in a school. For example, students can use writing centers to work on college application essays, grant and scholarship essays, workplace resumes and cover letters, writing for extracurricular activities like literary and poetry journals, and more. One hazard of writing centers is that they can be viewed as remedial spaces that students don't want to be associated with. In response, the most effective high school writing centers work diligently to craft student "buy-in" to the fact that all writers need sounding boards and support. Administrators and teachers can set the tone for how writing centers are received in their schools by closely considering how the mission of the center is portrayed in the school community. Proper training of writing center tutors also helps create a welcoming atmosphere and sense of community for a range of student writers.

Writing-Across-the-Curriculum (WAC) Programs

Writing centers often work in tandem with Writing-Across-the Curriculum programs. While writing centers work with student writers, WAC programs promote faculty involvement in the writing culture. As John Bean (2001), a leading expert, explains, successful WAC programs can bring "a new level of awareness and appreciation for the power of writing as a means of both engaging students and developing their thinking skills" (p. xvii).

The WAC movement emphasizes that students need more opportunities to write, and that more practice in writing makes them better writers and also better thinkers (Bean, 2001, p. xvii). In WAC programs, teachers learn to use writing-to-learn (WTL) teaching techniques that employ writing as a tool for critical thinking. Such approaches acknowledge that writing and critical thinking are often intertwined as cognitive processes. The techniques and strategies encourage teachers to use informal, short, and ungraded writing assignments to keep students writing and thinking. Some approaches include the use of response journals, writing buddies, learning logs, and problem analyses. They can be as simple as teachers handing out notecards and asking for students' questions or reactions, or as complicated as longer content-area reports. In the best of circumstances, schools hire in-house WAC coordinators who offer ongoing faculty training and support to schools in designing writing assignments, learning more about the teaching of writing, building better response strategies, offering writing center programs, and more. WAC programs can also play a role in developing curricular responses to digital literacy and oral communication skills, as part of a larger Communication-Across-the-Curriculum (CAC) approach. WAC coordinators can also assist fellow teachers with grant writing, serve as a sounding board for ideas and motivation, and provide feedback for professional writing endeavors that faculty undertake. The best WAC-trained teachers are knowledgeable about best practices at the secondary *and* college levels, because they are able to see how the demands shift across the grade levels.

In recent years, local resources for starting high school writing centers and WAC workgroups have been emerging across the country. Many national resources, like the International Writing Center and the WAC Clearinghouse, are open to secondary school WAC leaders, and they encourage the idea sharing and cross-institutional collaborations that have made these initiatives so powerful at the college level. I share a list of these resources at the end of the chapter.

Both writing centers and WAC programs can help schools create a kind of nerve-center for the writing initiatives in their buildings. These programs can become valuable resource stations for student and faculty writing concerns, composition theory and pedagogy, best practices, and more. They can serve as launching pads for school-wide literacy activities and events. For example, one school's writing program director held a speaker series that brought in a range of local creative writers, technical writers, and university writing teachers to meet with students and faculty. Each speaker offered a workshop for students and a workshop for teachers that helped broaden the investment of all the stakeholders. On another occasion, the director brought in expert writers to help teachers and staff with professional activities, like grant writing. The expressed outcome of these initiatives was to encourage all members of the school community to make the act of writing more visible. There were more visible writers, in and around students, talking about writing. In making writing more visible throughout the school community, teachers and administrators hoped to dispel the myth among students that only weak writers need support or struggle with writing tasks. Teachers and administrators aimed to create a school atmosphere that valued writing and also acknowledged that even the most experienced writers still need support and encouragement from others along the way.

TRANSFORMING EXTRACURRICULAR ACTIVITIES AND INITIATIVES

In an effort to provide more writing support for ELL student writers in our schools, we also need to find more opportunities to celebrate the writing that they are often already doing. Currently, so much of the research on ELL writers focuses solely on their academic writing. This research focus guides our classroom practices, and although such practices can be very successful, there are emerging concerns that one by-product of this emphasis on only academic writing is that ELL writers have few opportunities to engage with writing as a creative act. In our school, many ELL writers find themselves on the periphery of extracurricular activities like school newspapers, literary magazines, screenwriting clubs, and poetry groups. Some ELL writers may shy away, seeing these clubs and activities as being "owned" by other students in their schools. They may also shy away if they feel that their English writing is not good enough for these kinds of publications.

The truth is that, in many schools, ELL writers receive few invitations to write creatively, either in English or in their native languages. They have even fewer opportunities to publish their creative work. In response, though, teachers can establish more extracurricular spaces for ELL students to showcase their writing and language talents. Our ELL writers have stories to share, lyrics to express, and poetry to voice. We need them to know that their stories and their creativity are valued in any language.

One good starting point for teachers is to consider the creation of multilingual literary journals that encourage bilingual writers to submit their work in their home languages. Another option is to open a school's existing literary journals to multilingual submissions. Students can also be invited to play larger roles in the editorial process of such journals. At colleges and universities, there are many successful models of multilingual literacy journals that embrace the kinds of writing and stories that second language writers have to share. One example is the undergraduate journal, *mOthertongue*, at the University of Massachusetts, which publishes poetry and visual art in languages other than English with facing-page translations. Likewise, the College of Charleston's *Polyphony*, a multilingual undergraduate literary journal, offers online editions that teachers can use as models to establish similar publication venues for the multilingual writers in their own schools. These journals can serve as powerful and useful models for teachers and students interested in broadening the scope of their school's writing venues. In the Additional Resources section at the end of this chapter, I've included the web addresses for both journals.

Other options for opening up more creative spaces for ELL writers include multilingual drama clubs that encourage students to try their hand at playwriting. Screenwriting clubs are also becoming more popular, and students with a high interest in cinema and film could be approached about playing larger roles in these activities. Most schools also have a school newspaper, and this is another venue where multilingual writers could be more actively recruited. Learning more about the acts of reporting and writing for a newspaper are invaluable experiences for young student writers, and often our ELL writers find that they can gain access to stories and individuals that others cannot. At the same time, school newspapers could also consider how to create more editorial and leadership roles for these students. Finally, advisors might consider making sure that the newspaper, not just the staff, is a reflection of the school's student body and multilingual communities through its content. For example, some school editors have started to add bilingual components to their papers, particularly in the form of advice columns, community news briefs, and profile pieces.

THE IMPACT OF THESE INITIATIVES: WHY IT MATTERS

As students get older, the most valuable gift we can give them is a sense of confidence in their voices and their written expressions. Initiatives like writing centers and WAC programs, along with writing opportunities in the extra-curriculum, allow ELL writers to participate in a larger number of authentic, meaningful activities and conversations about writing. Programs like these provide ELL students with genuine moments to act and feel like real writers. These moments can confirm their gifts and competencies as language users and help move them from perceptions of themselves as beginners and novice language learners.

These kinds of initiatives also build larger networks of support for these writers. We can't always ensure that every writing experience will be a good one for ELL writers. But we can aim to replicate better principles and under-standings for working with ELL writers in as many pockets of our school as possible. Replication builds multiple strands of support, like a web. Even when one strand fails or breaks, the other elements of the web can continue to foster growth and confidence in these young writers.

FINAL THOUGHTS

My journey with Wisdom, Paul, Miguel, Therese, Ken-zhi, and Vildana ended after 2 years. The younger students were well into their sophomore years of high school, and Vildana had graduated.

By then, school had become more difficult for many of them. Therese, for one, struggled in her sophomore year when she was no longer eligible for the school-to-work program (a 1-year program due to funding) and she had tak-en the only heritage-language class available to students. Her English class that year had more than 26 students, and she felt anonymous. She fell silent in the classroom. When she struggled to complete assignments, she wasn't sure how to approach her teacher. She confessed that she sometimes contemplated drop-ping out as some of her friends had done. In the spring of her sophomore year, we met and talked. During that conversation, Therese, who 2 years earlier had dreamed of becoming a bilingual lawyer, remarked to me: "I don't think that I'm going to make it to college. I don't get things. I'm not as smart as you think I am."

But, despite setbacks likes these, all the students continued to strive and move forward. Upon graduation, Vildana completed a nursing program, first attending a community college, and later a small state college. Wisdom con-tinued to write passionately about his homeland in his music and in his note-books. He graduated, and though he had hoped to attend his state's flagship university, he was wary to apply. Instead, he was accepted at a smaller state college where he decided to study biology. He remained involved in the Boys and Girls Club and his local church. He will graduate from college shortly. Miguel's family moved out of state at the end of his sophomore year to join extended family in a larger city, and we corresponded briefly thereafter. School remained a struggle for him, and we lost contact before he began his junior year. Paul's family moved to Utah after he graduated high school. He intended to apply to college after his family was more settled. Therese graduated from Mill River North High School, but at the time of her graduation, she was still unsure if she would pursue any higher education. She had tentative plans to take classes at the community college. Ken-zhi was accepted to a music school in Canada upon his graduation, but his family decided to return to Taiwan to care for extended family. He is currently a performance arts student at a university in Taipei.

In many ways, the diversity of the students' outcomes captures the range of trajectories that adolescent multilingual writers can move toward. It also captures some of the limitations in those trajectories. At the end of the day, how we teach writing is of great importance if these students are to gain the confidence and writing prowess to pursue longer-range goals and dreams. If their experiences with writing are limited, then their trajectories and dreams can be limited as well. But I remain hopeful. By embracing the resources of these young writers, expanding our teaching techniques, and understanding the complexities of writing in a second language, we can broaden the scope of possibilities for these young and resilient writers. We can, indeed, make a difference.

ADDITIONAL RESOURCES

For more on secondary school writing centers, I recommend the following resources:

Fels, D., & Wells, J. (2011). *The successful high school writing center: Building the best program with your students.* New York, NY: Teachers College Press.

George Mason University's website on High School Writing Centers: http://writing-center.gmu.edu/highschoolwritingcenters/sites.google.com/site/hswritingcenters/index.php

Information on Writing-Across-the-Curriculum programs and development can be found at the WAC Clearinghouse: http://wac.colostate.edu/

National Writing Project's resources for high school writing centers: http://www.nwp.org/cs/public/print/resource/3584

Bean, J. (2001). *Engaging ideas: The professor's guide to integrating writing, critical thinking, and active learning in the classroom* San Franciso, CA: Jossey-Bass. Bean's best-selling book has innovative ideas for building writing-to-learn activities into all content-area classrooms.

Activity—Play, Write, Revise

Note: An extended version of this exercise is available on my website: http://pubpages.unh.edu/~ortmeier/about.html

Stretching Our Writing

We all have to start somewhere with our writing. Sometimes what we first put on paper, the first draft, is not as good as we want it to be, but we don't know what else to say. That is okay. Learning how to revise—*to play with your writing, to stretch it out, to make it more focused or more interesting*—is something that all good writers learn to do.

Try one of the following prompts to help you work on adding details and making your writing more interesting for your reader.

1. *Diving Deeper (Describing a Person/Place/Object):* Choose a person, object, or place that you mention in one of your writings. Then try the following directions to help you dig deeper into the details and memories that come with those details.
   a. *Person:* Write about that person in more detail. Write about the person's physical features, dress, smell, and mannerisms. Think about how they talk and how they act with other people. Help me as a reader to pick him or her out of a crowded room.
   b. *Place:* Take a very specific place within one of your pieces. Now write about it in more detail. Try to make me feel like I'm there. What would I see, smell, hear, taste, feel, and touch?
   c. *Object:* Look for an important object that you mention in one of your pieces. Now fully describe it, using all of your senses. What does it look like, feel like, smell like, and so on? For example, if I were writing about my wedding ring, I would show the cursive engraving on the inside, the cool metal against my skin, the way I play with it when I'm nervous, the slightly worn scratches on the gold, and so forth. I might even mention how it looks almost identical to my mother's wedding ring and how that similarity

brings her experiences and my experiences closer together in some ways.

2. *Unbury a Story:* Find a line in one of your pieces that seems to hide a story, and unbury that story. You might find a line that "tells" but doesn't "show." Open up that story. Some statements, such as "I can't write," often hold one or more stories within them. Choose one to share with readers. (I give thanks to Sue Wheeler and Rebecca Rule's book *True Stories* for this wonderful prompt.)

3. *From Vague to Specific:* Comb through your writing and add as many specific names and sensory details as you can. Change vague nouns (car) to specific nouns (Jeep Cherokee), general adjectives (red) to specific ones (metallic cherry), direct statements (my SUV handles well) to metaphors (When shifting across three lanes to get to my exit, my SUV handles like what I imagine a racecar to feel like, hugging the road while cleanly gliding to the next lane, and responding quickly to my every move).

Developing Meaning

1. *Looping:* Read through your draft. As you read, try to find a line or two that really speaks to you and gets your attention. It might be a line that seems to hold more meaning; maybe it is a line that confuses you or that seems to have more stories behind it. On a new piece of paper, copy this line at the top. Now freewrite using that line as a starting point. As you write, try to push further and develop more meaning as you go. After you write, read through this new piece of writing, find another line, and repeat the process. This is also a great technique to use when you feel stuck or like you have nothing left to say.

Transforming Our Writing

Sometimes we learn more about a piece of writing by changing it into something completely different. Take your piece of writing and change it into something new. Here are some ideas:

1. *Write a Letter:* Transform one of your pieces into a letter to a person who is significant to your story or to a good friend to whom you'd like to tell this story.

2. *Write a Poem:* Rewrite this piece of writing as a poem. Think about the ways this change brings out different aspects of your story or helps you use different words and images.

3. *Write a Play:* Rewrite one of your pieces as a short play, complete with a cast of characters, description of the setting, and stage directions.

4. *Write a Dialogue:* Create a dialogue between two people in one of your pieces. Choose a scene that briefly shows important information for your reader. Remember that people rarely talk in complete sentences. Try to make the dialogue sound as natural as possible. Use contractions and slang, when appropriate. Avoid small talk, and keep the dialogue crisp and brief.

Activity— Who are My Readers?

An Exercise in "Profiling" Your Readers

Your goals:

1. Identifying your readers
2. Thinking about your readers' expectations, values, needs, and attitudes (Johnson-Sheehan, 2010)
3. Setting goals for your next draft, based on your Readers' profile

Look over the assignment sheet for the essay we are working on. Then read through your draft. Now step back for a moment, decide who your readers are for this piece of writing, and then complete the chart on the next page.

Who Are Your Readers?	Primary Readers	Secondary Readers
Purpose*: What is your purpose in writing to these readers?		
Needs** (in terms of evidence, e.g., what counts as evidence for these readers?)		
Needs** (in terms of language expectations, vocabulary/language precision, and tone)		
Attitudes** (in terms of how the audience perceives your topic, your research question, or your purpose. What opinions do they already have?)		
Attitudes** (in terms of what your readers already know. What do they not know?)		
Values** (what do you know about what your readers values—genres, clarity, certain kinds of arguments, and so on?)		

*I preface this question by defining some ways that we may be interacting with our readers. We talk about what it means to persuade, inform, argue, convince, synthesize, recommend, and so forth, in order to help ELL students and other students distinguish these terms. I often share samples with passages underlined to identify certain rhetorical moves that authors make when they write for their readers. Graff and Birkenstein's *They Say/I Say: The Moves that Matter in Academic Writing* (2009) is a helpful resource for these kinds of discussions.

**Teachers will need to define and discuss these terms with the class in order to establish a vocabulary that all student writers can use. Many of these terms may be new or may be used in ways that seem new to English language learners.

Activity—Mapping Our Literacies and Resources

In this activity, students are asked to map out their social and academic influences with a particular emphasis on motivation, reading, and writing. (See illustration on next page.)

Step 1: Create envelopes filled with 10 colored cut-outs for each of the five icons (on next page)—individual people, groups of people, places, events, and things.

Step 2: Each student is given a large piece of poster paper, along with an envelope filled with a series of visual icons. The teacher explains each of the icons, and the class completes a few examples together to make sure everyone understands.

Step 3: Students then work independently for about 30 minutes, identifying these influences by writing the name of the influence on the series of icons.

Step 4: Next, students write their own names in the middle of the poster and paste the icons onto the paper, placing those with the strongest influence closest to their names.

Step 5: Students discuss and share the icons and posters orally with teachers.

Note: When I've done this activity with individual ELL writers, I have sat beside them, asking about certain icons or the map so that they orally explain the various elements to me. On occasion, I've also tape-recorded these conversations so that I can reflect upon what I've learned about a given student afterward.

171

FIGURE C.1. Key for mapping activities in Chapter 6 figures.

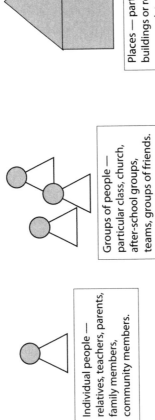

PROMPT: Which people, groups of people, places, events, and things influence you when it comes to schoolwork and school writing?

Places — particular buildings or rooms that you associate with writing or learning.

Things — books, technology, (computers, Internet, certain software, games) instruments, music, miscellaneous items.

Groups of people — particular class, church, after-school groups, teams, groups of friends.

Individual people — relatives, teachers, parents, family members, community members.

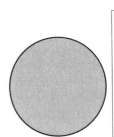

Events — events that took place over the past school year or in previous school years that have influenced your schooling, your attitude toward school, or achievement.

Sample Genre Tags for Genre Awareness Activity

Genre/Audience/Purpose Tag A

Genre: What kind of writing is this?

Audience: Who is it written for? Is the language formal or more personal? (Give an example.)

Purpose: What does this piece of writing do? (Inform, argue, share a story, entertain, persuade, etc.)

Design: What does it look like?

Genre/Audience/Purpose Tag B

Genre: What kind of writing is this? What do you notice about this genre?

Audience: Who is it written for? What do you notice about the language that is used for these readers? (Certain word choices, personal or more formats, etc.)

Purpose: What is the purpose of this piece of writing? (To inform, persuade, sell, share a story, create empathy, share good news, say "thank you," stay in contact with friends or family, etc.) Try to be as specific as you can.

Design: What does the text look like? (Colors or no colors, pictures, logos, lines, and boxes to separate information, text only, tables and graphs, etc.)

Building Rhetorical Fingerholds Into Our Assignments: Sample Questions

	ENTERING *(what students know, the "safe harbors" of their experiences)*	BRIDGING *(connecting what students know to what they need to learn)*	ADVANCING *(what students need to learn to stretch further)*
Writer's Position	What roles has the student already played in his/her various communities? *Examples:* son/daughter, sibling, grandchild, student; team member, captain, dancer	What are the roles that the student needs and wants to play within the school setting? How might the "safe harbor" roles connect to the roles students can play in their academic writing?	What are the roles that the student needs or wants to play beyond school? In which communities? For what purposes?
Audience (Primary, Secondary)	Currently, who does the student interact with (communities, groups, etc.)? What are the relationships?	What kinds of relationships does the student need/want to develop? Who does the student want to communicate with? How might the new relationships be similar to the relationships they already know well?	What kinds of relationships does the student want to develop in communities beyond their current school environment?
Topic/ Inquiry Questions	What does the student already know (e.g., current reading interests, current activities, personal experiences, etc.)? Are there any resources (e.g., family, community, language, technology, etc.) that the student already has easy access to?	What does the student need/want to know and how might that knowledge connect to knowledge s/he already has? Are there ways that students might deepen resources or expand on resources that they already have access to? Are there new ways that they may think of using those resources?	What does the student need/want to learn? What does s/he need or want to read? What other resources does s/he need or want to learn to use?

	ENTERING *(what students know, the "safe harbors" of their experiences)*	BRIDGING *(connecting what students know to what they need to learn)*	ADVANCING *(what students need to learn to stretch further)*
Genre	What genres have the students already used in her/his writing? What does s/he read for leisure? What does s/he read for daily practical purposes (e.g., brochures, newsletters, charts, newspapers, emails, etc.)? What are the characteristics of those genres?	What genres does the student need/want to learn? What are the characteristics of those genres?	What genres does the student want to learn? What genres will help them develop new roles in new communities (in school and out of school, workplace, higher education, civically, etc.)? What genres will open them to new opportunities? What are the characteristics of those genres?

A Discussion of L2 Writing, Assessment, and Computer Scoring

Assessment is a well-documented area of L2 writing research, since college-level international students often need to pass exams like the TOEFL (Test of English as a Foreign Language), and resident ELL students are increasingly required to take benchmark tests in local school districts. Hamp-Lyons (1991), Weigle (2002), and Crusan (2010), among others, have examined holistic approaches, scoring procedures, the norming of scores, placement procedures, and the construction of assessment tests. College-level assessment studies on multilingual writers are often fueled by considerations of placing L2 students in first-year writing courses, writing intensive coursework, entry/exit testing, and portfolio assessment. I encourage readers to look into the work of these individual authors if they are seeking information on broad-scale testing and placement procedures.

Concerns with Computers and Automated Scoring

Increasingly, we are seeing efforts to have computers evaluate student writing. There is a convenience factor for some teachers, and students value the prospects of immediate feedback. But the move to computerized writing assessment is fraught with concerns on multiple levels. First, machine scoring can penalize ELL writers for different approaches to prose or argument. Second, if we believe that writing is fundamentally a social and communicative act between a human reader and a writer, then machine scoring profoundly violates that principle. The CCCC Statement of Assessment maintains that

> automated responses may promise consistency, but they distort the very nature of writing as a complex and context-rich interaction between people. They simplify writing in ways that can mislead writers to focus more on structure and grammar than on what they are saying by using a given structure and style.

Middle and high school students are often just learning about the context-rich nature of writing, but scoring machines remove student writers from their audiences. Automated scoring undermines the very communicative aspects of writing that we are trying to teach.

References

Alsup, J., Emig, J., Pradl, G., Tremmel, R., & Yagelski, R. (July 2006). The state of English education and a vision for its future: A call to arms. *English Education 38*(4), 278–294.

Anzaldúa, G.E. 1987. *Borderlands/la frontera: The new mestiza.* San Francisco, CA: Aunt Lute.

Atwell, N. (1987). *In the middle: Writing, reading, and learning with adolescents.* Portsmouth, NH: Heinemann.

Au, K. H. (1993). *Literacy instruction in multicultural settings.* Fort Worth, TX: Harcourt Brace.

Ballenger, B. (2008). *The curious researcher* (6th ed.). London, United Kingdom: Longman.

Bazerman, C., Bonini, A., & Fiegueiredo, D. (2009). *Genre in a changing world.* Retrieved from http://wac.colostate.edu/books/genre/

Bean, J., Cucchihara, M., Eddy, R., Elbow, P., Grego, R., Kutz, E., . . . Matsuda, P. K. (2003). Should we invite students to write in home dialects or languages? Complicating the yes/no debate. *Composition Studies, 31*(1), 25–42.

Bean, J. C. (2001). *Engaging ideas: The professor's guide to integrating writing, critical thinking, and active learning in the classroom.* San Francisco, CA: Jossey-Bass.

Black, R. W. (2005). Access and affiliation: The literacy and composition practices of English language learners in an online fanfiction community. *Journal of Adolescent & Adult Literacy, 49*(2), 118–128.

Bomer, R. (2005). Meet our new students: English language learners in English Language Arts classrooms. *The Council Chronicle, 15*(2), 16.

Bosher, S., & Rowecamp, J. (1998). The refugee/immigrant in higher education: The role of educational background. *College ESL, 8*(1), 23–42.

Boyd, F. B., Ariail, M., Williams, R., Jocson, K., Sachs, G. T., McNeal, K., . . . Morrell, E. (2006). Real teaching for real diversity: Preparing English language arts teachers for 21st-century classrooms. *English Education, 38*(4) (Reconstructing English education for the 21st century: A report on the CEE Summit), 329–350.

Brisk, M. E., Hodgson-Drysdale, T., & O'Connor, C. (2010/2011). A study of a collaborative instructional project informed by systemic functional linguistic theory: Report writing in elementary grades. *Journal of Education, 191*, 1–12.

Callahan, R. M. (2005). Tracking and high school English learners: Limiting opportunity to learn. *American Educational Research Journal, 42*(2), 305–328.

Campano, G. (2007). *Immigrant students and literacy: Reading, writing, and remembering.* New York, NY: Teachers College Press.

Canagarajah, A. S. (2002). *Critical academic writing and multilingual students.* Ann Arbor, MI: University of Michigan Press.

Carson, J. G., & Nelson, G. L. (1996). Chinese students' perceptions of ESL peer response group interaction. *Journal of Second Language Writing, 5,* 1–19.

Chiang, Y-S. & Schmida, M. (2006). Language identity and language ownership: Linguistic conflicts of first-year university writing students. In P. K Matsuda, M. Cox, J. Jordan, & C. Ortmeier-Hooper (Eds.), *The critical sourcebook on second-language writing in the composition classroom* (pp. 95–108). New York, NY: Bedford/St. Martin's Press.

Chiang, Y-S., Perez, G., Wong, G., Nquyen, N., & Hernandez, Z. (2009). *Four voices from the contact zone of composition theory and linguistic minority.* Paper presented at Conference on College Composition and Communication, San Francisco, March 12.

Childers, P. (1989). *The high school writing center: Establishing and maintaining one.* Urbana, IL: NCTE.

Christie, F., & Derewianka, B. (2008). *School discourse: Learning to write across the years of schooling.* London, United Kingdom: Continuum.

Christofides, L. N., & Swidinsky, R. (2010). The economic returns to the knowledge and use of a second official language: English in Quebec and French in the rest-of-Canada. *Canadian Public Policy Journal, 36*(2), 137–158.

Conference on College Composition and Communication (2009). *CCCC statement on second language writing and writers.* Urbana, IL: NCTE.

Connor, U. (1996). *Contrastive rhetoric: Cross-cultural aspects of second-language writing.* New York, NY: Cambridge University Press.

Connor, U. (2003). Changing currents in contrastive rhetoric: Implications for teaching and research. In B. Kroll (Ed.), *Exploring the dynamics of second language writing* (pp. 218–241). New York, NY: Cambridge University Press.

Cope, B., & Kalantzis, M. (Eds.) (1999). *Multiliteracies: Literacy learning and the design of social futures.* New York, NY: Routledge.

Cox, M., Ortmeier-Hooper, C., & Tirabassi, K. (2009). Teaching writing for the "real world." *English Journal, 98*(5), 72–80.

Cox, M., & Tirabassi, K. (2008). Playing with revision. In M. Cox, A. Doyle, K. Evans, & E. Pezzulich (Eds.), *Embracing writing: First-year writing at Bridgewater State College* (pp. 55–59). Dubuque, IA: Kendall/Hunt.

Crusan, D. (2010). *Assessment in the second language writing classroom.* Ann Arbor: University of Michigan Press.

Cummins, J. (2001). *Negotiating identities: Education for empowerment in a diverse society.* Ontario, CA: California Association for Bilingual Education.

Currie, P. (1998). Staying out of trouble: Apparent plagiarism and academic survival. *Journal of Second Language Writing, 7*(1), 1–18.

Davidson, A. L. (1996). *Making and molding identity in high school: Student narratives on race, gender, and academic engagement.* Albany, NY: SUNY Press.

De la Paz, S., & Graham, S. (2002). Explicitly teaching strategies, skills, and knowledge in writing instruction in middle school classrooms. *Journal of Educational Psychology, 94*(4), 687–698.

Derewianka, B. (1990). *Exploring how texts work.* Rozelle, Australia: Primary English Teaching Association.

Devitt, A. (2004). *Writing genres.* Carbondale, IL: Southern Illinois UP.

Dutro, S., & Moran, C. (2003). Rethinking English language instruction: An architectural approach. In G. G. Garcia (Ed.), *English learners: Reaching the highest level of English literacy* (pp. 227–258). Newark, DE: International Reading Association.

Echevarria, J., Vogt, M.E. & Short, D. (2008). *Making content comprehensible for English language learners: The SIOP® model, third edition.* Boston, MA: Allyn & Bacon.

Edelsky, C. (1986). *Writing in a bilingual program: Habia una vez.* Norwood, NJ: Ablex.

Elbow, P. (1973). *Writing without teachers.* New York, NY: Oxford University Press.

Enright (Villalva), K. A. (2006a). Hidden literacies and inquiry approaches of bilingual high school writers. *Written Communication, 23*(1), 91–129.

Enright (Villalva), K. A. (2006b). Reforming high school writing: Opportunities and constraints for generation 1.5 writers. In P. K. Matsuda, C. Ortmeier-Hooper, & X. You (Eds.), *The politics of second language writing: In search of the promised land.* West Lafayette, IN: Parlor Press.

Enright, K. A. (2011). Language and literacy for a new mainstream. *American Educational Research Journal, 48*(1), 80–118.

Enright, K. A., & Gilliland, B. (2011). Multilingual writing in an age of accountability: From policy to practice in U.S. high school classrooms. *Journal of Second Language Writing, 20*(3), 182–195.

Fels, D., & Wells, J. (2011). *The successful high school writing center: Building the best program with your students.* New York, NY: Teachers College Press.

Ferris, D. (1999). One size does not fit all: Response and revision issues for immigrant student writers. In L. Harklau, K. Losey, & M. Siegal (Eds.), *Generation 1.5 meets college composition: Issues in the teaching of writing to U.S.-educated learners of ESL* (pp. 143–157). Mahwah, NJ: Erlbaum.

Ferris, D. (2002). *Treatment of error in second language student writing.* Ann Arbor, MI: University of Michigan Press.

Ferris, D. (2003). *Response to student writing: Implications for second language students.* Mahwah, NJ: Erlbaum.

Ferris, D., & Hedgcock, J. S. (2005). *Teaching ESL composition: Purpose, process, and practice, second edition.* Mahwah, NJ: Erlbaum.

Fillmore, L. W. & Snow, C. (2000). What teachers need to know about language. (Contract No. ED-99-CO-0008). U.S. Department of Education's Office of Educational Research and Improvement, Center for Applied Linguistics.

Fránquiz, M., & Salinas, C. (2011). Newcomers developing English literacy through historical thinking and digitized primary sources. *Journal of Second Language Writing, 20,* 196–210.

Freeman, Y., & Freeman, D. (1992). *Whole language for second language learners.* Portsmouth, NH: Heinemann.

Fu, D. (1995). *My trouble is my English: Asian students and the American dream.* Portsmouth, NH: Heinemann.

Fu, D. (2009). *Writing between languages: How English language learners make the transition to fluency, grades 4–12.* Portsmouth, NH: Heinemann.

Garcia, O. & Kleifgen, J. (2010). *Educating emergent bilinguals: Policies, programs, and practices for English language learners.* New York, NY: Teachers College Press.

Gebhard, M., & Martin, J. (2010). Grammar and literacy learning. In D. Fisher & D. Lapp (Eds.), *Handbook of research on teaching the English language arts.* Mahwah, NJ: Erlbaum/Taylor and Francis.

Graff, G., & Birkenstein, C. (2009). *They say/I say: The moves that matter in academic writing* (2nd ed.). New York, NY: Norton.

Graves, D. (1983). *Writing: Teachers and children at work.* Portsmouth, NH: Heinemann.

Grosjean, F. (1989). Neurolinguists, beware! The bilingual is not two monolinguals in one person. *Brain and Language, 36,* 3–15.

Halliday, M. A. K. (1985). *An introduction to functional grammar.* London, United Kingdom: Edward Arnold.

Hamp-Lyons, L. (1991). *Assessing second language writing in academic contexts.* Norwood, NJ: Ablex.

Hamp-Lyons, L., & Condon, W. (2000). *Assessing the portfolio: Principles for practice, theory and research.* New York, NY: Hampton Press.

Harklau, L. A. (1994a). ESL and mainstream classes: Contrasting second language learning contexts. *TESOL Quarterly, 28*(2), 241–272.

Harklau, L. (1994b). Tracking and linguistic minority students: Consequences of ability grouping for second language learners. *Linguistics and Education, 6,* 221–248.

Harklau, L. (2000). From the "good kids" to the "worst:" Representations of English language learners across educational settings. *TESOL Quarterly, 34,* 35–67.

Harklau, L. (2001). From high school to college: Student perspectives on literacy practices. *Journal of Literacy Research, 33,* 33–70.

Harklau, L. (2002). The role of writing in classroom second language acquisition. *Journal of Second Language Writing, 11,* 329–350.

Harklau, L. (2011). Commentary: Adolescent L2 writing research as an emerging field. *Journal of Second Language Writing, 20,* 227–230.

Harklau, L., Losey, K., & Siegal, M. (Eds). (1999). *Generation 1.5 meets college composition: Issues in the teaching of writing to U.S.-education learners of ESL.* Mahwah, NJ: Erlbam.

Heath, S. B. (1983). *Ways with words: Language, life, and work in communities and classrooms.* New York, NY: Cambridge University Press.

Hillocks, G., Jr. (2002). *The testing trap: How state writing assessments control learning.* New York, NY: Teachers College Press.

Hinds, J. (1987). Reader versus writer responsibility: A new typology. In U. M. Connor & R. B. Kaplan (Eds.), *Writing across languages* (pp. 141–152). Reading, MA: Addison-Wesley.

Hudelson, S. (1989). *Write on: Children writing in ESL.* Englewood Cliffs, NJ: Prentice Hall Regents.

Huot, B., & O'Neil, P. (2008). *Assessing writing: A critical sourcebook.* New York, NY: Bedford/St. Martin's.

Johns, A. M. (1999). Opening our doors: Applying socioliterate approaches (SA) to language minority classrooms. In L. Harklau, K. Losey, & M. Siegal (Eds.), *Genera-*

tion 1.5 meets college composition: Issues in the teaching of writing to U.S.-educated learners of ESL (pp. 159–171). Mahwah, NJ: Erlbaum.

Johnson-Sheehan, R. (2010). *Technical communication today, third edition.* New York, NY: Pearson.

Jordan, J. (2009). Second language users and emerging English designs. *College Composition and Communication, 61*(2), W310-W329.

Jordan, J. (2012). *Redesigning composition for multilingual realities.* Urbana, IL: Southern Illinois UP/NCTE.

Kaplan, R. B. (1966). Cultural thought patterns in intercultural education. *Language Learning, 16*(1), 1–20.

Kibler, A. (2011). I write it in a way that people can read it: How teachers and adolescent L2 writers describe content area writing. *Journal of Second Language Writing, 20,* 211–226.

Kittle, P. (2008). *Write beside them. Risk, voice, and clarity in high school writing.* Portsmouth, NH: Heinemann.

Kroll, B. (1990). *Second language writing: Research insights for the classroom.* New York, NY: Cambridge University Press.

Kubota, R., & Lehner, A. (2004). Toward critical contrastive rhetoric. *Journal of Second Language Writing, 13*(1), 7–27.

Lam, W. S. E. (2000). L2 literacy and design of the self: A case study of a teenager writing on the internet. *TESOL Quarterly, 34,* 457–483.

Lamott, A. (1995). *Bird by bird: Some instructions on writing and life.* New York, NY: Anchor.

Langer, J. A., & Applebee, A. N. (1987). *How writing shapes thinking: A study of teaching and learning.* Urbana, IL: NCTE.

Leki, L. (1991). Twenty-five years of contrastive rhetoric: Text analysis and writing pedagogies. *TESOL Quarterly, 25,* 123–143.

Leki, I. (1991/1992, Winter). Building expertise through sequenced writing assignments. *TESOL Journal, 1,* 19–23.

Leki, I. (1992). *Understanding ESL writers: A guide for teachers.* Portsmouth, NH: Boynton/Cook.

Leki, I. (2007). *Undergraduates in a second language: Challenges and complexities of academic literacy development.* Mahwah, NJ: Erlbaum.

Leki, I., Cumming, A., & Silva, T. (2008). *A synthesis of research on L2 writing in English.* Mahwah, NJ: Lawrence Erlbaum.

Liu, J., & Hansen, J. (2002). *Peer response in second language writing classrooms.* Ann Arbor, MI: University of Michigan Press.

Martínez-Roldán, C., & Fránquiz, M. E. (2009). Latina/o youth literacies: Hidden funds of knowledge. In L. Christenbury, R. Bomer, & P. Smagorinsky (Eds.), *Handbook of adolescent literacy research* (pp. 323–342). New York, NY: Guilford Press.

Matsuda, P. K. (1997). Contrastive rhetoric in context: A dynamic model of L2 writing. *Journal of Second Language Writing, 6*(1), 45–60.

Matsuda, P. K. (2006). The myth of linguistic homogeneity in U.S. college composition. *College English, 68*(6), 637–651.

Matsuda, P. K., Canagarajah, A. S., Harklau, L., Hyland, K., & Warshauer, M. (2003). Changing currents in second language writing research: A colloquium. *Journal of Second Language Writing, 12*(2), 151–179.

Matsuda, P. K., Cox, M., Jordan, J., & Ortmeier-Hooper, C. (Eds.). (2006). Second-language writing in the composition classroom: A critical sourcebook. Boston, MA: Bedford/St. Martin's.

Matsuda, P. K., & De Pew, K. E. (2002). Early second language writing: An introduction. *Journal of Second Language Writing, 11,* 261–268.

Matsuda, P. K, & Matsuda, A. (2009). The erasure of resident ESL writers. In M. Roberge, M. Siegal, & L. Harklau (Eds.), *Generation 1.5 in college composition: Teaching academic writing to U.S.-educated learners of ESL* (pp. 50–64). London, United Kingdom: Routledge.

Miller, S. M., & Fox, D. L. (Eds.). (2006). Reconstructing English education for the 21st century: A report on the CEE Summit [Special Issue]. *English Education, 38*(4).

Murray, D. M. (1982). *Learning by teaching: Selected articles on writing and teaching.* Montclair, NJ: Boynton/Cook.

Murray, D. M. (1990). *Write to learn* (3rd ed.). Fort Worth, TX: Holt, Rinehart, and Winston.

Murray, D. M. (2003). *The craft of revision.* Belmont, CA: Wadsworth.

National Clearinghouse for English Language Acquisitions (NCELA), U.S. Department of Education. (2008). *Educating English language learners: Building teaching capacity. Roundtable report.* Retrieved from http://www.ncela.gwu.edu/files/uploads/3/EducatingELLsBuildingTeacherCapacityVol1.pdf

National Commission on Writing in America's Schools and Colleges. (2003). *The neglected "R": The need for a writing revolution.* Washington, DC: The College Board.

The National Commission on Writing. (2004). *Writing: A ticket to work . . . or a ticket out: A survey of business leaders.* The College Board. Available at: www.writing-commission.org/prod_downloads/writingcom/writing-ticket-to-work.pdf

Nelson, G., & Carson, J. (2006). Cultural issues in peer response: Revisiting "culture." In K. Hyland & F. Hyland (Eds.), *Feedback in second language writing: Contexts and issues* (pp. 42–59). Cambridge, United Kingdom: Cambridge University Press.

Nystrand, M. (1997). *Opening dialogue: Understanding the dynamics of language and learning in the English classroom.* New York, NY: Teachers College Press.

Ogulnick, K. (2000). *Language crossings: Negotiating the self in a multicultural world.* New York, NY: Teachers College Press.

O'Malley, J. M., & Valdez-Pierce, L. (1996). *Authentic assessments for English language learners.* Menlo-Park, CA: Addison-Wesley.

Ortmeier-Hooper, C. (2008). English may be my second language, but I'm not "ESL." *College Composition and Communication, 59*(3), 389–419.

Ortmeier-Hooper, C. (2010). The shifting nature of identity: Social identity, L2 writers, and high school. In M. Cox, J. Jordan, C. Ortmeier-Hooper, & G. G. Schwartz (Eds.), *Reinventing identities in second language writing.* Urbana, IL: NCTE.

Ortmeier-Hooper, C., & Enright, K. A. (2011). Mapping new territory: Toward an understanding of adolescent L2 writers and writing in U.S. contexts. *Journal of Second Language Writing, 20*(3), 167–181.

Pally, M. (1997). Critical thinking in ESL: An argument for sustained content. *Journal of Second Language Writing, 6*(3), 293–311.

Peregoy, S., & Boyle, O. (2008). *Reading, writing, and learning, in ESL* (5th ed.). Boston, MA: Pearson Education.

Raimes, A. (1985). What unskilled ESL students do as they write: A classroom study of composing. *TESOL Quarterly, 19*(2), 229–258.

Reid, J., & Kroll, B. (1995). Designing and assessing effective classroom assignments for NES and ESL students. *Journal of Second Language Writing, 4*(1), 17–41.

Rief, L. (1991). *Seeking diversity.* Portsmouth, NH: Heinemann.

Reynolds, D. W. (2005). Linguistic correlates of second language literacy development: Evidence from middle-grade learner essays. *Journal of Second Language Writing, 14*(1), 19–45.

Reynolds, D. W. (2009). *One on one with second language writers: A guide for writing tutors, teachers, and consultants.* Ann Arbor, MI: University of Michigan Press.

Reynolds, D. W. (2010). *Assessing writing, assessing learning. A practical guide to evaluating and reporting on writing instruction programs.* Ann Arbor: University of Michigan Press.

Robb, L. (2010). *Teaching middle school writers.* Portsmouth, NH: Heinemann.

Roberge, M. (2009). A teacher's perspective on generation 1.5. In M. Roberge, M. Siegal, & L. Harklau (Eds.), *Generation 1.5 in college composition: Teaching academic writing to U.S.-educated learners of ESL* (pp. 3–24). London, UK: Routledge.

Roberge, M., Harklau, L., & Siegal, M. (Eds.). (2009). *Generation 1.5 in college composition: Teaching ESL to U.S.-educated learners of ESL.* New York, NY: Routledge.

Romano, T. (1987). *Clearing the way: Working with teenage writers.* Portsmouth, NH: Heinemann.

Romano, T. (2002). *Blending genres, alternating styles: Writing the multigenre paper.* Portsmouth, NH: Heinemann.

Rubinstein-Ávila, E. (2004). Conversing with Miguel: An adolescent English Language Learner struggling with later literacy development. *Journal of Adolescent and Adult Literacy, 47*(4), 290–301.

Rule, R., & Wheeler, S. (2000). *True stories: Guides for writing from your life.* Portsmouth, NH: Heinemann.

Scarcella, R. (1990). *Teaching language minority students in the multicultural classroom.* Englewood Cliffs, NJ: Prentice Hall Regents.

Scarcella, R., & Rumberger, R. W. (2000). Academic English key to long term success in school. *UC Linguistic Minority Research Institute Newsletter, 9*(Summer), 1–2.

Schleppegrell, M. J. (2004). *The language of schooling: A functional linguistics perspective.* Mahwah, NJ: Erlbaum.

Schleppegrell, M. J., & Go, A. (2007). Analyzing the writing of English learners: A functional approach. *Language Arts, 84*(6), 529–538.

Schwartz, G. G. (2004). Coming to terms: Generation 1.5 students in mainstream composition. *The Reading Matrix, 4(3),* 40–57.

Severino, C. (1993, Fall). The doodles in context: Qualifying claims about contrastive rhetoric. *The Writing Center Journal, 14*(1), 44–62.

Severino, C., Gilchrist, M., & Rainey, E. (2010). Second language writers inventing identities through creative work and performance. In M. Cox, J. Jordan, C. Ortmeier-Hooper, & G. G. Schwartz (Eds.), *Reinventing identities in second language writing* (pp. 174–194). Urbana, IL: NCTE.

Silva, T. (1993). Toward an understanding of the distinct nature of L2 writing: The ESL research and its implications. *TESOL Quarterly, 27*(4), 657–677.

Sommers, N. (1980). Revision strategies of student writers and experienced adult writers. *College Composition and Communication, 31*(4), 378–388.

Smith, M. W., & Wilhelm, J. D. (2002). *"Reading don't fix no Chevys": The role of literacy in the lives of young men*. Portsmouth, NH: Heinemann.

Smythe, S., & Neufeld, P. (2010). Podcast time: Negotiating digital literacies and communities of learning in a middle years ELL classroom. *Journal of Adolescent & Adult Literacy, 53*, 488–496.

Suárez-Orozco, C., Suárez-Orozco, M., & Todorova, I. (2008). *Learning a new land: Immigrant students in American society*. Cambridge, MA: Harvard University Press.

Swales, J. M. (2009). World of genre—Metaphors of genre. In C. Bazerman, A. Bonini, & D. Fiegueiredo (Eds.), *Genre in a changing world*. Anderson, SC: Parlor Press.

Tarone, E., Downing, D., Cohen, A., Gillette, S., Murie, R., & Dailey, B. (1993). The writing of Southeast Asian-American students in secondary school and university. *Journal of Second Language Writing, 2*(2), 149–172.

Tirabassi, K. E. (2007). *Revisiting the "current-traditional era": Innovations in writing instruction at the University of New Hampshire, 1940–1949*. Unpublished dissertation. University of New Hampshire, Durham, NH.

Tsui, A. B. M., & Ng, M. (2000). Do secondary L2 writers benefit from peer comments? *Journal of Second Language Writing, 9*(2), 147–170.

U.S. Census Bureau. (2009). *Origins and language: United States*. American Fact-Finder. Retrieved from http://factfinder.census.gov/servlet/ACSSAFFPeople?_submenuId=people_8&_sse=on

U.S. Department of Education. (2008). *New Hampshire: Rate of LEP growth*. Retrieved from http://www.ncela.gwu.edu/files/uploads/4/NewHampshire-G-06.pdf

Valdés, G. (1999). Incipient bilingualism and the development of English language writing abilities in the secondary school. In C. J. Faltis & P. M. Wolfe (Eds.), *So much to say: Adolescents, bilingualism, and ESL in the secondary school* (pp. 138–175). New York, NY: Teachers College Press.

Valdés, G. (1998). The world outside and inside schools: Language and immigrant children. *Educational Researcher, 27*, 4–18.

Valdés, G. (2001). *Learning and not learning English: Latino students in American schools*. New York, NY: Teachers College Press.

Valdés, G. (2003). *Definitions of giftedness: Young interpreters of immigrant backgrounds*. Mahwah, NJ: Erlbaum.

Valdés, G. (2004). Between support and marginalisation: The development of academic language in language minority children. *International Journal of Bilingual Education and Bilingualism 7*(2–3), 102–132.

Valenzuela, A. (1999). *Subtractive schooling: U.S. Mexican youth and the politics of caring*. Albany, NY: SUNY Press.

Ware, P. D., & Warschauer, M. (2006). Electronic feedback and second language writing. In K. Hyland & F. Hyland (Eds.), *Feedback in second language writing: Contexts and issues* (pp. 105–122). Cambridge, United Kingdom: Cambridge University Press.

Weigle, S. C. (2002). *Assessing writing*. New York, NY: Cambridge University Press.

Weissberg, R. (2006). *Connecting speaking and writing in second language writing instruction*. Ann Arbor: University of Michigan Press.

Wiggins, G. P., & McTighe, J. (2005). *Understanding by design* (2nd ed.). Alexandria, VA: Association for Supervision and Curricular Development.

Wilson, M. (2006). *Rethinking rubrics in writing assessment.* Portsmouth, NH: Heinemann.

Yi, Y. (2007). Engaging literacy: A biliterate student's composing practices beyond school. *Journal of Second Language Writing, 16*(1), 23–39.

Yi, Y. (2008). Relay writing in an adolescent online community. *Journal of Adolescent and Adult Literacy, 51(6),* 260–270.

Yi, Y. (2010a). Identity matters: Theories that help explore adolescent multilingual writers and their identities. In M. Cox, J. Jordan, C. Ortmeier-Hooper, & G. Schwartz (Eds.), *Reinventing identities in second language* (pp. 303–324). Urbana Champaign, IL: NCTE.

Yi, Y. (2010b). Adolescent multilingual writer's transitions between in- and out-of-school writing practices. *Journal of Second Language Writing, 19*(1), 17–32.

Zhang, Q. (1997). *Academic writing in English and Chinese: Case studies of senior college students.* Unpublished doctoral dissertation, Ball State University, Muncie, IN.

Zhu, W. (2001). Interaction and feedback in mixed peer response groups. *Journal of Second Language Writing, 10*(4), 251–276.

Index

About the Author

Christina Ortmeier-Hooper is an assistant professor of English at the University of New Hampshire. She began her career as a teacher of ESL reading/writing and English Language Arts in the public schools. She currently teaches undergraduate writing courses and graduate courses on composition theory, second language writing, and English education. Her work has been published in *English Journal, College Composition and Communication, Journal of Second Language Writing,* and *TESOL Journal.* Christina regularly presents workshops on multilingual students and writing at conferences throughout the United States.